NATURAL MAGICK

NATURAL MAGICK

THE ESSENTIAL WITCH'S GRIMOIRE

SALLY DUBATS

CITADEL PRESS
Kensington Publishing Corp.
http://www.kensingtonbooks.com

CITADEL PRESS BOOKS are published by

Kensington Publishing Corp.
850 Third Avenue
New York, NY 10022

All Kensington titles, imprints, and distributed lines are available at special quantity discounts for bulk purchases for sales promotions, premiums, fund-raising, educational, or institutional use. Special book excerpts or customized printings can also be created to fit specific needs. For details, write or phone the office of the Kensington special sales manager: Kensington Publishing Corp., 850 Third Avenue, New York, NY 10022, attn: Special Sales Department, phone 1-800-221-2647.

Citadel Press and the Citadel Logo are trademarks of Kensington Publishing Corp.

First Citadel printing: March 2002

10 9 8 7 6 5 4 3 2 1

Printed in the United States of America

Cataloging data may be obtained from the Library of Congress

ISBN 0-8065-2335-2

CONTENTS

NATURAL MAGICK

CHAPTER I

Natural Magick

There is a dance. The dance moves throughout the universe, throughout the galaxy, throughout the planets, throughout the Earth, throughout the Earth's creations . . . crystals, plants, trees, people, you. In this dance within you and within everything in the universe, there is a single energy, the music, creating a connectivity between the participants. The dance is joyous, and it's noisy!

Natural Magick is intended to show you ways that various gifts from the Earth combined with your natural talents dance together. Herbs, crystals, astrology, sacred tools, intuition, visualization, divination—together these create natural magick. The more intricate the music, the more divine the dance, the more wonderful the magick performed. Natural Magick is also intended to teach you how to use your intuition.

Because all things are connected, when you understand one magickal principle, the easier it becomes to understand the next. For example, since several forms of divination contain numerology, once you understand the basics of numerology and the meanings of numbers, you will much more quickly learn the Tarot and the meanings of the numbers on the cards. Likewise, studying the concepts behind elements of Earth, wind, air, and fire will enhance your knowledge of the Tarot *and* astrology, as both contain aspects of the elements. In other words, the basic knowledge of a few magickal principles will open the doors to many. Your magick will then become more intuitive based on the strength of these principles.

As your magick and Craftwork become more intuitive, you will learn to think about and intuit answers before trying to find them in a book or finding another source which is external rather than internal. Your internal sources already know the answers, and they already know how to perform magick. You will begin to ask yourself questions regarding how to understand a certain challenge rather than try to find answers elsewhere. Oftentimes you will find the answers that came from within you are repeated in other sources, and thus your intuition is confirmed. This process will allow you to begin the routine of trusting your intuition. Realizing that the answers come from within you and later seeing your solutions confirmed elsewhere is far more empowering than memorizing a book. It's a catch-22. If you don't trust your intuition, your intuition won't work.

Natural Magick will also show you some of the elements of Wicca and how they can be used together in the dance of the universe in order to bring about effective change in your life. The items in this book need not be performed in a circle, which is Wiccan ritual performed on various sabbats, full moons (and whenever the wind blows for some of us), but they are intended to be used to affect change. Our minds create matter (and change) before we do. You can't plan a trip, make a statue, write a letter, or build a house without first having thought of it in your brain or mind. You must first consider where you want to travel, or the materials for a statue, or to whom you're going to write, or where you want your house built. After your travel plans have solidified in your mind, your travel plans then become real. The intention is in place, and you suddenly have a flight booked for the Bahamas. This is the same way magick works. You create something in your mind, or on the astral plane, in order to affect physical change. The change doesn't have to be something solid, like a statue or a house. The change can be something abstract such as love, success, or prosperity.

Although adding ritual to your magickal work does enhance its efficacy, simply creating intention brings about change as well. Thought is a powerful tool. Thinking of a loved one who lives far away sends that loving energy out into the universe. That loving energy finds and perhaps comforts that person regardless of how the energy was sent, via random thought or with magick. How often has someone called you when you were recently thinking of him or her?

Lighting a candle for a loved one allows you to more consistently and consciously send them the same loving energy; carving their name in that candle sends thoughts to that person even more directly. Each step you take in focusing your intention creates a result in a more specific way. It is the difference between turning a light on in a room, or pointing a flashlight directly at an object. The focus is more direct.

Many of the things that we thought were magick a couple of hundred years ago are now being scientifically proven. It was once believed that willow was magick, and responsible for taking away evil spirits (or headaches) in the brain. Willow was slighted by the bulk of scientists for years as superstition. Aspirin is made of willow, and is now the most common pain reliever in use today. Here's another example: When we ingest chocolate, chemicals are manufactured in our bodies which are the same chemicals manufactured when we are in love. It's no wonder that chocolate is so popular in the first phases of the dating ritual. Although some of the mystery has been removed from the magick of the past, much of what we consider magick does come from our ability to visualize and then effect change. Ask any witch about how magick works, and you'll get as many different answers as there are witches. The more you work with magick, the more you will know your personal answer.

The writings in this book are not intended to be a magickal guide as much as a way for you to find how magick works for you and to point you in a direction of discovery that can send you into experiencing magick for yourself. No book is an answer. You can read all the books you want, but until you do the basic work with meditation, concentration, intent, and all the elements that comprise magickal workings, you are not going to find what you seek. If an item resonates with you, then it is right for you. If it does not resonate with you, certainly don't do it! There are books on hexing as a form of retaliation or revenge for wrongdoings that certainly don't resonate with the way many Wiccans perceive witchcraft. Many witches believe hexing sends negative energy into the world, and would not hex someone under any circumstance.

Whether you believe hexing is right, wrong, or neutral is up to you. This book is based on a connection with a divine force that works toward the good of All. Whether you call it deity, the Goddess, or God, or whether you simply want to call it Universal Energy, there is not a single right path to spirituality. Our diverse world culture shows us that. A respect for other belief systems is important to our strength in our personal belief systems. Certainly Christians light candles just as Wiccans light candles, and there are so many principles that are the same in every religion. Honoring our parents is a universal religious principle. Tolerance and love are the keys. We can work together toward realizing this.

If this book represents a seed, plant the thoughts and grow! As you learn new techniques and thoughts, and begin to work with other than your five senses, it is important to become aware of your responsibility to magick. . . . *And Ye Harm None, Do What Ye Will.* This is the Rede, the Golden Rule of Wicca and Witchcraft. The Rede is the only Wiccan tenet to follow when performing magick. If the action you are considering harms absolutely no one, including yourself, others, the Earth, plants, and animals, then the action is fair, just, and in line with the Good of All.

The materials covered in this book serve as a general introduction to the tools of modern Wicca, some forms of magick, the properties of common herbs and stones, and divination techniques. Natural Magick also contains a comprehensive list of common human traits or principles (e.g., love, anger, fear) for which magick is most commonly used, along with the elements, items, plants, and stones which will create change in your life, either combined with spellwork or simply used within your home to draw the desired results.

Learn about the tools before using them, and certainly learn about the tools before spending any money. Some tools or principles might sound strange or silly because, yes, they are steeped in Old World thoughts which seem superstitious, but remember that willow was once thought a superstitious placebo. Perhaps you picked up this book to reach beyond what you are normally willingly to believe as natural. Magick is natural. Take joy and delight in your willingness to open up and experiment. Most of all, take joy in your personal growth and your ability to effect positive change in your life.

Let's dance!

CHAPTER II

Ritual Tools

itual tools are physical symbols which help you to focus your thoughts and energy toward a specific magickal or sacred purpose. For instance, wands and brooms help you to direct your energy to create sacred space while one purpose of a cauldron is to transform your writing into magickal intention. Learn about tools and the meaning behind them to see how they will help you enhance your personal power prior to performing actual ritual. Some tools to consider collecting include a cauldron, broom, wand, ritual clothes and jewelry, and other items which will be discussed later in this chapter. Working directly and consistently with your tools will give them meaning and power for you. It is keenly important that you develop a relationship with your tools to find out what they symbolize for you and why they hold power for you. There is residual energy in the tools because of the energy and imagery that has been invested in them over the ages. For instance, it is the collective energy of all those before us who have worked with a cauldron which created our current concepts and perceptions of the cauldron. That same concept or perception, that feeling of mystery, will help you create power for your personal cauldron. Further, the energy you invest in your cauldron will help others who are using their cauldrons now, as well as future generations with the energy of their cauldrons. And so it is with all ritual tools.

Ritual tools contain energy because of their collective use over the ages and because of the energy you give them now. Consider how you will give energy with your personal power to the tools you obtain. As you look at pentacles in a store, one in particular will seem to jump out at you, and you will begin to receive certain feelings, an emotional response, about the pentacle regarding its beauty, size, or color. These feelings represent the energy that is already innate in that tool or symbol, but this is not only the collective energy in the pentacle, it is also the energy that is drawing you to that particular pentacle. Those kinds of feelings, or intuition, are what will help you select a particular tool.

Once you receive a tool, it is time to charge and bless the tool with your personal energy. This will bring your energies in line with the tool. Charging includes:

1. Understanding and knowing the purpose of a tool. You will then know what energy you want to put into the tool. Be very specific. For instance, know that your broom will be used to bless and cleanse an area and make it sacred for circle. At the end of this chapter are descriptions and purposes of certain tools to help you understand them.

2. Being able to consciously receive energy from the Goddess, the God, and the Universe into your body. We all have a spark of the divine within us, so we already naturally receive divine energy. The difference is being able to sense and become conscious of this divine energy, and then focus the energy for an intended purpose. One method of focusing energy is to fill yourself with Goddess light. First ground yourself to the earth by visualizing roots reaching from your spinal cord down through your legs and feet and down into the earth. Allow yourself to feel the warmth of the earth and feel connected to the earth. Next, visualize energy in the form of white light coming into your body through the top of your head, as though you are being fed white light to fill your body. With each breath, feel the energy of this light entering and filling you with greater and greater intensity. Feel the joy and loving power of this light and let it bathe you inwardly.

3. Passing the energy that has been collected into your body into the intended tool. Whether you are male or female, the left side of the body is Goddess, feminine, receiving energy. The right side of the body is God, masculine, sending energy. To pass energy into the tool, therefore, hold it in your right hand, the hand best suited for sending energy. Your body has been filled with white

light; allow the white light to move through your right arm, out your hand, and into the tool. Make sure every cell inside the tool has been filled with the white light and energy. Sense that the tool feels the same intensity of joy as you did as it is filled with the light of the Goddess.

4. Sealing the energy into the tool while blessing it so that it can receive energy at an exponential level each time you use it. This sealing will also work so that your tool will receive your energy, and your energy alone—not the energy of someone joining in your circle or someone picking up your tools. To seal the energy into your tool, imagine a velvety-blue light moving through the top of your head and filling your body. With each breath you take, completely fill your body with this blue light. Move the energy of this blue light to your right arm, and out your right hand, and visualize the blue *surrounding* the tool, but not moving inside the tool, on every side and angle, leaving no area open for penetration from the outside. This blue light is to protect your tool from picking up any unwanted energy.

☾ Care of Tools

Tools that you use for magickal purposes are sacred objects. Charge and bless them, then treat them as friends. Smile at them. These steps will empower your tools and allow you to develop a close relationship with them. The relationship you have with your tools will be reflected in the success of your magick. Use the full moon as a time of blessing and cleansing your tools. If you have an altar where most of your tools are kept, bless the altar and all the tools on it during the full moon.

To bless, or smudge, your altar, select herbs related to the purpose of your blessing (see Chapter VI, "Herbs"), or use a sage bundle. Bless the dried herbs and place them in a ceramic bowl or large shell used specifically for this purpose. Light the herbs or the bundle, and sweep the smoke toward your altar with either your hand or a feather. As the smoke moves against the altar, it will bless it and cleanse it of any impurities or negative energy, as well as empower it with the elements of the herb you are using. You might choose to repeat a verbal blessing several times while smudging your altar or tools such as, "I bless and cleanse this altar and all things on it, and I dedicate them to the light and love of the Goddess and of the God."

To anoint your altar, create an oil for the purpose of blessing as discussed in Chapter VI. Keep a small bottle of the blessing oil on your altar. To bless a tool, place a small drop on your finger and then consecrate the tool with it. Use words meaningful to you to bless your tool. For example, "I do bless and anoint this wand with the strength and purity of the Goddess and of the God for the purpose of directing my energy three-fold through this wand to do my bidding."

Family of Tools—Personality of the Altar

A good place to keep your tools is on an altar in your home. Having an altar as sacred space in your home will invite wonderful Goddess and God energy. Your altar doesn't have to be anything fancy. A small table will do. As the wheel of the year turns, change your altar to reflect the moods of the various sabbats and esbats. This could be as simple as changing the altar cloth and adding seasonal herbs or plants.

During each holiday, think about the energies available for your tools to absorb into their personalities. Bless your tools with the *feeling and mood* of the current holiday. Each holiday carries a different mood, and your tools and altar will gain the qualities and strengths of the various holidays and rituals as time goes by. The purpose of the following list of holidays is not to define Wiccan sabbats and esbats, but to offer ideas for tools and altars with regard to charging them with holiday powers:

> *Samhain* is on October 31 and is the Celtic New Year. This sabbat is wonderful for scrying and communicating with teachers, guides, spirits, as well as your own soul. Visualize each of your tools being able to assist you with truly hearing teachers, guides, and spirits. Visualize your tools assisting you with receiving messages from your own soul. Samhain

is also an especially favorable time to bless any scrying tools for strengthening their connection to you and your ability to use them for this form of divination.

Yule is during the Winter Solstice, between December 20 and 23, and is the joyous celebration of the Goddess giving birth to the Sun God. Permeate your tools with joy, light, and the ability to command successful beginnings.

Imbolc is the midpoint between Winter Solstice and spring, and is celebrated on February 2. It is a celebration of hope and the Sun God gaining strength, the bringing of light; there is literally more light during the lengthening days after the dark days of winter. Visualize the divine light of the universe, of the God and of the Goddess, moving into and strengthening your tools.

Ostara, the vernal equinox, is celebrated between March 20 and 23 and is the actual arrival of spring. The young God is growing, and light has returned to the earth with equal amounts of moonlight and sunshine. Give your tools the power of balance between feminine energy and masculine energy. Although tools are either masculine or feminine, balance is still required just as there is balance required in human beings who are either masculine or feminine.

Beltane is celebrated on May 1 and has traditions all over the world. The brightly colored May pole, a phallic sign of fertility, is erected in lots of countries! Beltane is a time of many kinds of fertility, so bless your tools with the ability to manifest gains in the material world.

Litha or *Midsummer* is celebrated on the Summer Solstice between June 20 and 23. An auspicious time for magick as the energy of the sun is at its highest, so charge your tools with the power of healing and loving energy.

Lughnasadh or *Lammas* is celebrated on August 1. A time of joyful celebration of the warmth of summer as well as a time for preparation for autumn and winter, so charge your tools with the strength of letting go. Just as there is strength in gain, there is strength in knowing when to begin the process of letting go. When your tools are given the gift of "letting go," you will be more in tune with your magickal workings and whether you should proceed with them.

Mabon is celebrated on the Autumnal Equinox on or about September 21, a time of introspection and endings. Begin to think about the New Year marked by Samhain, and the things you are ready to end. Give your tools the strength of endings. Doing so will give meaning to the words "So mote it be," which so often mark the ending of a particular spell. The ending of the spell also marks the beginning of the universe's ability to make it so!

✳ Working Without Tools/Astral Tools

If you haven't gathered all the tools you want to use in the Craft, working without them can be an effective way to learn to focus your energy until you do obtain the tools you desire. If you do have tools and have been working with them extensively, working without their physical presence is a terrific way to enhance your personal skills and powers.

Try doing a circle (as described in Chapter V, "Visualization and Ritual") with all astral tools. Astral tools are those that you visualize as being present without actually being physically present. This will increase your ability to apply your personal power. When creating the circle, visualize the energy in the form of blue light moving into the top of your head and filling your body as you inhale, and then direct the blue light out your hand and through your astral wand. All the energy will be directed and "concentrated" first in your hand, then in the wand and finally released outward to create the circle. Continue to cast the circle and work magick as though you have all your tools present. You might be surprised to find that the wand you later find actually looks like the astral wand with which you've been working.

✳ Minding Your Manners

As you begin to meet like-minded people, simply keep in mind that tools are specifically charged for individual or group use in ritual. A witch's tools and jewelry are considered very special, personal, and private. It's best to ask permission prior to handling any tools or ornamentation. Each person has his/her own energy field and that energy can be picked up by the tools of magick; many witches don't "seal" their tools as previously mentioned.

☾ Tools

The following tools are those you might consider collecting for your ritual work, magick, and altar pieces. Ideas on how to dedicate, cleanse, and bless them are included. Dedication of a tool creates a transition point marking the beginning of the tool's increase in power and use for your personal magickal intention. Blessing your tools within a circle ensures their purity of purpose; create a circle as you see fit, or as described in the ritual section of this book.

Cauldron

The cauldron is one of the tools intimately associated with women and feminine energy. It is associated with hearth and home and represents the womb and Mother Earth. It serves as a utensil for cooking and is thus seen as providing loving nourishment. Creation, abundance, and fertility are all connected to the history of nourishment that comes from the cauldron. The cauldron is used in modern Wiccan imagery and ritual to serve as a vessel to hold that which is holy, to hold elements of fire, water, incense (air), and earth. Diviners look inside the cauldron for visions of what is to be, and mixtures and brews are created within its brim.

If you are looking for a cauldron, try the local flea markets and antique shops for a bargain. Some metaphysical shops also carry cauldrons. Your cauldron will find you when the time is right.

To dedicate your cauldron, take it out at midnight on a full moon. As the cauldron is associated with the earth, gather a small amount of earth and bless it by holding it up to the moonlight and saying, "I do here and now bless and consecrate this earth by the light of the moon." Allow the energy of the moonlight to fill the earth for a moment, then gently sprinkle the blessed earth over your cauldron while saying, "I do bless and consecrate this cauldron, as well as dedicate her to the light and love of the God and of the Goddess. This dedication will serve notice that all work within this cauldron be born of the Goddess's womb for the good of All with harm to none." At this point, quiet yourself and continue with the dedication and sealing as described at the beginning of the chapter.

Chalice

Like the cauldron, the cup or chalice is a symbol of feminine energy and is sacred to the Goddess. It represents openness and receptivity. The chalice is a vessel for what is holy, and is symbolic of everything represented by the cauldron. This does not mean that the chalice and the cauldron are interchangeable. The chalice serves as an offering receptacle, as a communal celebratory vessel, for sharing of cakes and wine during ritual, as well as a receptor for the athame (ritual knife) during the Great Rite. The Great Rite is a significant moment during ritual when God (male) and Goddess (female) are joined via figurative movement of the athame into the chalice.

Chalices come in all shapes and sizes, from ornate jewel-bedecked goblets to a simple wineglass. Some chalices are simply a drinking glass from the kitchen shelf blessed before circle, but a particular vessel should be selected for ritual purposes alone. Rather than a glass plucked from the kitchen, repeated use of a chalice selected for the purpose of ritual creates energy that builds and stays with that particular chalice. Some see the Craft as a completely natural part of their everyday lives, and therefore want to treat ritual and magickal tools as naturally as they would any other aspect of their lives such as the evening meal.

To dedicate your chalice, take it to the ocean, or a lake, pond, or stream, at twilight. Dip your hand into the water and touch your forehead while saying, "Beloved Goddess, she who rules the deep blue waters of our earth, cleanse my sixth sense so that I might see and understand the wisdom of the chalice that is your gift." Next dip your hand into the water, and touch the chalice while saying, "I hereby bless, and consecrate this chalice that all who drink of it will receive and understand the wisdom of the Goddess." Continue with the dedication and sealing as described at the beginning of the chapter. Then take up the chalice, dip it into the water, and hold it up to the setting sun saying, "Behold, oh Lord of the Sun, the beauty of the Goddess fills this cup." Continue by pouring the water onto the Earth saying, "And her beauty also returns to the sun-kissed Earth." Hold the chalice to your heart saying, "As the cycle of fullness to emptiness represents the sorrows and joys of life, I am open to the wisdom of the Goddess and of the God to be shown to me in this my sacred chalice. So mote it be."

Athame

The athame is a double-edged knife or sword which is typically black, usually dulled, and used specifically for ceremonial and magickal purposes. It is *not* used for sacrifice. Sacrifice plays *no part* in Wicca, magick, or witchcraft! Athames can range from quite ornate tools to very unpretentious and simple blades. Some of the more ornate tools are crafted from gold or silver and inlaid with precious gems. The material an athame is made from does influence its personality and ability to direct power; however, it is certainly not a requirement to have an ornate tool. The more common athames can be quite simple blades which blend in with other kitchen items, but this is necessary only if a witch does not wish his or her practices in the home known or identified by guests.

The athame is a tool which is used for masculine aspects of power and is an extension of your personal energy and power. Further, just as your personal energy and power increase with use like muscles gaining strength when exercised, so does the energy of the athame become stronger the more you use it. The relationship between athame and witch is symbiotic. The more you interact, the stronger each of you becomes when working together.

An excellent way to feel and sense the growing relationship between you and your athame is to name your athame. Naming your athame will saturate the tool with new energy, further define its personality, and shape its power and energy. Perhaps the most famous named athame is the mythical Excalibur. Steeped in myth, the name alone conjures images of the truth and righteousness expected in King Arthur's round table.

During ritual, the common uses of the athame include casting and closing circle during ritual, invoking the Goddess and the God, directing energy for magick, and symbolizing the joining of male and female during the Great Rite. The lowering of the athame into the chalice represents the balance and perfect union of male and female which also acts to balance and temper the strong masculine energy of the athame.

Casting the circle is done by allowing universal energy, which is the energy that creates everything in the universe, to flow through you. Your body then becomes an energy conduit to the athame. While walking clockwise around the circle with the athame, allow the energy to move through the athame and visualize the circle being created. One method of channeling universal energy, even if you do not *sense* the energy moving through you, is to try to imagine breathing in violet light from the universe through the top of your head until your body is filled with the light, and then breathing that energy down your arm, and through the athame, while visualizing, or actually seeing, the light create the circle. To close, again move clockwise around the circle (some witches prefer to close counterclockwise, also called widdershins), taking the athame in hand, and see/feel the circle energy moving back into the athame, similar to a tape measure being drawn back into the case. The energy from the circle is collected in the tool, and each circle makes the tool stronger. This is also why the athame is usually black. Black is a color which collects energy.

To dedicate and consecrate your athame, first know the name you will give it during the dedication. As the athame is an air tool, awaken at dawn and go outside and kneel to the east, the direction of the element of air. As the sun rises, raise up your athame while saying, "Lord of the Sun, I thank you for and accept this athame which is your gift to me for doing work for the good of All." Slowly lower the athame and pierce the Earth saying, "Strengthened and blessed by the energies of Mother Earth, I do hereby name you _____. May the energies of our Mother Earth fill you with the strength of the universe." Continue with the dedication and sealing as described at the beginning of the chapter. Leave the athame in the Earth until noon to be given the strength of the sun and the love of the Earth, at which time you may remove it and place it on your altar.

Bolline

The bolline is a white-handled knife, sometimes straight, sometimes curved like a small scythe, which is used specifically for work related to the Craft. Unlike the athame which is a magickal, dulled ritual knife, the bolline is very sharp and used for "mundane" work such as cutting herbs, or shuffling coal around in a cauldron. Some use their bolline as an athame, or sharpen their athame to use as a bolline. Although there are those who would disagree with the practice of combining the function of the bolline and athame, the choice is yours. Be respectful of others who choose to keep these energies separate.

As with all tools, when you have found a bolline with which you would like to work, the blessing and dedication of this tool should include words that will ensure that it always be used properly, that it will harm none and, according to the Rede, be used for the good of All. In blessing your bolline in this manner, you will use it consciously, and plants and trees which participate in your herbal gatherings will sense your earnest, heartfelt work.

To dedicate and consecrate your bolline, an air tool, awaken at dawn, and go outside with your bolline and some incense which you have already blessed. Kneel to the east, the direction of the element of air. As the sun rises, thank the incense for its participation in your ritual and light it. Pass your bolline over the incense, saying, "I bless and dedicate this bolline to the light and love of the Goddess and of the God. I also dedicate this bolline to its being a tool used for the highest good of All, and that it harm none. So mote it be." Continue with the dedication and sealing as described at the beginning of the chapter.

Wand

The cauldron and chalice are feminine tools; the wand and athame are masculine. The wand is one of the older of the tools, and in many traditions it is seen as a shortened version of the sorcerer's staff and is likened to the king's scepter. It serves as an extension of the self, drawing and projecting energy and power. Because the wand is linked with the scepter, it can represent the power and authority of he/she who holds it. The wand can be made of various materials. Some prefer oak, birch, or willow, while others prefer copper, other precious metals, or crystal.

Traditionally the wand is made the length of one's arm from the bend of the elbow to the tips of the fingers, so the lengths of wands differ. But whether from a sacred oak, purchased in a store, or selected from a favorite tree, your wand should be a very personal and unique expression of yourself. You might choose to inscribe magickal symbols into your wand, or affix talismans, stones, or other items of power. Hand crafting and styling your wand while concentrating on the powers you wish to develop with the wand will make the power grow during its creation process.

The wand has various magickal and ritual uses, and again that may vary from tradition to tradition. Generally speaking, the wand is used to open and close circle, to direct blessings and energy toward specific objects, or to trace magickal symbols either in the air, on the Earth, or on other objects. It is a masculine tool, and can be used interchangeably with the athame. The wand, in the Tarot, is associated with the element of fire.

To dedicate and consecrate your wand, hold ritual at noon, the time of day sacred to the element of fire. If you can manage to wait until a sabbat, so much the better. You will want to select a date of power for dedicating your wand. Prior to ritual, select a gold candle to honor the God. Lightly carve words into the candle which pertain to the wand and which are meaningful to you ("power," "loving energy," "God energy," and "strength" are good examples). During ritual, anoint the candle, which now represents your wand, and light it saying, "I light this candle as a beacon for the God and the Goddess that they may know my intentions. I do lovingly receive and accept their gift of this wand to me." Take up the wand, and pass it several inches above the flame saying, "As my intentions for this wand are for [state the words you carved onto the candle], let the light and wisdom of these words forever shine in this wand. I bless and dedicate this wand to the light and love of the Goddess and of the God to be a tool used for the highest good of All, and that it harm none. So mote it be." Continue with the dedication and sealing as described at the beginning of the chapter.

Ritual Clothes, Robes, and Jewelry

Your appearance in daily life shows the world who you are and your attitude about yourself. When performing ritual, your appearance should reflect your magickal self. The clothes, robes, and jewelry you wear during ritual symbolize your magickal self, the self that is connected to the God and the Goddess, the self that makes magick! Clothes, robes, and jewelry specifically charged and used for ritual will help you to make the transition from the mundane world to the world of magick and the God and Goddess.

Of course you certainly have the option to do ritual in your mundane garb (preferably of natural fibers), and there are covens and solitaries who perform sky clad (nude), but even they often wear specially charged jewelry! If you are invited to a coven working, inquire as to their traditional method of dress. You don't want to be surprised when everyone is wearing their birthday suit.

Robes of any color can be worn during ritual, and it is best that your robe be of natural fiber to stay in tune with Nature. The most common vision of a witch's robe is the black robe with the large hood. Today, black is still a very popular color because it draws energy and assists with the creative and visualization process, but other colors are used for various purposes. Select the color of your robe based on what feels right for you, or what is in line with the energy you want to draw for that particular ritual. Some common colors for robes and their meanings are as follows:

Silver: Connects with the Goddess.
Gold: Connects with the God.
Green: Connects with the energy of the earth.
Blue: Connects with the energy of water.
Yellow: Connects with the energy of air.
Red: Connects with the energy of fire.
Pink: Connects with the energy of the heart.

Make your robe your personal piece of ritual clothing that is used only for ritual. The colors above can be used, or colors of your choice. Do investigate the meanings behind the color you select. The meanings associated with various colors are mentioned in Chapter III, "Magick and Candles." Also, colors have different meanings in various teachings. Whatever your selection, be creative when making your robe. Embroider symbols for the four elements, or your Sun Sign, or other personal astrological data onto your robe, all the while sending energy to the garment. Sew herbs into the hem for spiritual growth while wearing the robe. Do whatever makes your robe feel *magickal!*

Regarding jewelry, select rings, earrings, buckles, ankle bracelets, headwear, and other items to bring about the conditions you desire for your personal state of consciousness for ritual. Keep in mind that the left side of the body is for drawing energy, and the right side of the body is for sending energy. For instance, an amethyst ring worn on the left hand will facilitate the drawing in of spiritual energies, while a hematite ring on the right hand will magnify the ability to send loving energy during spellcrafting.

Broom

The broom is a sacred tool used for clearing energy and blessing the area where you are going to perform ritual. The broom is allied with the element of air (some say water). To bless and cleanse an area, use the broom as an extension of yourself, sweeping from the center area to the outside of the circle in a clockwise fashion. First near the ground, and then in the air above you for both physical and spiritual planes. It is not necessary to actually sweep the floor as this is a sweeping of energy, not literal dust. Imagine the negativity being swept away from the area while using a brief spoken blessing such as, "I dedicate and bless this space with the light and love of the Goddess," or one of your own. You might find that repeating this blessing over and over while cleansing the space will move you into a trancelike state. With practice, you will feel the Goddess energy moving through you to cleanse the circle.

There are numerous historical accounts of the importance of the broom to Witchcraft. Women would take their brooms, again a symbol and tool of a woman's role in an earlier society, and go into the fields. They would sit astride the broomstick and run through the fields to encourage the fertility needed to make the crops grow. Others would jump while running to indicate that the crops would grow to the height they could jump. It has been thought that this image is what conjured a fear-struck Europe to believe that witches flew on brooms.

✍ Altar Items

The following items are wonderful to have to add energy for your altar. Some of these items many witches find indispensable.

Candles or Statuary: Candles or statues representing the God and the Goddess help to align yourself with deity. Some candles are also statues! Some quite beautiful Egyptian or Greek artwork is available for relatively little cost.

Censor: A must to burn incense, although a cauldron can double as a censor. Some witches like the censors on chains that they can gently, but dramatically, swing through the air.

Blessing Oil: You can either make your own, or purchase oil for your altar. Blessing oil is contributive to candle magick, as well as necessary to have for blessing almost anything within circle.

Candle Snuffer: There are those who say that blowing out a candle with your breath offends the fire element, and therefore use a candle snuffer. The choice is yours.

Bowl or Shell: A special bowl or shell, one each for salt and water, would be necessary to do ritual circle.

Bell: Used for calling the quarters, watchtowers, or elements during ritual, as well as signifying the completion of a spell.

CHAPTER III

Magick and Candles

O f all the magickal workings, candle magick is perhaps the most beautiful. Seeing an altar alive with several delicately flickering candles reflecting their light off a bell, crystal, wand, and cauldron while incense is burning is a near mystical experience indeed. The world becomes more than quiet, and your soul is awakened to the deepest respect for and appreciation of the art and beauty of the Craft.

Candle magick consists of projecting the essence of an individual into a candle, and doing healing work for or drawing circumstances to that individual represented by the candle. There are several steps to take prior to that point, but candle magick is nonetheless very simple, very beautiful, and very rewarding. The steps to take during simple candle magick, and indeed for most types of magick, are as follows:

1. Decide on the magick you will perform.

This applies to any magickal undertaking and is trickier than it sounds. Choose your intent and desired outcome carefully and responsibly. As the Rede indicates, "And ye harm none, do what ye will." If you wish to gain employment, excellent. If you wish to gain employment at a particular establishment, be sure that your magickal working does not bend the will of the individual who will interview you. Magickal workings should be broad enough to give the Goddess room to work, yet narrow enough to be sure your desired outcome is *without bending the will of another*. For instance, in the case of gaining employment at a particular establishment, perhaps your magickal working could be focused on present-ing yourself with confidence and intelligence during the interview. This would preclude a sway during the selection process, and you would not bend anyone's will but your own. Then, if you don't get the job, you'll know that it truly wasn't meant to be and not a question of "faulty magick."

Performing magick for yourself is preferred, especially if it does not conflict with or change another person's will. If magick is for another, make sure you ask permission. It is tempting to perform magick for a sick friend, but odd as it seems, it is not for us to know the higher purpose of a friend's illness. If a friend asks you to perform magick specifically for him/her, for healing or for obtaining a job, by all means help your friend. Furthermore, the magick would be more successful if you *show* your friend how to perform the magick for him/herself or at least have your friend present for the ritual. However, if a friend wishes for a healing for someone *else*, then you must first get permission from the primary source. In other words, never do magick for someone without that person's permission. The final word in deciding to do magick is make sure that it is with permission directly from the source, and that it does not bend another individual's will.

2. Decide when to perform the magick.

Timing your magickal working with the phases of the moon will greatly contribute to a successful spell. Timing your magickal working with the moon *and* with astrological cycles in mind will produce even greater success in your magickal workings. Generally, to draw things to you, such as employment, prosperity, love, or something that you want to *add* to your life, do candle magick or magick of any kind when the moon is waxing. A waxing moon is when the moon is growing (think of dipping a candle in wax, as you "wax" the candle, it grows). To banish or get rid of things, such as a bad habit or to end a relationship, do candle magick or magick of any kind when the moon is waning, or disappearing. The full moon is for magickal workings of any kind.

If at all possible, further narrow the field. The moon travels through a sign in the zodiac in about two days. Select a time when the moon is in the appropriate sign to perform the magick. Find a good almanac which lists the astrological aspects of the moon and follow it. The astrology section in Chapter IV will help you to decide the best time to perform a specific spell. For instance, under Gemini you will find that this sign influences our ability to accept change. Therefore, if you're having difficulty accepting a new situation, the best time to do a spell to help you adapt to the new situation would be when the moon is in Gemini. Although a full moon is beneficial for any magick, a full moon corresponding with the magick you are doing is indeed a favorable time to perform magickal workings.

There is also a certain amount of cleverness that can be employed when deciding on a time to do magick. You can turn the intent of magick around to its opposite in order to find the closest time to do magick. As a hypothetical example, you are in a relationship that needs healing, and you wish to do a spell immediately to help the relationship. Unfortunately, you see that the next opportune time to perform this spell, during the waxing Taurus moon, isn't for another three months. Fortunately, you see that the waning Taurus moon is now. You can change the intent of the magick to banish negativity from the relationship. In other words, you can do a spell to bring love into the relationship during a waxing moon which is to draw something to you, or you can do a spell to banish the negativity in a relationship during the waning moon. The same can be done with any spell. Regarding prosperity, you can banish the lack you are experiencing during a waning moon, or draw prosperity during the waxing. Employing cleverness is part of magick!

3. Select the appropriate candle color.

What's your favorite color? What's your least favorite color? Your answers have meaning! The information regarding color is universal and applies not only to candle magick, but to all forms of magick, meditation, and visualization. Color is a relatively recent addition to candle magick within the last several decades. White candles were used for candle magick in Europe until recently. This addition of color to candle magick is a positive reflection of the ability to adapt to and learn from new information. As we come to recognize the power of color, creativity lends itself to our ability to integrate it into the powerful art of candle magick.

Our speech is rich with color references which show meaning

beyond merely the influence of the light spectrum. "He's green with envy!" "She's feeling blue." "They were tickled pink!" These color references also have specific correlations to energy centers in the body called *chakras,* a Sanskrit word meaning "wheel" (read more about chakras in Chapter IV, "Stones and Crystals"). Interestingly, in correlating these everyday statements with magick, you can see their influence. "Green with envy" pertains to matters of the heart, and green is the color you would use for healing the heart or healing jealousy.

Every color carries a specific type of energy. The major power colors are the seven colors of the rainbow. It is no mistake that the colors of the rainbow are also the colors of the seven major chakras or energy centers within the body. Colors do have different meanings in different cultures such as Native American, Eastern, or when working with the Kabbala. The colors listed below and their meanings have significance in traditional European and, consequently, American magick, but if these colors hold a different meaning for you, find what works for you.

Black: Black is the absence of all light and therefore the absence of color. Black is used for protection spells. Think of the protective cover of night. For some animals, the dark blanket is their best protection against predators. Black is also for banishing, repelling negativity, for bringing creativity, binding, and shapeshifting. (Literally, shapeshifting is changing into the shape of an animal. Figuratively, shapeshifting is taking on the consciousness of an animal to see things from its perspective.)

Blue: Blue is used in candle magick to better your communication abilities, to become aligned with spiritual principles, to seek wisdom, to seek peace and calm, and to perform protection spells. Blue also represents the element of water. As such, blue also helps us to move through obstacles, though be wary of using blue to move through obstacles. Think of a river flowing to the sea, whether it goes through a city or not! The same force of destruction could be the result of your magick to move through an obstacle if you are not careful. As blue is the elemental color representative for water, the water sign energies (Cancer, Scorpio, and Pisces) of intuition and emotions work particularly well with a blue candle.

Blue is the color of the fifth chakra which rules communication, and is therefore an excellent color to use when doing candle magick to heal the throat, vocal cords, bronchial passages, and lungs.

Brown: Brown is the color of our most basic element, Earth. As such, using a brown candle to very generally enhance the abilities of the Earth signs (Taurus, Virgo, and Capricorn) is quite successful. A brown candle would be beneficial for a general spell for a happy home. More specifically, a brown candle would be excellent for Earth-healing energies. Brown is also useful in spells involving friendship, favors, or influencing others.

Copper: Consider the hues within the color of copper, which include flecks of orange (passion), brown (earth and soil), a hint of gold (the God, wealth, winning). With these ideas in mind, copper is excellent for candle spells and other spells drawing money, creating goals, working for professional growth, and gaining prosperity in business. To meditate with a copper candle will also assist with contemplated career maneuvers.

Gold: The energy of the color of gold is similar to the energy of yellow. As with yellow, gold represents the God, the sun or solar energy, male energy, and personal power; however, there is a higher meaning to the use of gold rather than yellow. The color gold carries with it a reverential aspect of the divine, and when used to represent the God or personal power, work with your sense of the divine that is carried within yourself. Working with the color of gold during candle magick or any magick will also gain wealth, winning, safety, and happiness.

Green: Green represents Mother Earth and her healing properties. For the purposes of candle magick or other magick where color is used, green can be used for physical healing, healing of the heart in order to be open for a loving relationship, monetary success and abundance, fertility, tree and plant healing magick. Green is one of the preferred colors to work with when doing magick concerning the Earth signs of Taurus, Virgo, and Capricorn. These are the signs relating to the physical wants or needs mentioned above. Green is also the color of the fourth chakra, which is seated in the area of the heart and governs the well-being of the heart, blood, thymus, and circulatory system.

Indigo: Indigo is a deep violet-blue and takes communication a step further to psychic ability stemming from spiritual awareness, self-assurance, hidden knowledge, and vision magick including scrying. Indigo is the color of the sixth chakra, which governs the pituitary gland, the nervous system, lower brain, left eye, ears, and nose. Using indigo for candle magick or any magick will help to heal these areas of the body. Using a purple candle if an indigo candle is difficult to find is perfectly acceptable.

Orange: The energy of orange can be combined with any color if you need fast results or fast action. Using orange for candle magick is useful for ambition or goals of any kind, including career goals and general success. An orange candle is also excellent for finding the perfect home or buying or selling real estate or property deals of any kind. Creativity and creation as well as sexual awakening are other excellent uses for the color orange. Orange is also the color of the second chakra, which governs the reproductive system as well as your perspective on sex.

Pink: A pink candle is the traditional candle used for drawing romantic love to you. Some would say red is the proper color; however, red is a color of earth energy, while white is the color of spiritual energy. The combination of pink draws a life partner love, which includes friendship, affection, support, and caring. Red is for lusty love which could potentially burn out fast. Pink is also a great color to use for peace on the planet or sending the message to our planet that She is loved.

Purple: Purple has long symbolized the color of royalty and is also a symbol for leadership. One of the uses for purple in candle magick or any magick is to align yourself with those in high places. Although it can be used to influence those in high places, this is not recommended as it is not in keeping with the Rede. Purple also pertains to the third eye, which is the sixth chakra, and can be used in place of the more exact color of indigo. Purple is also used when seeking psychic ability, connecting with your spiritual self, creating self-assurance, and discovering hidden knowledge.

Red: Red represents our connection to the earth with regard to how we perceive ourselves on the physical level and how well we "fit in" here. This includes our strength and courage, as well as our motivation with regard to career goals. Red originally helped with our sense of survival, and now that means our ability to earn an income or be what is perceived as "safe" within our world. Red is also the color to be used when seeking passion and lust. Red is the color of the base chakra and governs the adrenals, as well as the spinal column and kidneys.

Silver: Like the metal, the color silver is used to honor the Goddess and to get in touch with Goddess energy. Silver candles can be used to seek telepathy, clairvoyance, clairaudience, and intuition, as well as to assist with remembering and interpreting dreams and working with personal astral energies.

White: White is reflected light containing all the visible rays of the spectrum. It is holy and sacred and is to be used for understanding your spirituality, seeking the Goddess, honoring and understanding your spiritual self, finding peace, and honoring female strengths. White can also be used in place of any other color as white contains all colors. White is the color of the seventh chakra, which is our spiritual center. The seventh chakra governs the pineal gland, the upper brain, and the right eye. Use a white candle to perform magick for healing these bodily areas.

Yellow: Use a yellow candle to honor the God and masculine strength represented by the sun. Yellow is also used for candle magick concerning memory, intelligence, logic, and learning. Yellow is the color to use to help you understand and then properly use your personal power. Yellow is associated with the third chakra, which is seated in your solar plexus and governs your pancreas, stomach, liver, spleen, and gall bladder.

4. Gather items for ritual.

For the best magickal results, perform candle magick during ritual. See Chapter V, "Visualization and Ritual," to gather the basic items for ritual. In addition to the items needed for ritual which are mentioned in Chapter V, you will need the appropriate candle, oil to bless the candle, an awl or other instrument for carving into the candle, and matches or a lighter. An awl is a tool for carving into the candle and can be as simple as a skewer from the kitchen, or an elaborate crystal-tipped tool you make and bless specifically for your candle magick. Other items you may wish to use are pictures, mirrors, an item belonging to the individual for whom you are performing magick, or stones and crystals. Pictures will help you visualize the individual. Mirrors help during banishing magick to reflect negative energy away from an individual. An item belonging to the individual will help you focus on their essence. Stones and crystals help to intensify the energy directed to the candle.

To select oil for blessing your candle, use oil that was specifically prepared with the magickal purpose in mind. You can create your own oils, or purchase the oil from a shop. Fortunately, oils are becoming easier and easier to find as the natural ways are becoming more and more popular. Some shops carry oils created for a specific purpose, such as love, prosperity, or protection. The next "step down," or less specific oil, is an oil created for the astrological sign under which you are performing the magick. For instance, if you are doing a love spell with candle magick, bless the candle with Taurus oil, less effective than oil made for love spells, but more effective than general blessing oil. Of course, you can also simply use oil made specifically for blessing, which is powerful, but less specific. Be aware, however, that the more exacting your magick is, the better the results will be.

5. Luxuriate in a ritual bath.

The ritual bath is for the purpose of purifying yourself, blessing yourself, aligning yourself with deity, becoming aware of your higher self, as well as getting in touch with your personal magickal energy. The ritual bath sets the tone for ritual and for the magick to be performed during ritual. You will find more about ritual baths in Chapter V, but it is important to know that this is the point to take purifying steps which will help you focus on the work at hand. If you lack time, you can bless yourself with incense, discussed in Chapters V, and VI.

6. Prepare the candle.

The candle must contain the essence of the person for whom you are performing magick or contain your essence if the magick is for yourself. There are several things you can do to personalize a candle in this manner. As you work with your candle, either focus on your intention for the magick, or remain in a meditative or reflective state for the duration of your work. It is important, while you are working, that you keep in mind the person for whom you are doing the magick and the desired magickal results, and that your magick is for the good of All and that it harm none. Using an awl or any tool available to you, lightly carve the name of the individual into the candle all the while visualizing the individual as you carve. Carve other items into the candle which would represent the individual, for instance the glyph of their astrological sign. Next, carve words or symbols into the candle which represent the purpose of the magick. For a love spell, carve the word "Love" and perhaps the symbol for a heart. Carve the words "Prosperity" or "Money" and perhaps a dollar sign to bring monetary prosperity to the individual. You can be as specific as room on the candle will allow. When you have finished carving the name and symbols into the candle, it is time to bless it.

To bless the candle, take up the oil you collected for this purpose. Lightly anoint the candle, bottom to top, with the oil. There have been various techniques suggested for blessing candles which also include anointing or dressing the candle from the middle to the top or wick end, and then again from the middle to the bottom. Another suggestion is anointing with oil toward the wick to draw energy to you, and away from the wick to banish or get rid of negativity. Select the method which works best for you, but the intent and the purifying and blessing energy you send into the candle are the most important.

Your verbal blessing while anointing the candle can be one of your choosing, perhaps something along the lines of, "I do bless this candle with the perfect light and love of the Goddess and of the God. So mote it be."

7. Create a magickal phrase.

You will need to create a statement which holds meaning and power for you in order to release the energy of candle magick. Writing your magickal phrase can be done during or after the time you carve and bless the candle, but your phrase should definitely be written prior to ritual. This statement is an affirmative magickal phrase and can range from a simple, single-word mantra such as "peace" to an ornate incantation modeled after time-honored poetic classics.

There are guidelines which apply to crafting affirmative magickal phrases. Although your intention and will are the most important magickal ingredients, your words also carry meaning and power and are a very significant contribution to the work at hand. Choose your words with care. Select a word or phrase which states that the magick is already taking place. As an example, let's say you are creating a spell for a friend, Judy, who has asked your help because she is experiencing a high level of anxiety. Judy's child is taking drugs, and she realizes that the parental anxiety and fear which she is choosing to experience isn't helping the situation. Judy has asked for your magickal assistance. In selecting a magickal phrase, choose one that includes the name, and the *positive aspect* that you wish to create. For instance, rather than saying "Judy is free of anxiety," you would do better to select "Judy is now peaceful and is surrounded by a peaceful atmosphere." The exception to selecting positive aspects is when you're doing the spell during the waning moon. You would then select "I do here and now banish any and all thoughts which keep Judy from experiencing peace." For the best magickal results, be as specific as possible while remaining as simple as possible. The simpler your phrases, the more they will speak to your subconscious mind in the form of images.

These rules of thumb also apply if you choose to create longer poetic incantations. Remember to see the *literal* results of your work to ensure that you are not projecting some strange magickal results. Flowery language can also create imagery which causes *literal* results. Amy wants a love spell in order to find a mate. You write an incantation something like this: "Amy now draws love, like a lovely morning dove, men will flock to her side, asking her to be their bride." Amy probably doesn't want to have to choose from a flock of males! Something slightly tamer yet concise would be more appropriate.

8. Perform ritual.

Continue with the ritual steps outlined in Chapter V, "Visualization and Ritual." In brief, you will be creating the sacred space for ritual, creating energy for circle, sealing the circle to create a protected space filled with energy, calling the elemental quarters, and calling the Goddess and the God. At this point in the ritual, you are prepared to perform magick, and you are ready for the final phases of candle magick, imprinting the candle and the release of energy.

9. Imprint your candle.

Prior to creating and releasing the magickal energy within the candle, you must first learn to imprint the candle with the essence of (1) the person for whom you are doing magick, and (2) the desired effect or outcome. Imprinting the candle allows the candle to truly represent the individual and bind the magickal intention to the individual. Imprinting allows the two essences, the essence of an individual and the essence of the magickal intention, to mingle together, perhaps for the first time. For instance, if an individual has never truly experienced prosperity, there is no prosperity intention within their essence. Imprinting allows the two essences to mingle together.

To imprint the individual's essence into the candle, you must first learn to sense a person's personality. It is much easier than you think, and it is something that most people do automatically. They simply haven't labeled the technique. Imagine how you feel when a dear friend walks into a room. Something happens to you physically and emotionally. Compare that physical reaction and emotional feeling to greeting a family member, or a coworker or classmate, or even a stranger in a grocery store. The differences in these feelings are actually caused by the individual projecting his/her uniqueness, or essence, onto you as a greeting.

To put her unique energy into the candle, create the details of the individual as clearly as possible. For instance, while gazing at the unlit candle, sense as much as you can about the person for whom you are doing magick. Include the facial features, color of eyes and hair, and perhaps a happy smile on her face. See the freckles or the radiance of her skin as vividly as possible. See her as animated as possible. If you can attach the fragrance she wears to that image, so much the better. Then feel that person's *essence*, just as you would if she were walking into a room. Once you have felt that person's essence during your meditation, allow it to move through you, through your hand, and into the candle.

Next, sense the energy that the person will feel when the magick takes affect. As with Judy, the woman who needed peace in her life, first sense her personality and essence, then *feel* the peace that she would feel when she chooses not to react negatively to her child's behavior. Create peace within yourself, then take that *sensation*, the sensation of peace, and imprint it into the candle. Allow the sensation of peace to move through you and into the candle. Feel it physically move from your hand into the candle.

You have now imprinted the candle with the essence of the person as well as the essence of her desire. It is very similar to giving a gift to someone. In Judy's case, you would literally be giving her the gift of peace by imprinting the candle with peace and with her essence, mingling those energies together. You are now ready to build and release the energy through any method you choose.

10. Various methods of releasing candle magick energy during ritual.

After moving through the steps to prepare yourself, the candle, the ritual space, and then moving through ritual, you are ready to create and release energy for the candle magick. There are several ways to build energy for candle magick or any magick. These include meditating, drumming or using music, chanting, gestures, dancing, or any combination of these. Find the method which best suits your personality and your talents.

To release energy through meditation, hold the unlit, imprinted candle in your hand. Focus and go deeper within yourself to your meditative state. Again visualize the person for whom you are doing magick (or visualize yourself if the magick is for you), and then see the desired magickal outcome. Visualize the *final* outcome of your magickal work. If the purpose of the magick is help someone get a job, see him happy and doing the work he's seeking. If the purpose of the magick is to heal someone, see her healthy. You need not visualize the job search for the one seeking a job, and you need not visualize the best doctor or herb or physical therapy for the one who is going to be healed. Leave the details to the deities.

When this aspect of your visualization is finished, set the candle in its holder. Light the candle while again blessing it and stating the magickal word, phrase, or incantation you wrote prior to ritual.

In the case of Judy, state the magickal phrase, "With my will, and the power of the Goddess and of the God and of the Old Ones, I do bless you Judy and give you peace. So mote it be." While gazing at the burning candle, move to yet a deeper aspect of your meditation. Hold the vision of Judy and see her peaceful as long as you can while gazing into the candle. Feel energy build while you are gazing. When you feel you have sent enough energy, and you may certainly use your best intuition in this regard, finish with a statement similar to, "This spell is for the good of All and intended to harm none. So mote it be."

Gestures are another form of magick which can be quite in depth or quite simple. For the purpose of candle magick, you would combine your meditative state with a gesture of your choice. One method of using gesture during magick consists of tracing a pentacle in the air, and then visualizing the pentacle moving into the object, a candle in the case of candle magick, and fortifying the object with its power and magick. While gazing at the candle, state your magickal phrase, trace the pentacle in the air with your hand or your wand, and send the image of the charmed pentacle into the candle. To finish the gesture, simply state, "This magick be for the good of All, and it harm none. So mote it be." Using your breath while gesturing and sending energy is also an excellent way to send your magickal intention into the candle. Simply gather pure, white energy at your third chakra. See the energy gathering power just outside your body, then literally scoop this ball of energy with your hands, just as if it were a literal "ball" of light, and forcefully push this energy into the candle while exhaling. You can do this several times, feeling the candle become stronger and stronger each time you send energy in this manner. Again, finish with a statement that this magick is for the good of All and that it will harm none.

Chanting is another excellent way to create energy for magickal purposes. Chanting is a relative of prayer and has a rich history dating back to the campfires of many ancient cultures. After imprinting the candle with the essence of the individual for whom you are doing magick as well as the magickal intention, place the candle in its holder, and light it. There are several methods of chant which can be used, and certainly you can create your own method. One method of chant is to begin by stating the magickal phrase you previously created while lighting the candle, and then continue to use that same phrase as the chant. Another method is to create a separate chant. Begin by stating the magickal phrase as you light the candle, and then continue with the new chant. In either method, begin slowly and quietly with almost a whisper while gazing into the candle. Quicken the pace of speech and volume until you feel you *must* release the energy you have created. When chanting energy is released properly, you will perceive a deafening quiet afterward. Sense the appropriate time to close with the statement similar to, "For the good of All and it harm none, so mote it be." It is also appropriate simply to use a one-word mantra while gazing into the candle. Begin saying the mantra slowly while gazing into the flame of the candle, and escalate as you feel the power building. As with the other methods, you will perceive a "tangible quiet" when the magickal energy is released, and you will sense the appropriate time to conclude your spell.

Drumming or using music will also build an extraordinary amount of energy for candle magick, or for any magick. Drumming is a primal language which is found within our own bodies as our heartbeat. Light the candle while stating your magickal phrase, mantra, or incantation. While visualizing the results of your magickal work, begin drumming. If you are a musician who keenly feels music, by all means use the instrument of your choice to build and release energy. As with the chanting, allow your drumming or music to build and crest to the point of release. You will perceive that "tangible quiet" when the magickal energy is released, and you will sense the appropriate time to conclude your spell with the statement similar to, "This spell is for the good of All and intended to harm none. So be it."

Dancing is another method to raise or build energy and power to release it. Dancing is your body's way of chanting. After imprinting the candle, set the candle in its holder, and light the candle while stating the magickal phrase or incantation. While gazing at the burning candle, begin to move in a manner which you have predetermined. If you move within a ritual circle, move clockwise. Your dance will begin to take a shape of its own which might have nothing to do with the predetermined set of steps you initially choreographed. Continue with the movement and allow it to carry you. As with the other methods of building magickal energy, you will sense when to stop. At that point you will perceive the power and magickal energy move outward and be released, and when it feels appropriate conclude with a statement similar to, "This spell is for the good of All and intended to harm none. As above, so below."

Any combination of meditation, gestures, drumming or using music, chanting, or dancing is acceptable. For instance, you might use the "ball of energy" gesture along with your selected chant, and use the chant to create more energy in the ball. You might carry a drum while you are dancing to keep the rhythm and allow the audio portion of your energy raising to help you to a more ecstatic state. You also might be surprised at yourself regarding what will come up during ritual. Remember that you have asked the Goddess and the God to assist with your work. If something new comes to mind that wasn't initially planned, go with it. It could very well be the Goddess or the God nudging you to successful spell work.

11. Finish the ritual.

Finish the ritual as stated in Chapter V, "Visualization and Ritual." The final note? Do not extinguish the candle. Allow the candle to burn and extinguish naturally. If you must remove your altar or cannot attend to the candle for the length of its burning, move the candle to a fireplace, bathtub, deep sink (not a standard bathroom sink), or somewhere that is absolutely, beyond a shadow of a doubt, safe to finish burning. Allowing the candle to finish burning will continue to release the energy of your magick.

☀ Simple Candle Magick

For very simple candle magick, an elaborate ritual is not necessary. Candle magick can become part of your everyday life. Simple candle magick includes changing the mood within your home, sending soothing or calming energy to a friend who needs it, motivating yourself in the short term, even sending a little positive energy to the world. Simple candle magick includes any other number of goodwill actions you would like to undertake. Simple candle magick pertains to general outcomes and requires far less emphasis on formal ritual.

Simple candle magick can be used for changing the general mood in your home, which can include banishing or clearing negativity directly after a resolved argument, creating a relaxing environment after work, creating a romantic atmosphere, creating a healing environment for a relaxing bath, or creating quiet time for children before they go to bed. Using the example of banishing negativity after a resolved argument, it is important to note that the energy from an argument will stay in a home, hanging in the air like cigarette smoke. To remove that energy, simply anoint and bless a candle, imprint the candle with peace, and light the candle. Gaze into the light of the candle and visualize the light generated by the flame moving swiftly to every part of your home. It is important to visualize the *light* moving to every part of your home, and *not* the flame! As the light reaches every corner and every person within your home, see it changing the energy. Allow the candle to burn for a short period. That's all there is to it.

Use this simple method of candle magick for any change in atmosphere that you wish to place in your home. For the romantic atmosphere, sense the romantic feelings, imprint them into the candle, and light the candle. For quiet time for children prior to bedtime, imprint the candle with the feeling of your children being content while coloring or some other quiet activity.

If you wish a more penetrating change in your home, to effect happiness for example, create a candle arrangement specifically for that purpose. Find a large, pink, pillar candle and bless and anoint it with oil. Create a wreath to fit around the bottom of the candle. Use wire and floral tape, as well as herbs or plants which are seasonal and appropriate to the essence of happiness such as apple blossoms in the spring, lavender in the summer, or juniper in the fall and winter. As you weave the plants into a circle, imagine your home being surrounded by happiness. Thank the plants for their help as you work. Imprint the candle with happiness. Visualize that as it is lit, it fills your home with the light of happiness. Next, place the candle on a plate and fashion the wreath to surround its base, light the candle, and enjoy the vibes! The wreath can be left to dry or replaced as needed; however, use the utmost caution in not letting the candle burn too near to the wreath as dried floral arrangements are flammable.

You can also surround a candle with stones for the same purpose. Simply place a pillar candle on a plate, and surround it with stones for your desired outcome. A pink candle surrounded by rose quartz sends a lovely vibration through your home. If you have a very large candle, you can affix the stones directly to the candle by warming the wax with a flame in a particular spot, and then carefully pressing the stones into the soft wax of the candle.

Simple candle magick has the distinct ability to help you focus on the truly important matters—your personal spiritual growth, the joy of your home, sending love to family and friends, and sending loving energy where strength is needed in the world. Seeing the delicate and fragile light in your home allows you to focus on and live with joy for all that is important.

CHAPTER IV

Divination

The root of the word "divination" is "divine," which is defined as "of or like God or a god." We all have a spark of the divine in us; it's merely a question of tapping into and trusting our own capabilities. Divination is information from the Higher Self, the aspect of self that knows all, the primary part of your soul which knows the answers.

We all have access to secret information. Our personal talents and abilities draw us to one form or another of divination. Some people have talent at dowsing; some have talent at the Tarot.

Divination has been accepted in all manner of religious traditions for centuries. The ancient Greeks and Romans, the Chinese and Polynesians turned daily to their oracles for signs and direction. The Old Testament is filled with references to divining practices.

As all things within the universe are related, there is a relation between astrology and the Tarot as well as a numerological relationship. Because of this, numerology, astrology, and the Tarot all work together, as do colors, the seasons, the wheel of the year; no thing in this universe works independently of any other thing in this universe. As you learn an aspect of one tool or form of divination, you will learn aspects of another. You will begin to learn many things at once. Your learning becomes exponential, creating a snowball effect of knowledge. When you learn about numerology, you are learning about the Tarot; when you learn about the Tarot, you are learning about numerology. As you learn about the energies, strengths, and weaknesses of the wheel of life and the wheel of the year, you are also learning about the energy of the Tarot.

Be receptive to your intuitive abilities. Have an open mind as to your abilities.

☾ Scrying

Scrying is the ancient art of looking into a surface or structure, and then receiving messages or images which can either be literal images or symbols which must then be interpreted. The great French prophet Michel de Nostradame, known as simply Nostradamus, used scrying for his famed quatrains in the 1500s. Gifted with prophecy, Nostradamus was a highly educated doctor and healer, and he was extensively studied and skilled in the occult arts and astrology. His intensive study led him to the use of a fourth-century method of scrying for his prophecies and divination. Nostradamus recorded this method, which includes privacy, evening time, and gazing into a bowl of water with candlelight reflected into its depths. Nostradamus would touch the water with a wand, and then the hem of his robe, acknowledge the presence of deity, and gaze into the bowl until prophecies came to him, prophecies including Hitler, the assassination of Kennedy, acid rain, great famines, and many more events which have come to pass and are still unfolding.

Scrying can be done in several mediums which relate to the elements of water, fire, air, and Earth. Although it is not absolutely necessary, it is best to scry on a night when the moon is within the influence of an astrological sign matching the element of the scrying you intend to perform. Do fire scrying when the moon is either in Aries, Sagittarius, or Leo. Do water scrying when the moon is in Cancer, Scorpio, or Pisces. Air scrying, which involves incense or smoke, works best for Gemini, Libra, or Aquarius moons. Do earth scrying during Taurus, Virgo, or Capricorn. Methods of scrying for each element are presented here.

Water: To scry with water, you will need a dark-colored bowl or small cauldron, water to fill the vessel, mugwort, a candle, blessing oil, a purple cord or ribbon (approximately 50 inches long), large enough to form a circle around the bowl of water and the candle, three crystals which have only one point each, and a match. Set aside time late in the evening when you will not be disturbed, and situate yourself at a table with a comfortable chair that allows your body to relax. Create a circle on the table with the purple cord or ribbon.

Take the mugwort in your left hand, covering it with your right, and bless it. To bless the mugwort, close your eyes and visualize white light moving from the universe or Goddess through your head, down your arm, and into the mugwort. Visualize that you are inhaling this white, purifying light, and sending the newly received energy into the mugwort. Bless the mugwort with words similar to, "I do bless this sacred mugwort and thank it for its use in empowering my scrying. This be done with the power of the Lord and of the Lady, harming none, and for the good of All." Sprinkle the mugwort within the circle on the table.

Anoint and bless a candle with oil which is beneficial to scrying or psychic awareness. To bless the candle, take up the oil and lightly anoint the candle, bottom to top, with the oil. A small dab of oil the size of a shirt button will suffice. Use words similar to, "I do bless this candle to illuminate the way to the future. This be done with the power of the Lord and of the Lady, harming none, and for the good of All." Place the candle within the circle on the table, toward the back edge of the circle.

Take up the bowl of water, and bless the water using a method similar to those methods used for the candle and the mugwort, and place the bowl of water within the circle on the table.

Take up the three crystals and bless them. Place the crystals around the bowl or cauldron of water with the points facing to the center.

Close your eyes and move within yourself to a meditative state. Inhale and become aware of your breath filling your lungs. As you exhale, allow the muscles in your body to relax. Use the meditation techniques described in Chapter V. When you have achieved a deep level of relaxation, visualize a deep blue light growing within yourself. Allow the blue light to move outside of yourself, escaping through your pores. Encompass yourself and the table within a great protective bubble of the blue light. It is a perfect sphere. Take several breaths, seeing the protective light becoming stronger and stronger. At this time, focus on Goddess or God energy. Invite this energy to fill the protected area. Now, begin to concentrate on the purpose for your scrying work. Is it for your future? Is it for a friend's future? The future decisions of our world leaders? The future of humanity? Allow yourself to go more deeply within yourself until you *know* you will achieve results. When you have reached that deep level of focus, open your eyes and light the candle. Touch a finger into the water, and then dab your forehead in the sixth chakra or third eye area. As you do this, mentally note that you are joining your psychic center with spiritual waters that can tell you what you wish to know.

With your eyes open, move again to that deep state of relaxation, empty your mind, and use your breathing to move yourself to that meditative place within. Gaze into the water that you have blessed. Expect no outcome; divest yourself of any results. It is time to simply let go, forget about time, and become receptive to the visions or symbols or even dissociated thoughts.

Fire: Fire scrying is far less formal than scrying with water, but can certainly be as effective. Fire scrying can be quite a spontaneous event, and range from quiet meditation with the light of a single candle to a social event of several people surrounding a full blazing bonfire.

To scry with a candle, sit comfortably in front of a candle; perhaps play some soothing instrumental music. Close your eyes, and allow Goddess energy to merge with you. As you inhale, breath in white light or energy of the Goddess, and feel the center of your being at your heart. To do this, move your area of thought from your head to your heart. Once there, open your eyes, and gaze into the flame of the candle. With this method, see the shapes in the flame. As an example of what to expect, perhaps you see a dome shape within the flame, and a female friend comes to mind whom you haven't seen recently. Suddenly you see a flame move within the dome shape. One interpretation is that your friend is pregnant, if that is the "thought" that comes to your mind. If the flame is moving quickly, your friend might be happy about the pregnancy, and "jumping for joy." Another interpretation is that your friend has issues or emotions "within her" that are greatly affecting her life. Be open and receptive to your thoughts. Be sure to check and record results.

Scrying with a large fire or bonfire can be done alone or with several people. If it is an outdoor pit-style fire and there are enough of you, it is an excellent practice for all those present to sit and grasp hands while circling the fire and then proceed with the scrying. As a group, you can either scry separately, holding the energy of the fire within the circle, or you can select an oracle, one who would scry for your group. If you work as a group with the intent to scry individually within that group, sit and grasp hands in a circle around the fire to create a space to build energy. Relax your bodies, and allow the energy of the fire to move you to a quiet, meditative space within. Focus on sending energy into the fire and within the circle. Once the energy has built to a sufficient level, let go of hands, and relax them to the sides with the palms facing toward the fire to send energy to the center of the circle. From this moment, focus on your internal questions, drop all expectation of any results (probably the most difficult step), and see what will come to you. Another group scrying situation includes drumming to build energy. Use the rhythm of the drums to send you deeper and deeper into a meditative state while gazing at the fire. The use of drums can actually quiet the mind's frenetic thinking patterns as you focus on the beat of the drums and release all other thoughts.

As mentioned, you can either scry separately within a group, or you can select an oracle, one who will receive the energy of the group for the purpose of divining for the group. If you as a group select an oracle, begin by seating yourselves comfortably around the fire and grasping hands to form a circle around the fire. Close your eyes and collectively move to a meditative state. When the oracle is ready to receive the group's energy, she (or he) should open her eyes, gaze into the fire, and then gently squeeze the hands of the two people sitting beside her. Those two should silently pass this signal to the two sitting beside them, and so forth, until all have received the indication to send energy to the oracle.

When you receive the signal to send energy to the oracle, inhale deeply, and as you do so, visualize universal white light moving through the top of your head, as though you are inhaling through the top of your head. Fill your body with white light with each breath. Next, begin to direct this energy toward the oracle by passing the white light from your hand to the hand of the person beside you. Move the energy in the direction closest to the oracle from your perspective. The oracle will begin to feel the energy and be filled with the collective group consciousness. Continue to inhale the white light, and send the energy to the oracle.

At this point, the person to the left of the oracle should ask the first question while the oracle focuses on the flame to give the answer. The questioning should continue clockwise until each person has had an opportunity to offer a question to the oracle.

Another method of fire scrying includes embers. As the flames burn down from a large fire and embers are all that remain, use the embers and quiet time to solo scry. You are likely to see many shapes including animals, insects, dragons, fish, birds, plants, or people. Use the image you see as a symbol which requires that you discover the meaning behind the symbol. You can either find the traditional meanings of these symbols through a book of symbols or animal totems, or you can discover your personal thoughts regarding a symbol. As an example, you see the shape of a large spider within the embers. Perhaps to you spiders mean poison and are therefore something to be avoided. You might interpret this symbol that there is something in your life that you should avoid. Yet the spider is a great huntress, artisan, and weaver, and in some traditions she also represents the stars in the sky. Therefore, the spider also has the meaning of mystery, creativity, hidden knowledge, and the Fates or weavers of life. It is up to you to intuit or discern the true purpose for you to have seen a spider, or any symbol, in the embers.

Air: If you scry with smoke, you are scrying with the element of air. Air is what carries the smoke to the ethers. Smoke from various sources can be used, including stick or cone incense, smoke from a fire, or herbs which you bless and use to create your own blend of incense. The method of scrying with these various sources of smoke is the same; the difference lies in the ingredients you use. As with water or fire scrying, first relax your body, move to the quiet and meditative place within yourself, focus on your purpose for scrying, invite deity assistance, let go of all expectations, then gaze into the smoke and listen with all of your senses for answers or visions which come to you naturally.

If you choose to scry with incense, the type of incense you use will have an effect on your work. Just as you would consider the astrological signs for the successful working of a particular type of spell, consider using various types of incense for a particular type of scrying. For instance, use lavender incense to help you scry for information regarding your own or a friend's love life. Basil is excellent for discovering the health situation of a friend or loved one. Study the properties of herbs and resins to assist your incense scrying. To intensify your incense-scrying experience, smudge an amethyst by holding it over the incense. Allow the incense to cleanse and mingle with the energies of the amethyst, and then hold that amethyst while you scry. The amethyst will magnify your intuitive capabilities.

Making your own incense of ground herbs and resins for the purpose of scrying is also effective, and actually preferred. The greatest benefit of making your own powder incense rather than purchasing stick or cone incense is that you know the exact ingredients as well as the intention with which the incense was made. There are hundreds of recipes for incenses that are made by grinding plants, herbs, and resins for a specific intention. Intentions include giving thanks, harmony, love, sensing the sacred, psychic ability, astral projection assistance, honoring sabbats, honoring particular deities—the list is endless. Any recipes you find for incense will also work for scrying, and will enhance your scrying work by adding the intention of the incense.

After working with incense recipes for a while, you will begin to notice inspiration to create incense from intuition rather than following a recipe. Follow that inspiration. Intuitive incense making offers great scrying results. When creating "inspired incense" for scrying, add some mugwort to assist with your psychic abilities. Raspberry leaf is also excellent to help you work from your heart, an important factor when scrying. Record your recipes and your results.

If you choose to scry with fire smoke, finding the right ratio of aged wood to green to create prolonged smoke is a bit tricky. You need enough aged wood to burn as well as enough green wood to create smoke. One way to coax enough smoke to scry from a blazing fire is to place a small branch of a green conifer, such as juniper or spruce or pine, atop a burning fire. This usually creates sufficient smoke; however, be certain that your fire is actually blazing. A conifer can just as easily put out a smaller fire which is not yet fully established. Some very good results can come of scrying on impulse when a fire has created smoke on its own. It will seem as though you have received a personal invitation from the element of air as it subdues the element of fire in order to give you a message.

Both steam and cloud scrying are methods of air scrying which bring successful results. In addition to the element of air, steam scrying also calls upon the elements of fire and water, and for this reason can be very powerful. Like scrying with smoke, scrying with steam can be intentional or quite an impulsive act. You can scry with the steam in a sauna, or use a pot of bubbling and steaming water. Scrying with clouds teaches us that there is a reason for the appearance of everything in our lives, if we are spiritually awake enough to listen to the teachings with which we are bombarded daily. To scry with clouds, give yourself permission to become like a child. Dissociate yourself from time and personal problems, and open your heart to possibility. The message will not be in the fluffy, white bunny rabbit that you see, but in the heartbeat of that bunny rabbit.

Earth: One method of Earth scrying uses the very famed crystal ball. In its natural state, the crystal ball is a gift from the Earth, which is her representative. As the Earth has the ability and generosity to give us everything we need, the gift of the crystal ball is ours to learn the lessons, secrets, and mysteries of the Earth. The secrets and mysteries revealed to us include the big questions as to why we are here, whether we are asking for a single soul's purpose or the purpose of humankind. The secrets revealed to us also include more mundane things like our future, but that would be akin to asking the Goddess who is buried in Grant's Tomb. Being receptive to meaningful messages without reducing the information from a gift from the Earth to mere fortune telling is keenly important.

To become more receptive, do an exercise to allow yourself to open up to deity, the universe, and the elements. Select a time when you will not be disturbed. Sit or recline comfortably, and close your eyes. Take a deep breath, hold it a short moment, and then exhale while relaxing your entire body. Repeat this twice, each time allowing your muscles to more deeply relax. Take three more breaths, this time inhaling blue light through the top of your head with each breath, and exhaling the same blue light through your pores to form a protective bubble around you. Take three more breaths, and this time visualize your body filling with healing, beautiful green light with the air you breathe.

After a total of nine breaths, visualize a door on the front of your body. If you were to see the door opening from an outer perspective, the inside of your body, or your inner world, would be an infinite pool of healing green light. See the door swing open. Visualize an entire forest inhabiting your body. Allow your inner world to be filled with forest. The forest that fills you is an entire ecosystem including trees, plants, animals, decaying leaves, fertile soil, insects, and birds.

Close the door to completely enter your inner world, and bask in the endless forest. Feel the balance. Feel the love of the Earth. Become receptive to the gifts of the Earth. Note how you feel. Do you sense a release of worry about time? Do you sense a release of expectation? Do you sense a feeling of peace and a place where it is not necessary to take action because all is as it should be? Allow yourself to fully feel and understand the beauty of Earth energy. When you are finished, gently open the door for the forest to leave, allowing the green light to remain. Move to your inner world of green light within your body, close the door, and begin to sense your physical body. Sense the room around the physical body. Take in a deep breath and then slowly exhale. When you're ready, open your eyes and jot down your notes.

You can do this receptivity exercise with various ecosystems spanning from desert terrain to snowy, mountainous terrain. Do the same meditation with lakes and oceans for the water element. Bring a candle to your inner world for the fire element. Bring space or sky for the air element. If you're feeling adventurous, you can try some not so peaceful natural settings to truly understand receptivity. A stormy sea, a raging forest fire, or even a tornado for the air element.

In Summary: Give away the idea that you contain personal power. You do or will have a unique way of allowing the gift of power to move through you. You cannot scry without the aid of the elements and the Goddess or God or Universal Energy; believing the power or energy to scry is singularly yours is the surest way to make

scrying *not* work for you. To believe that you personally are collecting wisdom and knowledge rather than realizing that the elements
are sharing their information with you is your ego at work. This
is the reason it is important to remain *receptive* when scrying or
doing any divination work; receptivity allows you to receive the
gifts of the elements. Envision looking into a crystal ball and trying
to perceive an image or a message. You are sending energy, not
receiving, and not being receptive. How can you receive messages
when you're sending energy? Allow the crystal ball to send its
message, its gift, to you.

The elements have gifts to offer. Water realizes its relation to
all water, as well as its cycles. The bowl of water you scry with
shares its consciousness with the streams and rivers, which are the
veins of the earth. The bowl of water you scry with is part of the
oceans of our earth. The bowl of water you scry with is part of the
water that is in our atmosphere. When you scry with a bowl of
water, you scry with the wisdom of all waters. Water is our force
of life. We cannot live without it. Consider that we take in this
spiritual "blood of the Earth" daily. It is the wise person who
realizes that the "waters of life" can be held in a bowl to tell us
mysteries that we alone cannot see. And so it is with each element.
As you scry with a crystal ball, you scry with the wisdom of the
Earth. As you scry with fire, you scry with the fires of the world,
even those which burn in the hearts of humankind. As you scry
with incense, you scry with the airs we have been breathing since
the beginning of time.

Runes

Runes are a set of twenty-five symbols used for divination and
insight. The actual rune artifacts, which were carved into wood,
bone, or clay, date as early as the third century, with references to
runes as early as the first. Warriors would inscribe these sacred
symbols onto their armor and weapons to ensure protection and
victory in battle. Runes were carved onto entryways to bless the
home or on cribs to bless the newborn. There were runes for the
whole of life, and gifted diviners were able to cast the runes and

interpret their lesser-known meanings for rulers and country folk alike.

Some runes eventually became letters in the Anglo-Saxon alphabet, but in and of themselves runes never became a spoken language. Instead, the language that evolved was mystical, and the runes became symbols for a wealth of information for any aspect of life. The mystical language of the runes was for clergy and gifted seers. Like looking at a painting, the runes became symbols to tell the entire picture of the future or the depths within the heart of the self.

One legend of how the runes came to be tells of the Norse god Odin moving through pain and selecting the not-so-easy path to culminate in his personal growth and receipt of the runes. Odin, the king of the gods, hung upside-down from the tree Yggdrasil for nine painful days without food or water. Yggdrasil is the great world tree which exists outside of space and time. Beneath the roots of Yggdrasil is the Fountain of Mimir, which contains secrets and wisdom. On the ninth day, Odin spied the runes and knew their secrets and then gave them to the people so they would know and learn truth. Odin was also the god of wisdom, poetry, and magick. For those who know their meanings, the runes carry with them wisdom. The word "rune" can also be synonymous to a poem with a mystical theme, and runes can be used for a focal point for Earth magick. Each of Odin's gifts became a function of the runes.

The runic function of wisdom is linked to very simple lifestyles including harvest, home, and family. The runes represent simple human qualities, ideals, emotions, and desires. This simplicity can remind us that even our most complicated problems or challenges will boil down to twenty-four basic qualities, as well as an eternal, all-knowing quality represented by the twenty-fifth rune which is blank. Educating yourself of the runic teachings will allow you to understand these basic human principles. Understanding the reason for these principles (e.g., desire for prosperity, a relationship, or spiritual growth) will in turn allow you to begin to understand yourself and how to achieve resolution of obstacles that arise.

Runes can be made of any material, and a variety can be found at occult or magickal shops. Create your own runes made of stone, clay, or wood; bottle caps can even be used. Stones can be painted or carved. Wood can be a series of sticks or chips which are painted or carved. Regardless of the style of runes you make or purchase, the symbols carry with them an element of magick because of the energy projected onto them over the centuries. Runes can be valuable to your personal growth, both magickally and spiritually.

There is not a singular, exact interpretation of the runes. The history of runes and their direct meanings have not been proven, but rather interpretations have been given through ancient poetry and writings which are open to speculation. Runes have been divided into three categories, or families, called Aett or Aettir, which have been likened to characteristics of particular Norse gods or families of gods. If you are of the understanding that all things, humans, animals, earth, waters, deities, are of one Universal principle or mind, another way to study the twenty-five runes is to break the categories into Maiden, Mother, and Crone. These are the three aspects of the Goddess. The runic families can also be termed as the three Fates, or the Muses. This is not to say that the runes are feminine; a patriarchal or masculine aspect would be to regard the runic families as Father, Son, and Holy Spirit. The number three has long been associated with divinity; it is a way for us to categorize and understand deity.

If you look at the runes as a trinity, a set of three which forms one unit, the first eight runes represent late adolescence, the Maiden aspect of the Goddess and the waxing phase of the moon. Imagine a young adult moving into his or her adulthood. The world is wide open with decisions, opportunities, desire for partnership, desire for material gain, sexuality, and creativity. The late adolescent is embarking on a journey. It is a time to learn how best to communicate with others. It is a time for young adults to test their wings. The first eight runes can be seen as the seeds of awareness.

The second set of eight runes represents the Mother aspect of the Goddess, the full moon. The Mother aspect of the second set of runes is movement into responsibility to others and the self, and full adulthood. It is coming into personal efficacy, validity, and capacity. It is illumination. In this role, the runes represent the ability to provide protection and nourishment, and begin to understand the meaning and fullness of silence and what can be gained by it.

The third set of eight runes represents the Crone, the waxing moon. The Crone is wise, having lived through a lifetime of love, sacrifice, fear, joy, magick, and pain. It is a time of having accumulated knowledge, and turning that knowledge into wisdom.

The blank rune is the culmination of the trinity of runes. It is the symbol of All that unifies the runic trinity into one. There is not a wise Crone who cannot learn from the Maiden.

The Maiden/Mother/Crone method of studying rune divination is simply a means to opening a new path to becoming intuitive with the runes. It is not a traditional way of studying or interpreting the runes, but it is helpful to see them from a new or fresh perspective.

Runes can be used for magick. Fire and Earth magick work well with runes. For Fire magick, select an appropriate rune symbol, and carve it into a twig or stick. Burn the twig or stick to release that energy on the astral plane in order that it can become real on the physical plane. If it is healing magick, Earth magick works well. While visualizing the person who requested the healing as healthy, carve the person's name into a twig or stick along with the appropriate rune symbol. Bury your magickal talisman in the Earth to be healed by the Earth's energies. Wearing jewelry with a rune carved into it can draw to you the energy of that rune, whether it is the energy of prosperity, love, work, or protection.

There are several ways to use runes for divination purposes. You can create a layout of your own design. You can use a design similar to a Tarot card layout. You can pull one rune from a bag for a specific answer to a specific question. You can pull three runes to represent past, present, and future. You can cast or throw the runes by making a circle from a cord or use a round cloth, and cast the runes to the circle. The runes that fall right-side-up within the circle are those that you will use to divine. In this last method you might want to note the number of runes from a particular trinity which fall into the circle to help you understand the aspect of the reading. If there are several from the first eight (Maiden), perhaps you are setting out on a new adventure or beginning something new such as a job or partnership. The remainder of the runes will tell you how to deal with that new beginning. Use your intuition and devise a method of casting that works for you.

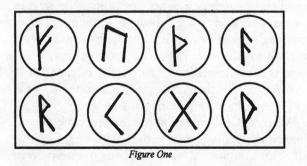

Figure One

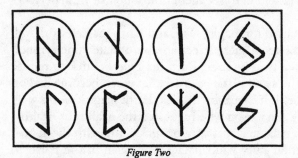

Figure Two

The All

Figure Three

The Maiden Runes in the first family of runes in Figure 1 are the following:

> *Top Row:* Earthly Wealth, Sexuality and Wildness, Discipline, and Awareness.
>
> *Bottom Row:* Journey, Openness and Creativity, Partners, and Happiness.

The Mother Runes in the second family of runes in Figure 2 are the following:

Top Row: Disturbance, Hardship, Reflection, and Harvest and Full Cycle.

Bottom Row: Transformation, Magick, Protection, and Power and Healing.

The Crone Runes in the third family of runes in Figure 3 are the following:

Top Row: Victory, Growth and Clearance, Forward Motion, and the Self.

Bottom Row: Emotions/Intuition, Balance, Satisfaction, and Integration.

The last rune represents the All.

Pendulums and Dowsing

Dowsing or using a pendulum are ancient methods of divination. Dowsing consists of using a divining rod to find an object or water within the earth. A pendulum is an object suspended above the palm of the hand or above paper which provides yes or no answers. There are still common uses for dowsing in this country today. Rural communities are quite comfortable with the use of a pendulum to determine the sex of poultry, and many communities use "water witches" as the preferred method of discovering where to place a water well. These dowsers divine the location of underground water by using a forked bough of willow, apple, or pear to guide the point to the exact spot that a well should be dug. Feed store employees will sex poultry by holding a pendulum above a selected bird. If the pendulum swings side to side, it's a cock, and a circular motion denotes a hen. These practices are current and common. Even those who doodlebug, another term for dowsing, for underground sources of oil and natural gas have been known to dowse for a spot to drill. Pendulums and divining rods are used for discovery of metals, power centers or Earth grids, and even in assisting the police in unsolved cases of missing persons.

The use of a pendulum for divination is uncomplicated and natural to most. Simply attach an object, such as a crystal, stone, ring, or pendant, to a string or chain. Hold the string or chain in your right hand so that the object is suspended over your left hand. Ask the question, "What is the motion for yes?" The pendulum will move either in a circle or back and forth. Ask the question, "What is the motion for no?" The pendulum will move in the motion that remains. The oracle is ready to be asked questions with these predetermined responses in mind.

Using a pendulum could be said to create an ideomotor response—unconscious movement of the body in response to an idea or thought. Consider the possibility that the unconscious movement is the result of the Self that knows everything giving a little nudge. Divinatory tools allow the reader to channel energy and resulting knowledge into meaningful answers.

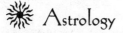 Astrology

This section contains basic information regarding how to use astrology for magickal purposes as well as for learning about the elements which help you understand other forms of divination. It is best to perform magick during astrological phases of the moon which enhance a magickal spell. For example, it is best to do spells involving the home while the moon is "in" Taurus. Although doing spells for specific purposes within the movement of the moon is not necessary, magickal workings will be much more effective if you work within that movement. Seek out books and calendars available which chart the moon's influence.

Now, imagine the moon's influence extending itself as a sign of the zodiac personified, and this personification is a friend who visits periodically specifically to help you! Create an image and, importantly, a personality for each of the signs of the Zodiac to help solidify your relationship with and understanding of that sign. It is important not to confuse this with knowing a person within a sign, as in knowing someone named Debra who is a Virgo, and attributing all characteristics of Virgo to that person named Debra. This is a persona that *you* create to help you understand how each sign can influence any magickal workings you perform. Each of these personalities within the Zodiac belongs to a family within the realm of the elements—Earth, Air, Fire, and Water, and are also known as masculine or feminine. Getting to know these families via their elements, genders, colors, and identifying personality traits will facilitate learning each individual sign, their power and influence, and which type of magick is best suited to that sign. As the moon travels through each of the signs approximately twice per month, take a couple of weeks to work with each of the personalities to get to know them.

Fire Family

Understand the attributes of fire, which are perceived as both positive and negative, and you will better understand the Fire Family within the astrological realm. Think about it. Fire can offer warmth and comfort from the hearth of a house, and a spark from that same warm fire can burn down the house within a matter of minutes. The members of the Fire Family—Aries, Sagittarius, and Leo—display characteristics of positive and negative with the quality of being fast to burn or offer warmth. Aries, Sagittarius, and Leo help with swiftness of action and have hot tempers, yet can also offer comfort in matters of the heart. Truth and honesty are methods of emotional cleansing attributed to Sagittarius. Fire also shines brightly, and no one likes to shine like a Leo onstage! Fire is also associated with the Phoenix, the mythical bird who rose anew from the ashes. Aries is the first sign of the Zodiac and very definitely a sign of rebirth. What other characteristics can you attribute to fire to give you a clear mental picture of the Zodiac personified?

Aries (March 21 to April 19). Aries is a masculine fire sign ruled by the planet Mars, named after the Roman god of war. The symbol for Aries is the ram, the gemstone is the diamond, and Aries is associated with the color red. With this in mind, your Aries ally would be a tall, attractive male in a red robe wearing a large diamond ring. Perhaps his hair would curl from his forehead like that of a ram's horns. Aries is an aggressive leader who is filled with the passion of fire. For magickal purposes, Aries assists in your magick under an Aries moon for rebirth or new beginnings (for example, starting a new life after a move or the loss of a job), assistance in following through with a goal, resolving disputes between two people, and self-confidence. Because Aries rules the face and head, doing magick for these purposes is also fruitful (i.e., headaches).

Leo (July 23 to August 22). Leo is a masculine fire sign ruled by the sun, the life-giver of the inhabitants of the Earth. The symbol for Leo is the lion, the gemstone is the ruby, and Leo is associated with the color gold. With this in mind, your Leo ally would be a vivacious, bossy male perhaps with a muscular upper body in a gold robe wearing a large gold and ruby crown (after all, the Lion has long been King!). Perhaps his hair would be like the glorious mane of a lion. Leo's attitude is that of a stereotypical, elite, pampered movie star filled with all the exuberance of theatrics and very willing to show you how to be attentive to yourself as well as pamper yourself while being authoritative to others. For magickal purposes, enlist Leo's assistance in your magick under a Leo moon for situations involving confidence, authority and courage, anything theatrical, as well as healing the heart in both physical and emotional matters.

Sagittarius (November 22 to December 21). Sagittarius is a masculine fire sign ruled by the planet Jupiter, the planet of growth, good luck, and an optimistic attitude. The Sagittarian symbol is the centaur and archer, the gemstone representing Sagittarius is topaz, and Sagittarians are associated with the color purple. With this in mind, your Sagittarian ally would be an exceedingly intelligent and well-built male with curly, dark hair, wearing an elegant purple robe who carries a topaz-studded bow to shoot his arrows. Sagittarius is optimistic and jolly, scholarly, but very blunt. He will also believe in you no matter your undertaking. For magickal purposes, Sagittarius assists in your magick under a Sagittarian moon for travel, prophesy, truth, and luck. Because Sagittarius rules the thighs and liver, doing magick for these purposes is also fruitful.

Air Family

The characteristics of the element of air, which are both positive and negative, are also true of the astrological Air Family. Close your eyes and concentrate on the qualities of air for a moment. We require air in order to live, yet breathing is an involuntary function. Perhaps during meditation we focus on air and breathing, and because of this, we can go to higher spiritual and meditative levels. When we are healthy and busy, we take breathing and life-giving air for granted. Air can bring a cooling and gentle breeze, or hurricane-force winds. The members of the Air Family—Gemini, Libra, and Aquarius—display the positive and negative qualities of air. They can either be highly aware of each moment and be enthusiastic about life, or they can become so focused mentally that their analytical natures override intuition. Gemini is an excellent communicator with keen mental capability. Libra is the sign of justice, order, and balance, and that balance includes the balance between body, mind, and spirit. Aquarius typifies the scientific method, but is also open to the creativity which the scientific mind requires. Create vivid pictures of the qualities of air to help you personify the Air Family.

Gemini (May 21 to June 21). Gemini is a masculine air sign ruled by the planet Mercury, represented as the messenger of the Gods. The symbol for Gemini is the twins, the stone is agate, and Gemini is associated with the color yellow. With this in mind, your Gemini ally would be a well-toned, aerobically fit male (from all that messenger servicing to the Gods!), wearing a yellow robe inlaid with an extraordinary display of agates. He might look like an exquisite ancient statue come to life. Gemini's eloquence cannot be matched, and his quick intellect will show you various solutions to your dilemma. For magickal purposes, Gemini assists in your magick under a Gemini moon for communication, adapting to change, new ideas, and writing. Because Gemini rules the arms, hands, and lungs, doing magick for these purposes is also fruitful.

Libra (September 23 to October 22). Libra is a masculine air sign ruled by the planet Venus, the planet of beauty and love. The symbol for Libra is the scales, the gemstone is the opal, and Libra is associated with the color lavender. With this in mind, your Libra ally would be a male who is certainly lovely to behold, wearing a lavender robe, carrying the balancing scales with chains inlaid with opals. Libra is an understanding and charming friend replete with social graces and the ability to see all sides of any disputes. For magickal purposes, Libra assists in your magick under a Libra moon for unions, artistic endeavors, harmony, balancing of body, mind and spirit, and legal matters. Because Libra rules the lower back and kidneys, doing magick for these purposes is also fruitful.

Aquarius (January 20 to February 18). Aquarius is a masculine air sign ruled by the planet Uranus, the planet of change, the unexpected, and science. The symbol for Aquarius is the waterbearer, the gemstone is the amethyst, and Aquarius can be associated with an electric blue color. With this in mind, your Aquarian ally could be a quirky-looking gent who cares more about finding purpose and meaning and delving into the mind than his personal appearance. Because Aquarius likes to be different, he doesn't mind wearing an electric blue robe and carry a beautiful water vessel inlaid with amethysts. Aquarius is an intensely friendly intellectual who is eager to share his knowledge and vision. For magickal purposes, Aquarius assists in your magick under an Aquarian moon for science, friendship, seeking visions, and breaking addictions. Because Aquarius rules the calves, ankles, and the health of your blood, doing magick for these purposes is also fruitful.

Earth Family

The element of Earth is the epitome of the feminine, creative forces, domesticity, contentment, hearth, home, and family. The Earth also shows us how to deal with the cycle of life in the renewal of spring, the abundance of summer, the changing fall, and the contemplative and restful winter. The members of the Earth Family—Taurus, Virgo, and Capricorn—certainly embody the characteristics of Earth. Each knows abundance, yet acknowledges within itself a colder side. Steady Taurus will move through the seasons, watching them change, and decide that it means things are consistent and not changing. Virgo emulates nature—everything is as it should be, but appears somewhat chaotic to a skeptical eye; therefore, Virgo is constantly trying to bring order to this seeming chaos. Capricorn takes her signal from the changing seasons, and saves for winter in a steady rhythm of preparedness. Make note of any other characteristics that come to mind which will give you a clear image of the Earth Family.

Taurus (April 20 to May 20). Taurus is a feminine Earth sign ruled by the planet Venus, Roman goddess of beauty. The symbol for Taurus is the bull, the gemstone is the emerald, and Taurus is associated with the color mauve. With this in mind, your Taurus ally would be a physically fit, exceptionally strong, attractive woman wearing a mauve robe and an emerald necklace. Perhaps she would have long, flowing hair the color of rich, dark earth. Your Taurus ally would be stable, reflective and patient, offering practical advice. For magickal purposes, Taurus assists in your magick under a Taurean moon for love and permanence in love or marriage, acquisition, the arts, and pleasure of any kind. Because Taurus rules the throat and neck, doing magick for the purpose of healing these is also fruitful.

Virgo (August 23 to September 22). Virgo is a feminine Earth sign ruled by the planet Mercury, represented as the messenger of the Gods. The symbol for Virgo is a virgin, the stone is the sapphire, and Virgo is associated with the color navy blue. With this in mind, your Virgo ally would be a slender, aerobically fit female wearing a navy blue robe and an emerald crown. Virgo's face reflects purity and her eyes reflect a wisdom beyond her years. Because of her intelligence and ability to reason, Virgo will bring an impartial fact-based solution to any emotional issues. For magickal purposes, Virgo assists in your magick under a Virgo moon for dieting and overall health issues, bringing order to your home, and stopping procrastination. Because Virgo rules the intestines and nervous system, doing magick for these purposes is also fruitful.

Capricorn (December 22 to January 19). Capricorn is a feminine Earth sign ruled by the planet Saturn, named after the Roman god of agriculture. The symbol for Capricorn is the goat or sometimes sea-goat, the gemstone is the garnet, and Capricorn is associated with a dark green color. With this in mind, your Capricorn ally would be an unwaveringly stately woman, with a secret heart of gold, in a long forest green robe wearing a large headdress bedecked with garnets. Capricorn is a matriarch who will ensure that you learn discipline or pay the consequences. For magickal purposes, Capricorn assists in your magick under a Capricorn moon for discipline, motivation, ambition, career, and money, which are all the things needed to "prepare for winter." Because Capricorn rules the knees and bones, including the teeth, doing magick to heal these areas is also fruitful.

Water Family

The feminine element of water has many qualities, both positive and negative. The most important thing to remember about water is that it takes the easiest course, flowing gently to meet with the sea, but it can also be devastatingly destructive in doing so. Because it knows how to flow and that its final outcome will be to meet the sea, water is connected with knowing, and therefore connected to intuition. Cancer, Scorpio, and Pisces demonstrate these water qualities time and again. Cancerians can display that intuition, but if they feel threatened by that intuition, their outer crab "shell" can turn to frozen ice in the form of protection. Scorpios are famous for their water sign extremes; they'll be the first to "go with the flow," and the first to turn around to let the dam break and the flood waters loose. Pisces, on the other hand, can be so sensitive to others' feelings via their intuition, it can get the better of them and cause them to drown in their own sorrows, real or imagined. What other characteristics of water can you apply to the following personalities?

Cancer (June 22 to July 22). Cancer is a feminine water sign ruled by the Moon, which influences emotion and intuition. The symbol for Cancer is the crab, the gemstone is the pearl, and Cancer is associated with the color silver. With this in mind, your Cancerian ally would be a woman perhaps with a robe of pearls, perhaps with long, flowing silver hair. Her eyes might be the blue of the ocean, and represent deep pools of wisdom beneath the surface. Cancer will be receptive and sympathetic, and then offer you shrewd, intuitive advice which will not let you feel sorry for yourself! For magickal purposes, Cancer assists in your magick under a Cancer moon for spells involving the home and letting go of unwanted emotions. Be careful, however, as spells might not work exactly the way you think they will; the crab moves sideways to get to its destination! Because Cancer rules the chest/breasts and stomach, doing magick for these purposes is also fruitful.

Scorpio (October 23 to November 21). Scorpio is a feminine water sign ruled by the planet Pluto, named after the god of the dead, the end also the gift of a beginning. The symbol for Scorpio is the scorpion, the gemstone is aquamarine, and Scorpio is associated with the color crimson. With this in mind, your Scorpio ally is a sexy woman wearing a crimson robe, with a band around her head with a large aquamarine stone at the third eye position. Her long, red hair curls mischievously around her face, sometimes hiding secret expressions. Scorpio is not afraid to let her intense emotions show in order to bully the best out of you. For magickal purposes, Scorpio assists in your magick under a Scorpio moon for power, psychic abilities, and bringing passion back to your sex life. Because Scorpio rules the reproductive organs, doing any healing magick for prostate, ovaries, uterus, etc., is also fruitful.

Pisces (February 19 to March 20). Pisces is a feminine water sign ruled by the planet Neptune, named after the god of the sea and filled with illusion and mystery. The symbol for Pisces is two fish, the stone is the bloodstone, and Pisces is associated with the color of sea foam. With this in mind, your Pisces ally would be an almost other-world creature in a robe the color of sea foam, perhaps wearing a dolphin necklace made of bloodstone. Pisces is a highly spiritual being who can see beneath your masks and armor if you have the courage to ask. For magickal purposes, Pisces assists in your magick under a Piscean moon for spiritual matters, telepathy, and dreams, as well as for musical endeavors and intellect. Because Pisces rules the feet, doing magick to heal the feet is fruitful.

Putting It Together

Once you have a feel for how the elemental families interchange within their own group, continue to further your insights by visualizing how the families interchange with one another. Begin with Air. What affect does Air have on Fire? It can either harmonize with it, or extinguish it. Air can exist without Fire, but Fire cannot exist without Air. What affect does Air have on Water? On Earth? Move through each of the elements, and see their relationship to the others in this manner.

Air: Fire
            Water
            Earth

Fire: Air
            Water
            Earth

Water: Earth
            Fire
            Air

Earth: Water
            Air
            Fire

☾ Numerology

Numbers have meaning. Each number, One through Nine, represents an aspect of a basic sociological trait such as cooperation, work ethics, family values, or spirituality. Each person has a Destiny Number, and by discovering your Destiny Number, you will have a better understanding of your life's direction. Just as you used your intuition to discover more about the elements, so too can you use your intuition to discover more about numbers. If you already understand the basics of numerology, think about what you have already learned regarding each of the numbers, and contemplate how these concepts might have come about. The number One, for example, represents confidence and leadership. If you consider that one person heads a group with confidence in order to lead it well, the number One begins to make sense. If you are new to numerology, think about the numbers One through Nine, and write down the possible meanings of the numbers. See how closely you come to the traditional meanings.

In order to determine your Destiny Number, you must reduce the numbers in your date of birth. To do this, first add the numbers together. For instance, if you were born January 1, 1960, your birthday would be reduced like so:

01 (The month of January)

+   01 (The first day of the month)

+   1960 (The year you were born)

1962

Next, add the result as follows:

$$1 + 9 + 6 + 2 = 18$$

Add the remaining results as follows:

$$1 + 8 = 9$$

Your Destiny Number is 9.

There are many aspects to numerology, and your Destiny Number is merely one aspect. Using only your Destiny Number to define your numerological self is like using only your Sun Sign (the commonly defined sign, i.e., "Leo" or "Aquarius") in astrology to define your personality when other planetary aspects and the moon comprise more than half of your horoscope. Knowing your Destiny Number, however, is still moderately definitive and useful. The following are some aspects of your Destiny Number:

One: One is the number for leadership, creativity, confidence, and attainment. Ones must learn to lead while at the same time understanding their unique qualities make up the substance of the whole. For example, a group of ten people is considered a group, but there are individuals within the group. One represents the single seed for planting. A lesson for Ones is that you needn't carry a burden alone. Ones also must learn that each ending is also a beginning. One is the Magician in the Tarot, and represents mastery over the elements.

Two: Two represents balance, duality, and the light and the dark. Twos must learn balance between male and female, between being receptive and giving. Cooperation and association with others is a lesson. Often, Twos are learning the lesson of balance so intimately that they cannot see that they are out of balance. Two is the High Priestess in the Tarot and is a number which resonates the need for awareness and intuition.

Three: Three represents manifestation. It is the single seed of One plus the balance of Two. Combining these creates unity and completion. Threes enjoy social situations and do well in jobs that involve work with people. Being social, however, leaves Threes open to being hurt, and a lesson for Threes is to know that they cannot control other peoples' thoughts or actions. Threes are excellent at manifesting through patience. In the story of the Tortoise and the Hare, the Three would be the Hare. Three is the Empress in the Tarot and represents fertility and hearth and home.

Four: While Threes manifest through patience, Fours manifest through setting their eye on a goal and doing the background work to achieve that goal. Fours are solid pillars of society. The lesson a Four must learn is to not throw himself entirely into his work or to sacrifice himself working for others. Four in the Tarot is the Emperor who stands his ground and surveys his kingdom.

Five: Change will follow Fives wherever they go. This constant change brings the lesson of adaptability and acceptance. Fives must adapt to new circumstances, whether they consciously bring change to themselves or it seems outside of themselves. Change also comes from their own boredom. Discipline, therefore, is a lesson that will follow them, and lack of discipline will create lack of freedom, something Fives dearly treasure. The Hierophant is the Five in the Tarot and represents spiritual study as well as control.

Six: Six is a number of balance and responsibility. It is also a number which will teach strength in unity. Two pillars holding up a building work better than one; four work better than two. Sixes will fight their ground rather than join with the masses, but joining with the masses is usually the better answer for them. The Lovers is the number six Tarot card and represents people with differences moving through difficulties to find strength in their differences.

Seven: This is a highly spiritual number which resonates to solitary activity. Sevens must understand their uniqueness in life, and appreciate the strength of their wisdom. It is the place where spirit and matter meet. Seven is a sacred number and comprises the musical scale, the colors of the rainbow, the days of the week, the seven chakras. Seven is the Chariot in the Tarot, riding through everything alone while seeking balance.

Eight: This is the number of earthly knowledge and strength. Eights have an amazing knack for finances, mortgages, business, real estate, and legal matters. This can be a trap, however, if used improperly. It is difficult for Eights to learn valuable lessons if they become too comfortable. Strength is the eighth card in the Tarot, representing the ability to overcome fear in order to find truth.

Nine: This number is the culmination of a long journey and represents wisdom from knowledge. Nine is the full circle and, like One, represents leadership. Whereas One represents leadership for earthly matters, such as business, Nine represents leadership in spiritual matters. The Hermit with his guiding lantern and completed journey represents the Nine in the Tarot.

This is merely a broad paintbrush approach to numerology, and intended to serve as a basis for the Tarot and other number-based tools. Further studies in numerology are definitely suggested.

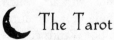 The Tarot

The earliest form of Tarot is believed to have come out of Egypt. The carriers of the cards, wanderers who were fortunetellers, musicians, and performers, were called Gypsies, who were earlier known as Gypcien, which was short for Egipcien. There is some obscurity, however, as Gypsies are also thought to have originated from India. The result is the same, however, as the Tarot spread throughout Europe in various forms, with varying levels of popularity. During the Inquisition, Tarot cards and even playing cards were forbidden to the common class.

The modern deck consists of seventy-eight cards. Twenty-two cards comprise the Major Arcana, with influence in our culture with well-known cards such as the Wheel of Fortune, The Hanged Man, and The Fool. Fifty-six cards comprise the Minor or Lesser Arcana. The fifty-two common playing cards and their suits can be found within the Minor Arcana.

The Tarot, however, is not intended for play. The Tarot is an excellent way to communicate with a part of you that is more psychic, more loving, more understanding, and a part of you that has more answers to life's lessons. The Tarot can give you a means to communicate that is far beyond your normal skills. Use of the Tarot to enhance your psychic and intuitive abilities is comparable to the use of weights to strengthen your muscles. It is very important, therefore, because you are in communication with an aspect of yourself that is in touch with the Divine, that you treat these cards with utmost respect and responsibility. The purpose of the Tarot is not mere fortune-telling. The purpose of the Tarot is to unite with an aspect of yourself that leads to showing you the purpose of the life lessons you are learning, and eventually to enable you to help others through their lessons.

You already have a basic understanding of the elements and numerology. When you apply this knowledge to the Tarot and combine it with your intuition, you're halfway home. There are four suits in the Tarot comprised of Cups, Swords, Wands, and Pentacles (or Coins). Each of these suits has a corresponding element.

The Suit of Cups corresponds with the element of water, and is therefore related to movement, change, feminine energy, and spiritual energy. The Suit of Swords corresponds with air, which sustains life and is related to taking in or breathing in information all around us so that we can internalize. The Suit of Wands corresponds with fire, representing passion, fast action, energy, speed, and warmth. The Suit of Pentacles corresponds with Earth, and therefore each card in that suit relates to prosperity, warmth, femininity, domesticity, family.

Once you learn the elemental correspondences to the cards, tie the numerological values to the elemental qualities. The Ace of Pentacles would represent a "One," which is leadership and the seed of new things, and would be combined with the element of Earth, which is prosperity. Therefore, drawing an Ace of Pentacles would tell you that there is a strong possibility of a new adventure on the horizon which is beneficial and could bring prosperity.

It becomes much easier to learn the cards as a whole. There are seventy-eight cards in the Tarot deck, and to remember the classical meanings of all seventy-eight cards as disjointed from one another is difficult. When you learn that there are four suits within the Minor Arcana, and the Major Arcana can be read intuitively, you are then learning how to integrate five pieces of information rather than seventy-eight pieces. This is much easier for the brain to categorize!

It is important to learn the classical meanings of the Tarot; however, balance is suggested. Learning to see the Tarot intuitively is an excellent way to hone your perception skills. To use your intuitive skills, go through the Major Arcana and look for symbols that speak to you. Even if you do not know the traditional meanings, write down the impressions you have of each card. Write down the mood of the card. Write down the colors in the card and what they mean to you. Examine every aspect of the card. When you are finished, compare your thoughts with the following insights into the Major Arcana, and compare your intuitions with these classical meanings. Notice whether your answers illuminate the meanings of the cards for you. See if you can more readily identify with the cards once you have finished this exercise. See if you draw life lessons from the cards, and see what the cards have *told* you.

Asking yourself questions when you look at your cards or read the following descriptions, especially about the finer details of the card, will illuminate the reason for the card being included in your reading at this moment. Why are candles in the card? Are they lit or extinguished? What time of day is it? If it is daytime, is it sunny or cloudy? What is the significance of weather in the card? Why are these symbols pertinent for this reading at this time? Asking point by point questions about the details will hone your intimate knowledge of the cards. The following observations of the Major Arcana, drawn from the Robin Wood Tarot deck, are not mere descriptions of the cards, but an attempt to illuminate the symbols which are communicating with your Aware Self.

1. The Magician: There is a strong-looking man, a Magician, who *appears* to have power over the elements as the four suits, or elements, are represented in the card. His robe has white roses on it which represent death and rebirth. Behind him are two lit candles, one black and one white, representing balance or moving between the worlds. He is wearing antlers, and perhaps possesses the quality or secrets of the Shaman. The Magician has levitated the symbol for eternity, the Alpha/Omega, the beginning and the end, and it is glowing. Interestingly, the look on the Magician's face is one of confidence; this is a man who understands the use of all in his realm.

2. High Priestess: A confident woman presents a book and a crystal ball beneath a full moon. She wears a robe, a pentacle, and a crown with a crescent moon. There are two trees behind her— one is in shadow and appears black; the other is in moonlight and is white, representing balance. The moon represents mystery, yet she apparently has the knowledge to tap into the mysteries of the moon with her book and crystal ball.

3. The Empress: A content and happy woman sits spinning. Her apparel is rich, made with expensive cloth in the royal color of purple and the color of heart and earth of green; she wears a jeweled crown. This woman personifies royalty. There is abundance around her—green valleys, summertime, a time of plenty. The spinning wheel represents cycles, and this woman is fertile and very pregnant. There is an ankh, the Egyptian symbol of life, hanging on the tree above her. She is patient in her "expecting" time, and there is an air of patience in the entire card. Things are as they should be.

4. The Emperor: A strong man is depicted clutching the arm of his throne, wearing armor and lavish purple jeweled robes and holding a scepter with an ankh at its tip. No one is moving this man from his throne. The throne itself has two birds carved into it, perhaps ravens. Perhaps these are the birds of myth which accompanied Odin on his journeys. There is also a drinking horn resting on the chair, which could symbolize the water of knowledge, or moving to a higher state of awareness through drink (not recommended). The throne is placed high on a mountain with an eagle

flying in the distance, and the Emperor's feet are symbolically resting on the world.

5. The Hierophant: The Pope with a large gold crown bedecked with jewels. His body is totally covered in fine robes of gold and red. He wears white gloves and carries a gold scepter. This is a somber man. He is pale. Two young boys kneel in front of him as though receiving blessing and instruction. The three stand within pillars in a cathedral. The pillars are carved with a female and a male (balance) and have a traveler depicted as well as an agricultural community. It doesn't appear that the Hierophant has actually seen the carvings in many, many years. He appears oblivious to anything but sacred texts and learning.

6. The Lovers: A man and a woman are naked, arm-in-arm, walking in front of a tree which is half oak, half apple. The apple tree and the woman are on the left side of the card, the female side. The woman happily carries the moon, the symbol of the Goddess, and is therefore content with carrying the feminine aspect of deity as well as the mysteries of the moon. The man is on the right side of the card, the masculine side, in front of the oak tree. The oak tree is a masculine symbol of strength. The man carries the sun, the symbol of the God. Both the man and the woman are content in their joining, moving forward together fully knowing that their union creates a whole. The sky is blue, and there are fertile valleys below them.

7. The Chariot: A handsome, fair, young man sings while playing a harp and riding a chariot drawn by two unicorns, one white and one black. The man wears the clothes of someone wealthy, and has the symbol of the sun on his breastplate. The chariot has the yin/yang symbol on it for balance. The chariot could be moving so fast so as to move through any obstacle. The downside is perhaps the chariot is moving so fast, it could be drawn by runaway horses and impossible to dismount without injury.

8. Strength: A maiden, pure and content, and dressed in white with a wreath of flowers in her hair has seemingly tamed a lion. There are flowers in the lion's mane, and the lion looks content in her arms, as she looks content holding the lion. The flowers in the mane of the lion and in the hair of the woman show a correlation between the animal and the woman, and perhaps a similarity that has removed fear and put trust in its place. The sky is blue, and

the two are under an oak tree, a sign of masculine strength. The paw of the lion is raised, as though it has been hurt. Perhaps there is an element of the "Androcles and the Lion" story, and the woman has gained the lion's trust by pulling a thorn out of its paw, and the lion allows the woman to soothe him.

9. The Hermit: A very old, white-bearded man in tattered robes carries a lantern. He stands at the apex of a tall mountain, holding the lantern and looking downward with a slight smile on his face. It appears to be a smile of understanding, wisdom, and accomplishment. His bony hand clutches a walking staff with a red feather at its tip. Red is the symbol for earth and heart, while the feather is the symbol of flying to greater heights. It is as though he is showing the light to someone else who is waiting at the bottom of the mountain, perhaps ready for their own journey. It could also be that he is content having left behind the world below.

10. The Wheel of Fortune: There is a wheel, with a silver ball traversing the outside like a roulette game, which is a gambling game, and therefore a game of chance. There is one woman who is depicted in varying stages of emotion around the wheel. This seems to signify the wheel of the year with its eight sabbats, and the cyclical nature of life. The woman starts out happy, surrounded by stars, perhaps lucky stars, and then becomes increasingly sad and depressed, but comes out of the cycle as again joyful. This card represents a beginning and an end, and a beginning again. Because the ball is shown as in motion, there is forward movement.

11. Justice: A stern and determined woman in a red robe holds a gleaming sword and scales of balance. The sword represents swift action and intellect, and the scales represent intellectual balance. Her look is wise and knowing. She stands between two pillars, and pillars hold up buildings. This woman is grounded, and she knows what she is doing. The scales are also representative of Libra, the sign of balance and harmony. Behind the woman is fertile, lush, green land and blue skies. Once her words are dispensed and justice has been served, the fertile land beyond is obtainable.

12. The Hanged Man: A man hangs on a branch between two trees with his hands behind his back. It is not known whether his hands are tied, but if he let go with his legs, he would drop to the ground. He is literally suspended, and seemingly has no choice but to hang there. Perhaps this is related to Odin hanging from the tree

to obtain the runes and their knowledge, and is therefore similar to tempering steel. The greater the heat in which steel is forged, the stronger the steel. The sky in this card is gray, but there is a white light emanating from the man's head that indicates illumination.

13. Death: A figure in a hooded red robe stands in a forest holding a large, black flag with a white rose on the flag. There is a butterfly just in front of the figure. The time of year is spring, and new plants abound in the forest. The soil is rich and brown, seemingly very fertile. It is not known whether the figure is male or female. White has long meant purity, and the rose and white trees give a feeling of renewal and regeneration. The butterfly also is a symbol of renewed life. A caterpillar could perhaps think that its cocoon was all there was to life, until it breaks loose and miraculously becomes the butterfly. As all of life is in cycles, death represents life.

14. Temperance: A man with wings, perhaps an angel, is standing with one foot in water and one foot on solid ground. He has a triangle emblazoned on his white robe. He is effortlessly juggling three shiny round objects. Sun is breaking in the distance. The water represents the spiritual aspect of this being, while the ground represents understanding how to incorporate the spiritual into the earthly realm. This man or angel incorporates both into his being. The triangle could represent the triple aspect of the Goddess— Maiden, Mother, and Crone—or because it is enclosed in a square, it could represent the base chakra and our connection to the Earth, although the symbol is upside down. The angel's ease of juggling teaches us to relax about all things, and take them as they come.

15. The Devil: While many decks depict a stereotypical devil acting as puppeteer to a man and woman, the Robin Wood Tarot deck depicts a man and a woman playing "tug of war" with a treasure chest of jewels and gold. There are monkeys carved onto the treasure chest. The man and the woman pull with all their strength to take the treasure in their direction, but the treasure chest is bound to its place with thick chains which the man and woman apparently do not see. They are in a dark tunnel with a way out. They merely need to let go of the treasure. Perhaps this up-to-date interpretation of the Devil card shows us that when faced with an obstacle that *seems* outside our control, *we do have a choice*. This leaves more room for personal growth than the traditional "chains that bind" Devil card.

16. The Tower: A tower which is many stories high is the central theme of this card. The tower has been struck by lightning and is on fire, and is apparently going to crumble. People are leaping from the top of the tower to escape its fiery grasp, yet they certainly leap to their deaths in the crashing waves of ocean water below them. They seemingly have no choice but to escape one form of death to leap to another. The sky is dark and foreboding, and it could be anticipated that the waters will not calm anytime soon.

17. The Star: A beautiful, nude, young woman with long, flowing hair kneels and pours water from two vessels into a stream. She is illuminated by a very large, bright star, which seems to symbolize guidance or divine light. Seven smaller stars encircle the main star. As with the Temperance angel, this woman has one foot in the water indicating a knowledge of the occult and all things mystical. The woman's nudity indicates purity of thought with no masks or ornamentation.

18. The Moon: A dog and a wolf stand by a pond howling at the moon. A small water creature is also acknowledging the moon in some manner. The moon, which symbolizes secrets and mystery, is being acknowledged by both a domestic dog that is wearing a collar, and a wild beast, which traditionally holds dominion in the dark night forests. The dog is known as "man's best friend" while the wolf has long been feared because of its ferocity, although cultures are now appreciating the roll of the wolf. The animals are between stone pillars and seemingly oblivious to their natural enemy nearby, indicating balance between the two. There is a path leading away from the dog and the wolf.

19. The Sun: A carefree, smiling child with blond hair rides a white pony. The sun shines brightly down upon the child, casting a golden light. Sunflowers grow large in the distance. The child has a red feather in his hair, and carries a red flag with an eagle at the top of the flag pole. The horse also represents our ability to journey farther than we could on our own. However, for all this happiness and joy, there is still a stone wall behind the horse and child, and therefore there are limitations to this joy and to the child's journey.

20. Judgment: The phoenix rising from the fire is depicted in this card. The fire is within a large cauldron, which represents the earth and the womb, where new things are created and born. The

phoenix appears to be made of flames, and there is a triumphant woman rising from the flames with the phoenix as her shadow, seemingly protecting her. The fire is so intense, it appears to be sunshine rising from behind the phoenix. This is the Self rising from lessons. This is moving through a cleansing period or difficult time to be reborn fresh and new, with new wisdom.

21. The World: A woman carrying batons in a victory pose is leaping through a wreath which appears to be another dimension. Stars light her way. The four elements of the Earth, air, fire, and water are depicted as this victorious woman's domain. She apparently can control it all, and is happy to do so. Victory and winning are hers; she has left one realm and moved successfully to the next.

0. The Fool: A young adult plays the flute and is so carefree, he walks on tiptoe just about at the edge of a cliff. The tiptoe symbolizes a lack of walking firmly on the ground. A white dog barks playfully at his heels, but holds back a bit as it probably doesn't want to go over the cliff with the Fool. White roses form a wreath around the Fool's head, again the symbol of renewal. Butterflies play about, again a symbol of renewal. It is a warm, sunny day with a pleasant breeze. The Fool represents the end of the journey, moving through each of the phases of the Major Arcana without learning a lesson. The Fool therefore represents the beginning and the end, just as the Magician does. The Fool also shows us that we shouldn't take life so seriously; after all, there will always be another beginning. (*Note: At one time, some Tarot decks had two Fool cards, one at the beginning and one at the end.*)

Use the above descriptions as well as your own descriptions to gain intuition while using your cards. For instance, the Chariot "could be moving so fast so as to move through any obstacle. The downside is perhaps the Chariot is moving so fast, it could be drawn by runaway horses and impossible to dismount without injury." How could this be applied to a reading? If you draw the Chariot in a reading, could it mean that your life is moving so fast that you are not paying attention to what is happening around you?

Once you have learned to intuit the cards, feel free to use popular layouts given with instructions with any set of Tarot cards, but see how learning how to read symbols will make an incredible difference in your ability to get true depth from your efforts.

CHAPTER V

Visualization and Ritual

Effective magick and ritual depend upon effective visualization. Visualization is a powerful tool, an anchor in magickal endeavors. It is the art of relaxing your mind enough to see situations, items, or events as you would like them to be. Visualization is limitless. You can see a friend who is not well as healthy. You can see yourself as more prosperous. You can see adverse or difficult events in your life, or even in the world, as successfully resolved. You can see your favorite parking spot at a mall. Visualization is understanding how a situation would best be resolved with effective results, and seeing those results in your mind.

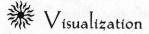 ## Visualization

Visualization is necessary for ritual so that you can create an effective circle, to be able to create a place between time and space, as well as being able to see events as you wish to have them happen. In order to learn visualization, there are a few things you have to keep in mind. The first thing that you have to learn is to relax your body. Once your body is totally relaxed, you can finally slow down your mind enough to create the pictures that you want to create. The mind literally does slow down. It has several facets of consciousness that it moves between. There are brain frequencies which differ at various levels of consciousness. The beta level is when you are actively awake doing your normal routine, and the brain frequencies associated with beta level are 14 to 21 pulses per second.

The alpha level, which is the desired level to be in while doing visualization and magickal work, is 7 to 14 pulses per second. During alpha, your body is in a relaxed state, your mind is in a relaxed state, and yet you are completely alert. The theta level is 4 to 7 pulses per second. Theta is the relaxed twilight state you experience prior to deep sleep, and it is the level you are taken to when surgery is performed. Deep sleep is the delta level which is less than 4 pulses per second.

The various levels of brainwave activity have various levels of function and use. The delta level, which is the deep sleep level, helps you to solve problems and helps you to sort through events of the day through dreams. The alpha level is the level to visualize and make things happen on the astral plane prior to them happening on the physical plane.

There are various methods for getting yourself into a relaxed state in order to move to the alpha level. Some of these methods include counting backward while consciously relaxing your body, or relaxing your body first, and then taking your brain to alpha. In order to relax your body, which is the first phase in moving to alpha, get in a comfortable position. Either sit comfortably with your back relaxed but straight, or lie down and relax, whichever is your personal preference. Sitting straight up might be best at first so that you don't fall asleep, which is easy to do until you are accustomed to alpha. Another method is to actually tape record the following paragraph so that you can have a focal point for learning and relaxing. Tape recording is beneficial as you don't have to remember as much, and you can deeply relax while listening to yourself move you into alpha and have complete trust as to what will happen next. If you choose to record the following, pause at length between sentences in order to allow your mind to catch up with your words.

First, select a spot on the wall as a focal point. Allow your body to relax completely. Take a deep breath and slowly exhale. As you exhale, relax your muscles and body. Take another deep breath and exhale. Again, totally relax your body. As you inhale, inhale clean, healthy air as a cleansing system to your body, and inhale peaceful thoughts. Allow your body to relax. Relax all your muscles. Continue breathing softly. Consciously relax your toes. Allow gravity to help you sink back into the chair or bed. Relax your heels. Relax your shins and calves. Allow your breathing to further calm you. Relax your knees, your thighs. Consciously relax the pelvis area, and all the muscles in your abdomen, and the muscles in your back. Relax your shoulder muscles. Become aware of your breathing, and allow your body to sink deeply into the chair, or bed, or floor. Let your body continually become more relaxed. Relax your shoulders and your neck muscles. Relax your upper arms and your forearms. Relax your fingers. Totally relax. Relax your facial muscles, the muscles around your eyes. Relax your forehead. Relax your scalp. Continue breathing, and with each breath continue to more deeply relax your body and allow gravity to pull you to the ground.

This is the method to totally relax your body. Recording the above paragraph will also keep your mind busy so that it doesn't drift away from the focus of relaxation.

The next step after relaxing your body is to relax your mind to a point where you can effectively visualize. This relaxed state utilizes the right side of the brain, which is the creative, intuitive side. The left side rules logic. There are many methods you can use to get to the alpha level, which is the slowing down of the brain waves. One of the methods is to count backward from ten, and allow yourself to become more and more relaxed. Another method is to use color to take you to another state, using the colors of the chakras. A method that is also nice is to visualize a rosebud. Make sure the rosebud is out and away from you, not within your own head. See the rose, a beautiful red rose. See it clearly: the stem of the rose, the leaves, the thorns, and the rosebud tightly shut. Visualize the rose beginning to bloom. With this bloom, each time the petals open, it will open another part of your brain and relax it. As each petal opens, you will feel it wash your brain and mind in total beauty. As another petal opens, it washes your brain with the wonderful, glorious scent of the rose. The flower continues to bloom, slowly opening, filling your mind with beauty.

Once the rose has fully bloomed, allow yourself to put the rose into a bud vase, and know that your mind is in alpha when you have that rose perfectly visualized. Later, when you become more adept at moving to alpha, you can simply close your eyes and visualize the rose, and it will take you immediately to alpha. This is the point you need to be at to begin doing circle, where you can visualize the rose blooming, calming your mind, slowing down your mind, totally relaxing, to the point where you have a screen within your head where you can see things happening, the magickal work you are doing. When you can be in your mind and completely make a circle.

Practice these things until you can get to that point of alpha so that you can focus on your candle magick, and you can focus on moving the energies from stones and crystals within you, so that you can focus feeling the energies of the herbs and plants that you use for healing and magickal work of any kind. Once you are good enough at achieving alpha quickly and effectively, you can move to actual ritual.

An important factor to feed your brain while you are in alpha level is that you are healthy, that you are filled with love and draw loving energy to you. You have the determination to continue with your goals, and you can literally program your mind while you are in the state of alpha to achieve any of the goals that you wish. You can also program your mind while you are in alpha to know how to do the things that will bring about successful magick intuitively. You can even talk to people on the alpha level by summoning their presence, and discussing difficult matters with them. Oftentimes, disputes can be solved in this manner.

Magick takes focus, and once you have achieved this focus through attaining the alpha level several times through discipline, your mind becomes stronger. The more you meditate, visualize, and relax your mind, the stronger you are, and the stronger your spell work becomes using visualization. You should be able to move to a state of alpha while in your waking mind. The body relaxation is a wonderful tool, but continuing to do your meditation homework will make you aware that being in alpha can come even while jogging.

Alpha can even be part of your jogging or exercise program. You will be able to jog farther simply by moving to this state. Any exercise will become easier with the proper application of your mental focus to alpha. While in alpha, you can also suggest to yourself that you will not have sore muscles as a result of "going for the burn." Other applications of alpha include talking to people. If you have a challenge in a relationship, simply move to the alpha state by visualizing the flower, or any other method which suits you best, visualize the person in front of you, and talk to him from your heart. Talking to someone from your heart will preclude any feelings of anger that accompany challenges.

☾ Ritual

There is a school of thought that says you must do ritual and magick perfectly in the traditional manner, and this magick is a scientific method by which you achieve what you desire if all the steps are taken. There is also a school of thought that the mind creates the magick, and that moving through the steps of ritual helps you to focus in order to get your mind to do the things it needs to do to create the magick. In the first method, grinding up the proper herbs and going through ritual, and burning herbs to release them into the ethers during the correct phase of the moon, are what make magick work. In the second method, each of those steps merely assist your mind to create and hold the vision necessary to achieve the same effect. There are also Wiccans who work in between the two extremes. Your personal experimentation and intuition will help you to decide which works best for you. To draw a comparison, some chefs would never go into a kitchen without their favorite recipes, following them with exacting measurements and skill. Some chefs wouldn't dream of using a cookbook, believing their intuition in the kitchen will create their best recipe yet. Both create wonderful dishes. And so it is with magick. Results of magickal spells, whether a success or failure, have been achieved by the solitary novice as well as the practiced High Magician.

Regardless of your belief in either of these two schools, your ability to visualize successfully is of utmost importance in continuing with magick. Regarding ritual, there are several major keys to performing effective ritual, and they can be broken down into the larger part as understanding why you are going to do ritual, for instance celebration of sabbat, initiation, or to perform magick. You will also have to decide how you are going to go about performing your ritual. Make a summary of what you wish to do, and create a ritual that has meaning for you. If you decide to use a ritual from a book, and something doesn't make sense to you or "ring true" for you, then it isn't a valid statement coming from your mouth. Wicca is a beautiful way of life because everything is to make *you* feel at home with the universe. So by all means . . . create a ritual that has meaning for you.

Gather the items that you need. Make sure that all the items you have collected have been blessed in order that everything within your circle, including you, is consecrated and sacred. If you use some of these items strictly for magickal purposes, they need not be blessed again. However, if you use some of the items for mundane things, they should be blessed each time you use them. These items are spoken of in Chapter II, but a partial list for your altar is as follows:

Goddess symbol, which can be a candle or statue.
God symbol, which is also a candle or statue.
A bowl of water to represent the water element.
A red candle to represent the fire element.
A bowl of salt, just a little. Perhaps it can be sea salt for the Earth element.
A cup or chalice filled with some form of liquid such as wine, water, or juice.
A pentacle (one drawn on paper is even sufficient).
Incense to represent air.

Other items which are helpful include a wand, a cauldron, a bell, an athame, and some oil for consecrating and blessing. These are bare necessities. Also, depending on any magickal workings, gather together the necessary items to perform the magick or divination, for example, Tarot cards or candles which you have prepared.

The next step is to prepare your body for ritual. In order to cleanse the body, you might want to try fasting the day of ritual. Some witches fast, but it is important to make sure that you are healthy with no disorders which would prevent you from fasting comfortably. Even a four-hour fast is helpful.

A ritual bath is also a manner in which to cleanse, bless, and prepare your body and mind for ritual. Draw your bath water, and collect incense, a little sea salt, a candle, and oil you have prepared as well as a small bit of blessed water.

Hold the incense and say, "I bless and consecrate this incense that it may cleanse my body, mind, and spirit." Then imagine energy from the Goddess or universe flowing through you to the incense as you light it. Hold the incense over the bath, visualizing it cleansing the water. Bless the water with words similar to, "This water be blessed and cleansed of all impurities with the element of air that it be fit to cleanse my body of its impurities." Let the incense burn.

Bless the salt, which represents Earth in the same manner as the incense. Sprinkle the salt into the bath water. Bless the candle, which represents fire in the same manner, light it, and pass it over the bath water with words of blessing. Bless the water and sprinkle it into the bath water. When you add each of these to your bath water, be keenly aware of what each is for. The incense is for the air, the east, and being clean and light and spiritual. The salt is for connection to our Mother Earth—and treading softly over her. The water is for the mystical elements, and represents the west and is a strong spiritual cleanser. The candle represents the fire element and the south, and is to purify you and your thoughts, and give you energy. Lastly, pour a small amount of the consecrated oil into the bath.

During your bath, concentrate on your upcoming ritual, thank each part of your body for the work it is doing for you, and bless each chakra. (More information about chakras is in Chapter VII.) Each person experiences a slightly different ritual bath. Mostly it is a time of purifying and cleansing. And chiefly, it is a time for blessing and loving yourself. You can also place crystals or stones in your bath water to help you meditate and achieve alpha level.

In lieu of a ritual bath if time is short, you can bless yourself or smudge yourself with incense, which you can make for this specific purpose, or you can certainly purchase common incense at a store, or use a small sage bundle. It is best to use the ritual bath rather than incense for regular sabbats or full moons, as the cleansing has to do with bathing yourself in the waters of intuition and fully relaxing your body and releasing the tensions of the mundane world.

The smudging process is simple. Bless the incense or sage, and then bless and cleanse yourself by smudging, which is fanning the smoke from the incense toward you. The following concentration points for smudging are the seven chakras. "Lord and Lady" are used with respect to requests to bless yourself, but feel free to use any deity or idea with which you feel comfortable. Deities named can include Diana, Cernunnos, Isis, or even God or Jesus the Christ if you are so inclined. If you feel more comfortable with an idea rather than a deity, feel free to say, "the wisdom of the universe," or "the wisdom of the All." All entities or religions stem from the same creative force of the universal energy. While guiding the smoke to the seven major chakra centers, state the following:

While guiding smoke to the top of your head, the location of your seventh major chakra, say words similar to, "I bless and cleanse my seventh chakra so that I will be open to the wisdom of the Lord and Lady, as well as to understand how to best use this wisdom."

While guiding smoke to just below the center of your forehead, the location of your sixth major chakra or third eye, say words similar to, "I bless and cleanse my third eye in order that I be open to the visions of the Lord and Lady, and will see what I need to see."

While guiding smoke to the throat, the location of your fifth major chakra, say words similar to, "I bless and cleanse my throat chakra, in order that I communicate to the Lord and Lady that which I need to communicate, both in words expressed and wisdom to be heard."

While guiding the smoke from the incense to the heart, the location of your fourth major chakra, say words similar to, "I bless and cleanse my heart chakra, in order that I express the love of my highest good and do work from the highest good of my heart, in order that this love be felt by the Lord and Lady, and that I feel the love coming from them."

While guiding smoke to the upper abdomen, the area of the third chakra, say words similar to, "I bless and cleanse my power center in order that I manifest and go forth with an understanding of the purpose of my personal power, which is an aspect the Lord and Lady manifested in me."

While guiding smoke to the area below the naval, the area of the second chakra, say words similar to, "I bless and cleanse my creative and sexual center in order that my creativity best represent that aspect of myself which is the Lord and Lady."

While guiding smoke to the base of the spine, the area of the first chakra, say words similar to, "I bless and cleanse my base chakra so that I might better understand my relationship to our Mother Earth."

Words similar to these can also be used to meditate upon while taking your ritual bath as a means to moving you to the alpha state.

After your bath or smudging, prepare yourself in whatever manner makes you feel different from your daily self. In other words, don any ritual garb you made for the event, or wear something that is made of natural fiber or any natural clothing that makes you feel really good about yourself and different from how you feel every day. Perhaps enhance yourself with jewelry, or a different perfume from your usual one. Use items or perfume that you save separately which is especially for ritual.

After you finish preparing yourself, you are then ready to bless and make sacred the area where your circle and ritual are going to be performed. The steps to making your sacred area include selecting the area for your circle, sweeping the area clean of negativity, marking the quarters, physically creating your circle, and then bringing energy to your circle. The circle is a magickal and sacred place between time and space. There is a marked difference between the boundaries of that which is inside and that which is outside of a circle. The four cardinal points represent the elements, archangels if you wish, and the marking of the seasons. The aspect of the four quarters being the seasons accounts for the "between time" aspect of a circle. Physically completing your circle within the confines of the four quarters represents the totality of universal energy and also represents our Mother Earth, and completes the aspect of the circle being between space.

In selecting the area for your ritual, it's nice to be outside so that you can be in touch with the natural forces, but if you can't make it outside, simply clear enough space inside. If you are outside, be safety conscious. Select an area relatively free of tall grasses or plants, and clear away any loose stones. You will need to be able to walk in your circle without tripping. If you are in an unfamiliar area or campground, dowsing for a power spot can be beneficial. Simply use a "discarded," small branch shaped in a Y. Delicately hold the ends of the two branches and point the long end of the branch down toward the ground. Take your mind to the alpha level, then walk until the branch seems to be lightly tugging toward the earth. This light tugging sensation will indicate you have found your space for ritual. If you cannot be outside for ritual, find space inside where you will not be disturbed. Don't forget to unplug the phone or turn off its ring. Being disturbed by a loud ring that you have no intention of responding to can be highly aggravating while performing ritual.

Once you find your sacred place, sweep the area clean of negativity with your broom. If you don't have a broom, use your hand just as you would a broom. As your right hand is the hand which sends energy, your right hand is the preferred hand to use. Move into the alpha state, and visualize the area being gently swept clean of any negativity with your broom or hand. Continue with the sweeping of your sacred ritual space as mentioned in Chapter II.

After you have swept your ritual space of negative energies, mark the four cardinal points of the compass with items of your choosing. Gather four larger stones for the quarters, and place the stones at due north, south, east, and west. The quarters can also be marked with flowers, pinecones, or fist-sized crystal clusters if you have them. It is important that you find due north, as that is where your north stone should be, and due north marks the direction your altar should face. If it is absolutely safe, you can use candles for the elemental directions. Green for north, yellow for east, red for south, and blue for west. If colored candles are lacking, use white. Incense can be used, or you can use crystal clusters the size of your fist to mark the quarters, which adds considerable energy to your circle. Use items that suit your personality or the occasion to represent the quarters. The quarters have been represented by everything from sticks to elaborate standing altars honoring the elements at each cardinal point. The end result, however, should be that your altar and the north stone face due north.

The remainder of the circle can be created from a cord which you have made specifically for that purpose, or draw a circle into the earth, or form a circle with flowers, stones, or crystals you have collected. Pinecones or any other natural item available to you can be used. The circle should be within the four cardinal points.

It is time to build energy for the circle. You are about to make an energy grid on the earth which is the approximate area of your circle. Energy within the circle is created by walking the circle with blessed items representing each of the elements— salt for the earth, incense for air, a red candle for fire, and water for, well, the water element.

The first item is salt to represent Earth. Move into alpha level, then take up the salt, and lightly sprinkle it around your circle. It doesn't have to be a thick line as you might have seen in a movie. Moving in clockwise fashion around the circle, say something similar to, "In the name of the Lady and of the Lord, I do bless this circle and create this protected area filled with the powers and energies of the Earth with this salt of the Earth." Continue to walk the circle repeating that statement several times.

Next, take up the incense which you have blessed, and walk around the circle creating further energy and building energy, stating, "I do here and now walk this circle with the element of air to protect my circle with the properties that air has to offer. I bless this circle with the element and powers of air."

Next, take up the red candle which you have blessed, and light it. Walk the circle again. Each time you walk the circle, feel energy building within the circle, creating your personal universe, a universe between space and time. Walk the circle with the candle, and say something similar to, "I do here and now bless this circle with the element of fire." You can use any other words that honor fire in order to continue to feel the circle's energy building.

Next, pick up the water which you have already blessed, and lightly flick the water from your hands, or use an oak leaf or pine branch. Move around the circle while stating, "I do here and now bless this circle with the energy of the sacred waters of the world."

You have well prepared your sacred space, and it is time to actually seal your circle. Once you seal the circle with your athame or wand, do not leave the area until the seal is broken, or until you cut a doorway with your athame which you can again seal after you have completed your business outside the circle. To seal your circle, move into alpha and take up your athame or wand, and walk to the north stone or crystal. Create the circle by feeling the energy move through you. Visualize the energy. Feel the energy move through the top of your head, down to your arm, and through the wand. Walk clockwise while visualizing a strong, bright white or neon blue ring around the circle created by your wand. Watch the circle grow until the final outcome is like a bubble that completely surrounds you. It's not a dome that is over the area you are working, but a bubble that also penetrates the ground and is beneath you. As you walk, state the following words or words like, "By the power of the Goddess and of the God, I do hereby create this place of perfect love. This circle does here and now represent all the loving powers of the Goddess and of the God and of the universe. This circle does here and now form a protective circle in which no harm can spring from nor enter into. By the powers of the Goddess and of the God, this circle is now sealed." When you are finished sealing your circle, place the wand back on the altar.

The next step is to call the watchtowers, which are the four cardinal directions of north, east, south, and west. There have been many beautiful rituals written to call the quarters. Most of them are very poetic and conjure images of beauty and strength from our Mother Earth. The watchtowers protect and help us during our works of magick. Use the following words or create your own, but use your knowledge of the elements gained from the astrology section to learn the energies of the quarters and create your own words to call the quarters.

Move to the north. The north represents our Mother Earth and her strength. When you call the watchtowers of the north, you are calling the same energies as Taurus, Virgo, and Capricorn. These are the energies of love, integrity, particularity, and success and money (money merely being the form of energy used on Earth which suggests well-being). Green is the color which predominantly represents the Earth, which is the color of the heart chakra. With your wand in your right hand, raise both hands in a V high above your head. Visualize the color green. Call the north watchtowers with words of your own, or the following words:

Guardians and watchtowers of the north, come to us from the mystic midnight of your soft, green, fertile fields. Bring us the energy of Earth from your rolling hills, towering mountains, powerful stones, loving crystals, and secret caves. Be sentry to us as we celebrate this [sabbat or full moon or other event].

Feel the energy move to the northern part of the circle. Once you have sensed the presence, which will feel something like someone with a very, very strong character having walked into the room, lower your wand and move to the next quarter.

Move to the east with your wand, and visualize the color yellow, which is the color representative of air. When you call the watchtowers of the east, you are calling the same energies as Gemini, Libra, and Aquarius. These are the energies of communication, balance, intellect, the mind, and the future. Call the east watchtowers with words of your own, or the following words:

Guardians and watchtowers of the east, come to us from the mystical dawn on your quiet, gentle breezes. Bring us the energy of air from the lofty clouds, dancing through green trees, hissing through the great plains, and swirling across this field. Be sentry to us as we celebrate this sabbat.

Feel the energy move to the eastern part of the circle. Once you have sensed the presence, lower your wand and move to the next quarter.

Move to the south. Hold your wand high and visualize the color red, which is the color representative of fire. When you call to fire, you are calling the same energies of Leo, Sagittarius, and Aries. These energies represent passion, quickness of action, optimism, pride, spiritual endeavors, and prophecy. Call the south watchtowers with words of your own, or the following words:

Guardians and watchtowers of the south, come to us from this spellbound midday with your passionate red flames. Bring us the energy of fire from your scrying embers, playful candles, healing hearth fires, and raging forest infernos. Be sentry to us as we celebrate this sabbat.

Feel the energy move to the southern part of the circle. Once you have sensed the presence of the watchtower, lower your wand and move to the last quarter.

Move to the west with your wand. Hold the wand high and visualize the color blue, which is the color representative of water. When you call the west, you are calling the same energies of Pisces, Cancer, and Scorpio. These energies are intuition, change, creativity, mystery, power, and intensity. Call the west watchtowers with words of your own, or the following words:

> Guardians and watchtowers of the west, come to us from the enchanted twilight of your gentle blue waters. Bring us the energy and intuition of water from your kindly streams, tame rains, lovely falls, and tumbling oceans. Be sentry to us as we celebrate this sabbat.

Calling the quarters brings to you the energies of (1) love, integrity, particularity, success, and money from the north, (2) communication, balance, intellect, the mind, and the future from the east, (3) passion, quickness of action, optimism, pride, spiritual endeavors, and prophecy from the south, and (4) intuition, change, creativity, mystery, power, and intensity from the west. These are brief summaries of the energies of the quarters, and you haven't even called the Goddess and the God yet! This is the power that is available to you from the universe. Use it wisely. After you have called the quarters, return to the altar in order to call the Goddess and the God.

Center and balance yourself by meditating on the energies of the Goddess and the God. The Goddess can be a nameless female figure, as the God can be a nameless male figure if you wish to honor them simply as God and Goddess. You can also select a pantheon for this purpose, which is any order of deities within a specific system. You can choose from the Greek or the Celtic pantheon, or you can select the Egyptian pantheon. You can use whatever feels comfortable to you. If you have a candle set up for the Goddess and a candle set up for the God, you will be lighting these candles in order to align yourself with the light and love that is the Goddess and the God.

Bringing the Lord and Lady into the circle is simply asking

them to come and help you with your ritual, and let them know that you enjoy their company and want to work with them. It is a good time to feel how they enter the circle and how you feel they are entering into the circle. Just talk to them and let them know that you want to feel their presence. You can create your own poem honoring each of them for this purpose, or you can use one from a number of books. Creating your own poem will help you get to know them and build a relationship with deity. You will feel a lot of joy and love from doing your own work rather than reciting someone else's. You will also feel comfort and strength.

Light the candle representing the Goddess, and then meditate a moment on Her presence. Stating anything from your heart for the purpose of your circle. Repeat this procedure with the God. You can also become as dramatic as you like. If you are out in the middle of the woods and no one can hear you, you can call to the God and the Goddess at the top of your lungs. Yes, the treetops might stir a bit with unexpected breezes during this procedure!

Once you have called the Goddess and the God into your circle, let them know what you're here to celebrate, whether it be Midsummer, Samhain, or the full moon. Also, introduce yourself. Let them know, "It is I, _____ [use the magickal name which you have selected for yourself]. I honor you and celebrate this sabbat with you, and am here to work magick of the purest intent for the good of All."

At this point you can celebrate if the purpose of the circle is for sabbat or to acknowledge the full moon. If it is for sabbat, research the purpose of the sabbat and write a poem honoring it. If it is a full moon, find out which moon it is, and write a poem or create a chant or do some drumming to honor the purpose of that particular full moon.

Now it's time to work the magick. It might be candle magick or stone magick or knot magick, or any kind of magick that you feel is appropriate to the outcome you desire. To put your thoughts in order, the first magickal working should always be to visualize yourself becoming stronger and more in tune with the universe. It helps you to become more psychic, intuitive, and loving. While in alpha, bless and light some incense for yourself, saying something like, "This incense represents all that I am, and all the good of which I am capable. I send this as a message to the Goddess and the God that I am ready for my happiest of blessings, and to receive further gifts of intuition and capacity for talent, for the good of All and by the will of me. So be it." Meditate on the incense as it burns. Know that it represents your will moving into the universe to unfold your highest good.

Any magick or divination work can be performed now, followed by the raising of power and energy. Raising power can be done by dancing, chanting, or even meditating. Release the energy into the universe when you feel the moment is appropriate. Let yourself feel the energy drift away and move outward.

After your magickal workings, it is time for cakes and wine (or juice or water). Bless the juice or wine, stating it is representative of the waters of the Earth, and a token of our faith that we will never thirst. Pour a little into the Earth to represent that you will always give of yourself to the Goddess and the God. Bless the cake stating it represents the Earth, and leave a little behind. Cakes and wine will help to ground you. After drifting about in meditation, alpha, and magickal workings, you need something to pull you back to the Earth plane!

Once you are done with cakes and wine, you can thank the deities, the Goddess and the God, for joining you. Bid the Goddess farewell, and extinguish her candle. You can use words you choose, or something similar to, "Thank you, Lady, for joining this circle and for the blessings received in our work together. I bid you farewell." Bid the God farewell by extinguishing his candle in the same manner, using similar words or words that you create.

Close the circle by saying farewell to the quarters. Move to the north quarter and say something similar to, "Mystery of midnight, energy of north and Earth, return ye to your home. We thank you for your watchful work and bless you as you go." Move to the east quarter and say something similar to, "Mystical dawn, energy of east and air, return ye to your home. We thank you for your watchful work, and bless you as you go." Move to the south quarter, and say something similar to, "Spellbound midday, energy of south and fire, we thank you for your watchful work, and bless you as you go." Move to the west quarter, and say something similar to, "Enchanted twilight, energy of west and water. We thank you for your watchful work, and bless you as you go." Each time you make the statement of departure to the quarters, sense the energy leave the area.

Physically close the circle by taking your wand or athame to the north again. Pierce the circle's "wall" at the waist level, and move clockwise around the circle. Some witches move counter-clockwise or widdershins—do what feels right for you. Visualize the power being sucked back into the wand or athame, literally being pulled back into the wand or handle of the athame as you walk. Sense the circle moving right inside either tool in order that the outside world can reclaim its dominance in the area. As you walk, say words similar to, "I do here and now open the seal of this circle which was a place between time and space. As this circle is opened, the power remains with this wand. Blessed be." When you arrive at north again, the circle is no more.

Once the circle is done, you wash any plates and glasses and put away any of the tools that you used for circle.

🌿 Astral Circles

Some of the most effective circles actually take place in other than the physical world! During meditation, move yourself to a special place that you have created, perhaps in a woods or near the ocean. Visualize an entire altar, and either bring the tools from the physical world with you or create astral tools. Use these tools to bless yourself, bless the ground, create a circle, call the quarters and elements, invoke the God and Goddess, work magick of any kind, have cakes and wine, say goodbye to the God and Goddess, say goodbye to the elements, and close the circle. You will see how this empowers you to better understand and use your tools on the physical world. While you are doing this, see the elements, see the boundaries of the circle as laser light, smell the incense, taste the cakes and wine, see the energy leave to do your bidding as you do magick and work with your tools on the astral level.

☀ Visualization and Magick

Learn as much as you can about the mind and how it works. Learn as much as you can about magick and how it works. Some witches treat magick like a science to be learned as a series of steps; some treat magick like an intuitive art. Both methods have brought stunning results. An example of the difference between science and intuitive art is the Tarot. If you study the Tarot, you can learn the classical meanings of seventy-eight cards and your Tarot readings will be very effective. However, you can also learn to read symbols, and become intuitive about what the symbols within the cards mean when applied to a certain individual. Your Tarot readings will still be highly effective.

The most important aspect is to begin a library for research and recording. Discover for yourself which method works best for you. Many witches have extensive libraries containing everything from grimoires (spell books) and herbals to books on various religions. Witches are students of the universe and take their studies seriously. Whether you are drawn to Wicca as an expression of religion or spirituality, or to magick as a tool to assist with success and happiness in life, it is very important to create your personal system of study.

An important method of keeping your records is to keep a journal of your magickal workings listing results, astrological phases, sabbats, and any other record-keeping information. Journals and record keeping can be kept in separate volumes of three-ring binders with a separate binder for herbs, a separate binder for spells, a separate binder for meditations, or any other workings in which you are involved. These journals and binders will become your Book of Shadows, your witch's spell books, and the legacy of your life in magick.

CHAPTER VI

Herbs

In ancient times, there would be one person in a community who was experienced with herbs. This person would know how to use plants and herbs for physical healing of maladies from the common cold to more mysterious, threatening diseases. The herbs would be taken internally as medicine. The town herbalist would also employ a distant cousin to aromatherapy, popular in the Middle Ages, to create much-sought-after oils intended to help the body, mind, and spirit. This person would also, however, know how to use herbs for magickal workings, creating incenses or tinctures in order to bring love or prosperity into someone's life, or to help him or her obtain a good year of crops.

Today there are three distinct areas involved in the study of herbs and plants. These include herbalists who work for physical healing, aromatherapists who help with physical healing as well as the mental and spiritual aspects of life, and the magickal herbalist, who uses herbs and plants in a variety of ways to bring about positive change. As with many fields, specialization has evolved in the herbal realm. The physical herbal practitioner, the aromatherapy practitioner, and the magickal practitioner all have quite different views of the use of herbs.

The herbal practitioner is likely to give you echinechea for a cold or other internal remedies for serious illness, as well as advise on diet and lifestyle in order to help you achieve optimum health. The aromatherapy practitioner is likely to give you an aromatherapy massage for relaxation and to relieve stress, offer treatments for physical healing, and even to use essential oils to open spiritual centers within your consciousness. The magickal practitioner is likely to give you a poppet (doll) which has been charmed and filled with particular herbs which represents your body being filled with the healing herbs in order to heal your body, bring prosperity, and even change your life.

Bringing herbs into your life for any of these purposes is an excellent way to begin to have respect for our Mother Earth and become more connected with Her. We within the human species are varied and have respect for each other's talents, such as acknowledging our differences. Compare the different feelings when thinking about a doctor, an actor, a teacher, or a carpenter: each of these individuals provides a vital service to our community. Regardless of this soul's purpose on earth, there is respect for each purpose. So too can you gain respect for the talents, abilities, and purpose of each plant within the plant kingdom. As we each have our own specialty or purpose, so too do the plants. Awakening to these other abilities will help you to see the plant kingdom with new eyes. Not only are they beautiful and furnish us with oxygen, but they also teach on the body/mind/spirit level.

If your intention to work with herbs is to become more familiar with their healing properties from taking them internally, there are certainly many herbals available for your benefit in learning these techniques. A new term has come to light—*complementary* medicine. Herbal healing work and other ancient practices which are not mainstream scientific medical practices have become known as *complementary* rather than *alternative*. This term suggests the combining of ancient and new methods for healing rather than selecting one over the other. Combining the scientific knowledge of the modern physician with the wisdom of the ancient herbalists and healers can offer a broad range of choices and give you a high sense of involvement during your healing path. Although it is your choice, *complementary* healing techniques for any illness can be used by both seeing your doctor and treating any illness with herbs. Because these are *complementary*, be sure to tell your doctor the herbal procedures you practice in conjunction with his or her procedures.

The following contains information on sachets, poppets, pillows, wreaths, oils, and incense. These are the most common uses for herbs and plants within the magickal spectrum, and can work with or without ritual. Any work you do with herbs, however, should be done with a loving spirit, for the good of yourself, and for the good of others, and definitely with reverence and thanks to the herbs and plants you are using. Chapter VI deals with the magickal level, although there are some physical tips for the most common of ailments.

☀ Charming, Charging, or Enchanting

Regardless of the herb you are working with or the purpose for the work, any magickal working should include the first step of infusing the herb with your personal purpose for the use of the herb. This is called charming, charging, or enchanting. To charge a plant or herb, first hold the plant or herb in your hand, and send it thanks and let it know that you appreciate its help in your magickal endeavors. Move yourself to the alpha level. Allow your body and mind to relax, and become receptive to the universe. Visualize universal loving energy and power, which can be in the form of white light moving through the top of your head or your seventh chakra and filling your body with the white light. Mix the intention of your charging the herb with this light within your body. If you are charging an herb for prosperity, fill yourself with the feeling of being relaxed and prosperous. Allow this energy to move out your arm, through your hand, and into the herb. Sense the herb growing with your intention and energy. This can be accompanied by a short phrase such as, "I fill this ginger with the light and love of the universe, and with the specific purpose of sending my intention for prosperity into the universe. This will complete my magickal intention."

Each herb or plant you work with should be filled with this magickal intention, and charged with it using an incantation to accompany your intention. The process should be the same for each, including, (1) giving thanks to the herb, (2) moving to the alpha level and filling yourself with light and intention, (3) allowing this light and intention to move into the herb for your personal purposes, and finally, (4) accompanying that intention with your incantation. If you are using more than one plant or herb for any magickal working, each herb and plant should be charged individually. This technique can also be used in the kitchen to bless herbs used in cooking. Your food can become a source of spiritual nutrition and energy.

☾ Sachets

The sachet in general is a bag of herbs which can be either a drawstring bag or one that is sewn. Sachets have become readily available in small boutiques and card shops, sewn in cute little hearts with lace around them and filled with flowers and aromatic plants. A close relative of a sachet is simply potpourri, which is left in an open bowl rather than enclosed in cloth. Both sachets and potpourri mixtures can become more than their original intent of creating a nice scent for your home. The herbs and plants that you choose to fill either a sachet or a bowl with can have meaning, significance, and alter the vibrations in your home.

Sachets can be made for a variety of reasons limited only by your ability to imagine. They can be made to draw luck, to bring love, to make your cooking turn out well, or to create a pleasant atmosphere in your home. Sachets can be very simple, or quite elaborate decorations. Their magickal intention is of a broad, sweeping nature, and therefore they have less specificity to their magickal purpose. For example, creating a sachet to lighten the environment in your home will not necessarily prevent two toddlers from fighting over toys; however, the tense atmosphere in the home after the fight will dissipate more quickly.

To make a sachet, simply find a piece of cloth with the color to correspond to the intent of your sachet—for instance, pink for peace in the home—and find some corresponding herbs or plants which would work for peace. These herbs or plants should be dried properly prior to making your sachet. Dried roses, gardenias, and basil work well for peace. Charge these herbs and plants. Place the dried herbs and plants into the center of the cloth. Pull all the corners together, and wrap ribbon or string around the joining part of the cloth. While wrapping the ribbon around the sachet, visualize your desired goal. For instance, if you wish love in your life, as you wrap the string around the cloth, visualize yourself being surrounded in love. Your final product will look like a small sack. The size of this sachet can vary from something that you can carry with you in your pocket, to a larger sachet that can also work as an unobtrusive decoration in your home.

A more complicated sachet can take the shape of the effect that you intend to achieve. If you want to have a more peaceful atmosphere in your home, you can do a bit of quilt work, and make the symbol for peace on a sachet and fill it with the appropriate herbs or plants, such as gardenia or rose petals. If you want to bring more love into your life in general, you can make a heart-shaped sachet, sew the ends of it, and even trim it in lace. Fill this sachet with lavender, raspberry leaves, strawberry leaves, or any combination thereof. To create a sachet for power at work, you would sew together two yellow circles to represent the sun (power), and fill them with cinnamon, gardenia, and pine. Sachets work just as well out of sight, such as in your desk drawer at work, in case you don't want them noticed.

Poppets

The poppet is a small, simply sewn doll, as simple looking as a gingerbread cookie. The poppet can be as small as six or seven inches, and is sewn out of material corresponding to a color to achieve the effect that you wish, such as green for healing or love, or yellow for power. The doll is then filled with charmed herbs and plants in order to achieve and draw to you the effect desired. It is important to note that poppets are not voodoo dolls. As with any magickal working, the Wiccan Rede should be fresh in your mind: "And ye harm none, do what ye will." Although poppets and voodoo dolls are sister forms of magick, the intention is entirely different.

Use the poppet for a focal point to send your intention to the doll while creating the magick. As you cut the material into human shape, visualize the person who needs the magick. See the person as clearly as you can; see their facial features, their hair, the kind of clothes they wear. As you sew the poppet, visualize that which you are trying to attract being sealed within the person. If you are doing healing magick, visualize while sewing that you are actually sealing in good health and creating a protective shield around the person. Leave a small area open at the top of your poppet. Charge the herbs appropriate to the magick that you are doing, and fill the person with these herbs. While you fill the poppet, build energy by visualizing this person being filled with the energy it takes to heal, the energy it takes to draw love, the energy it takes to be prosperous, or the energy it takes to become powerful.

If you are using more than one type of herb or plant, there are a couple of methods with which to do this. You can individually put the herbs into the poppet, and concentrate on the intent of those herbs as they go into the poppet. For instance, if someone wants you to do magick for them to have many aspects of their lives changed, you can stuff the poppet with power, love, and peace. Visualize each of these qualities with each herb as you stuff the poppet. The other method is to mix the herbs with a mortar and pestle, and crush them prior to putting them into the poppet, but stirring them together for a unification of these qualities within one person. While you put the herbs into the poppet, visualize the qualities desired. Both methods are effective. Some prefer one over the other. It is your experimentation (preferably on yourself) and notes which will help you decide which method works best for you.

An excellent love poppet, for yourself or a friend who requests it, consists of pulling together ingredients representative of the person whom you want to attract. This is not intended to draw a particular person whom you've set your eye on, but rather to draw a person who is supposed to be with you, a person who shares your interests and lifestyle. In fact, ensure that your spell does not attract any one, single person toward you, but rather allows the Goddess room to work to find and bring to you the One who is right for you. The draw for love should be specific, yet ambiguous; your results will be beyond anything you could possibly have imagined. This particular love poppet takes quite some doing, as you have to eat a lot of strawberries over a period of time to get plenty of strawberry leaves.

Begin in the late spring, which is the beginning of the season for strong magickal workings to bring things to you. Each time you eat strawberries, make a mental note that you are bringing fruit into your body which will attract love. Save the leaves that form the tip of the strawberry, and allow them to dry somewhere where they will not become brown or bruised on one side. Perhaps you can place them on a small screen or rack which allows air to flow through to the leaves evenly. You can also place them on a paper towel, as they tend to curl enough to allow air through them naturally.

Also collect for your poppet herbs representing the person you wish to attract. An important feature of this spell is knowing exactly what you want. A joking comment regarding love spells is that people can easily determine what they don't want. It is just as important to know what you do want. This form of magick, if you are performing it for yourself, works on the principle that you are filling yourself, meaning the poppet, with the aspects you want to draw to you. If you want the relationship to be passionate, put a little ginger root into the poppet. If you want a spiritual partner, use some gardenia petals. If you want someone who is a leader, put a little frankincense into the poppet. If you would rather have the creative type, stuff the poppet with some benzoin. The basic ingredients of this poppet should be the strawberry leaves that you collect over a period of time. Of course, if you're in a hurry, you can have strawberries every night for a month, serve them to guests, or do anything imaginable to collect the strawberry leaves!

The next step is to select green or pink material, which represents the heart. Make a cutout of a human shape, which doesn't have to be any more elaborate than something that looks like a paper doll or a gingerbread cookie. This cutout of material will represent you or the person for whom you are working magick. Move into alpha, and cut the shape out while visualizing yourself, and also visualize each aspect of yourself that you feel strongly about. In doing so, you are also sending the message out stating the kind of person you are in order to attract the person who will like your qualities as well. Fill the poppet with the items which represent who you want to draw to you while visualizing this person. Alternate the herbs and plants with the strawberry leaves, and focus on each aspect of the person as you fill your poppet. For example, do a layer of pine needles if you are attracting wealth or a person who is looking for growth (you can make this spiritual growth, personal growth, etc.). Make sure that you focus on the purpose of the herb or plant for the particular purpose you wish, as herbs have many focal points. Place in the poppet a layer of strawberry leaves. Next, place a layer of chamomile if you want to attract a gentle type, and then another layer of strawberry leaves. Each time you add a layer, focus on the aspect of the personality you wish to draw which corresponds to the herb.

Another aspect of poppet magick is to put the type of plant or herb that corresponds to the body near that body part of chakra. For instance, if you want a very passionate relationship, you can put ginger or lavender near the second chakra area of the poppet. Follow with the layer of strawberry leaves. If you want to draw someone to you who is artistically talented or in an "artsy" profession, place ground orange peel near the hands as a symbol to you of artistic pursuit. If intelligence is important, fill the head of your poppet with horehound, sage, or benzoin. (See Chapter VIII, "Guide to Spells," for more ideas.) The point is to fill your poppet with the intent of drawing to you aspects of a personality that you would like for a long-term companion. You can create the poppet prior to ritual, and then bless the poppet during ritual and place it in a prominent place within your home to send energies to it. You can also choose not to do ritual, but merely send your energies to the poppet on a daily basis.

To make the poppet symbolize yourself, dress it with something representing a symbol for you. If you are a female who wears bows every day, place a bow on the head of the poppet. If you wear skirts much of the time, make a skirt for the poppet. If you are a male who wears a ponytail or an earring, sew some yarn onto the poppet and tie it in the back for the ponytail and place an earring on the poppet (no, your ear won't start to bleed if you pierce the poppet!). You might sew or draw your astrological glyph onto the poppet. Make this poppet personally represent you, and give it some personality of your own. This process will also allow you to visualize more strongly that this doll does, in fact, represent you. If the poppet is to represent someone else, give the doll at least one characteristic of that person or the person for whom you are creating the doll.

Poppets can be made for a variety of reasons. The love spell poppet was an example of how to fill a poppet with the intention that you are drawing to you. If the poppet's purpose is to heal, place the strongest healing herb in the area of the poppet that requires healing. For example, place chamomile in the head if the person is suffering from headaches.

Your reasons for making poppets and performing poppet magick are only as limited as your ability to conceive new purposes for this magick. You can even create a spherical poppet to represent the world and fill it with healing herbs. You can send healing energy to the earth poppet with a group. You can create an earth poppet for world peace and attach forwarding instructions as to your intention for the earth poppet. Perhaps your instructions can be to send peace energy to the poppet for a week, and pass it to a friend, to pass to a friend, to mail to a friend, and so on. The instructions can have a list of where the poppet has been, such as, "This poppet started in Hometown, USA. Please list your town if it isn't already noted." Millions, perhaps billions, pray for world peace at one time or another. Your poppet for the Earth is another way for that prayer to make it around the world. The possibilities for healing with poppets are endless.

The poppet can remain in your home and help to remind you of your magickal intention. The poppet can be given to the individual for whom the magickal work is intended. Once the magickal affect has been completed, you can bury the poppet with the intent of sending the energies back to the earth and into the earth for the purpose of being distributed to someone else who needs that energy. Thank the energies of the poppet for doing its work. You should also inform anyone to whom you give the poppet of this manner in which to complete the magick.

✳ Pillows

A pillow is similar to a sachet, although there is more specificity and direct purpose involved. A pillow can be made as a square envelope made of material, and filled with the intention of being able to solve your problems while you dream. With a pillow, a three-inch square piece of material in the color of the idea that you are trying to draw to you is sufficient. Simply stuff the pillow that you make with equal parts of three pillow aspects, (1) a calming herb for sleep such as chamomile or lavender, (2) an herb for dreams such as gardenia or jasmine, and (3) an herb representing your desired magickal accomplishment. For instance, if you are trying to muddle your way through a creative endeavor but are "stuck," add some orange peel to the pillow for creativity.

Your pillow should be comprised of equal parts, one for sleep, one for dreams, and one for the drawing aspect. An example is that if you have an interview the following day for a job you would like, add one part chamomile for restful sleep, one part lavender for dreams, and one part bay for employment. You can use any herbs for the last part of the spell ingredients as long as they correspond with your magickal intention for the pillow. Visualize the desired outcome while you charge the three herbs. Place the herbs in the pillow, sew it shut, and simply fall asleep with the pillow by your regular pillow. If you wish for superior results, bless the pillow during ritual within a circle.

☀ Wreaths

The wreath represents the eternal circle, the feeling of that which is magickal. It represents the Earth and the universe. It also represents the magickal circle which comes from the Earth and the universe. The purpose of the wreath is also to surround an object or person with the intention of the wreath. If you make a wreath for your front door, the intention is to surround your home with love, protection, or any aspect of the plants and herbs you use. A wreath for a home can be made of healing herbs with the intention to heal the person who dwells within that home. Beltane wreaths as crowns for maidens can be made of specific flowers charmed to bring love to the person wearing the wreath; beltane wreaths as crowns for men can be made of leaves which send the magickal message of the personality of the male who wears the crown.

To make a wreath for your home, you can use a round wooden ring such as found at craft shops, and use floral tape and wire to create a wreath. Use the herbs or plants best suited to the magickal intention of the wreath. Wreaths are especially nice in cities to help you adjust to the changing season. Examples of seasonal wreaths include beautiful spring wreaths of dried lilacs, dried flower wreaths for the summer, beautiful fall leaves for an autumnal wreath, and of course the ever-popular pine or juniper wreath for winter. Creating wreaths for the season not only attunes you to the earth, but helps you learn about the elements and internalize the messages and intelligence of the seasons. Wreaths on your front door serve several purposes. Not only will the scent be pleasing to all who enter, but it will serve as a blessing and a cleansing to anyone who passes through your front door. You can also charge the wreath at your front door to invite only those who bring love and friendship into your home.

☾ Oils

Aromatic oils used for ceremonial and sacred purposes have their origin among the Hebrews, Egyptians, and early Greeks and Romans. Priests and magicians of ancient times anointed their bodies with oils to heighten the senses and induce visions. Oils were used for purification and for offerings to the deities. These traditions continue today. In magickal workings, essential oils and blends are used to anoint people, candles, and talismans, and to heighten and intensify any spell being done. Using essential oils is relatively recent as technology has grown. Availability has come to mass marketing proportions, and essential oils have made quite a stride in being used with magickal workings. To create essential oils, it is best to purchase and blend them with other oil bases such as sunflower, jojoba, almond, or olive oils. Creating your own essential oils is costly, time consuming, and space consuming. Essential oils require huge quantities of fresh plants as part of their ingredients. Combining the essence of the oil with your own various base oils is effective; however, make sure that your purchased oils are pure. Many synthetic oils are on the market which smell great but have no magickal value.

If you are of a purist nature, a method to create homemade oils is to put the *suggestion* of a plant's energy into a base oil of your choice. This oil cannot be used for aromatherapy, and it will not carry the aromatic value of the essential oil mixed with your base oil, but your homemade oil will carry the magickal intention, spirit, and properties of the herbs, resins, and plants. To blend your own oils, you will need:

1. Bottles with tight lids, stoppers, or corks (small quantities work best as oils generally do not "keep" well).
2. Herbs, plants, flowers, or resins (dried or fresh).
3. Oil bases (olive oil, jojoba, sesame, almond, etc.).

Charge your selected herbs with the intention of the oil you wish to create. For instance, if you wish to create prosperity oil, charge the herbs with the *feeling* of prosperity. Fill the bottle three-fourths full with the herbs. Bless the oil you are working with, and fill the remainder of the bottle with the oil. As you do so, say words similar to, "Herb and oil, mix your energies well. Herbal spirits to the oil go. Oil be receptive to the herbal flow. Work as partners to create that which is blessed, clean, and pure, and for the highest good of All." As with incense, using a bit of a corresponding resin or gum such as frankincense or myrrh in any of your mixtures works well and helps to add a slight scent. Close the bottle tightly, and place in a dark cupboard for three days. Strain the oil through a cheesecloth into another container. Remove the herbs or plants from the original bottle, and rinse. Make sure the bottle is completely dry, then pour the oil back into the bottle. As a side note, some mixtures of oil look so lovely in the bottles with the herbs or flowers floating about, it isn't necessary to remove the plants to strain the oil. You may also use the oil just as it is, with the herbs or plants remaining. The oil generally does not last as long if you leave the plants in, although some oils can last quite long with this method. The best test is to keep an eye on your oils to make sure they aren't spoiled before you use them.

Incense

Incense is likely the fastest way to take yourself to an altered state. Incense has been burned on altars and in churches and syna-

gogues for more than 5,000 years. The scent can take the practitioner, the priest, and the layman alike to spiritual places, leaving
the mundane work-a-day world far behind. For magickal purposes,
incense is used to create sacred space, cleanse the area, create a
circle, invite deity, and work herbal magick. Herbal magick consists
of deciding on the type of magick to be performed, selecting the
herb that corresponds with your endeavors, charging the herb with
the energies specific to your needs, and then lighting the herb to
change it from an Earth substance to an air substance. As you light
the herb and its scent and smoke fill the air, the herb becomes
ethereal. Visualize the smoke forming into your magickal intention
in the astral plane. As above, so below. The herb that was transformed to an ethereal and eventually astral thought is strong
enough to set into motion the changes necessary to complete your
magickal working on the physical plane.

The burning of herbs can be magick in and of itself by chanting,
building energy, and releasing the energy just as you would with
candle magick. It can also be used to amplify any other type of
magick. For example, you can bless a candle with an incense made
specifically for the candle magick you are performing, or bless a
poppet with a portion of the herbs inside which were held aside
specifically for this purpose.

Incense can be made from age-old recipes which have been
handed down through the years, or can be made through your
own intuition to create incense for a particular magickal working.
A basic knowledge of plants, herbs, resins, and gums (including
frankincense, myrrh, benzoin, and others) will give you an idea of
the herbs that can work together. Write down the incense that you
are creating so that you know whether its results were effective.
Along with writing down the incense that you are creating, make
sure that you also write down the aspect of the moon or other
pertinent magickal data.

To create incense, the tool you will need is a mortar and pestle.
To burn the incense, you will need charcoal which is found in round
discs at most magickal supply stores. Charcoal discs are now also
found at other types of craft shops. Simply prepare the amount of
incense you would like—a little goes a long way—by pulling a healthy
pinch of each type of herb (dried), gum, or resin, charging the
ingredients, placing them into the mortar and pestle, and grinding

the ingredients as you visualize the intent of the herb. You should first experiment, some of the herbs and plants that you would think aromatic actually create near offensive odors when being burned.

Adding frankincense to your herbal recipes can help to heighten your magickal success as this resin is highly spiritual. Frankincense will help you when blessing the herbs, enable you to focus on and see clearly your magickal intention, and ensure that you are doing magick for the good of All. Although it is not necessary that you add frankincense to your magickal workings, it is highly effective for these reasons.

Once you have ground all of the incense into a powder or very near powder form, it is ready to be used for any purpose that you desire. Your incense can be used during ritual or simply burned within your home in order to remind you of the purpose that it was created for in the first place, such as to draw love, to draw protection, or any other purpose.

Incense can be as simple as one herb, plant, resin, or gum. Incense can be burned at any time for the purposes that have been indicated in Chapter VIII. For instance, you can simply burn frankincense if you wish to have higher spiritual vibrations in your home; however, you should not burn any incense just because it smells nice, unless you have made an incense for that general purpose.

General incense recipes include:

Altar or Blessing Incense
Equal parts frankincense, myrrh, and rosemary.
Love Incense
Equal parts frankincense, strawberry leaves, and raspberry leaves.
Prosperity Incense
Equal parts benzoin, cinnamon, and sandalwood, with a pinch of mustard seed. In this incense, benzoin will act to banish previous attachments to lack of money.
Healing Incense
Equal parts frankincense, raspberry, and allspice with some ground orange peel. The orange peel is to add good attitude to the individual who needs the healing.
Meditation Incense
Equal parts sage, gardenia petals, mugwort, and benzoin.

☀ Guide to Plants and Herbs

The body, mind, and spirit sections of the plants and herbs listed below apply to magickal workings which would be beneficial for incenses, oils, poppets, etc. The body section applies to magickal workings that would best benefit the body. If "health and healing" are indicated, the herb or plant can be used for any magickal work with regard to healing the body. The mind section applies to areas where magickal work can be performed to change one's thinking to bring about the desired change. The spirit section applies to magickal workings to enhance spiritual growth or principles. Occasionally, you will note some duplication with regard to, for example, "love" appearing in all three categories of body, mind, and spirit. This would indicate three different types of love.

1. *Body:* Indicates that a spell using the herb or plant would be good for an individual learning to *love* and accept her body as it is.
2. *Mind:* Indicates the spell would be helpful to an individual's ability to open their mind to a relationship involving romantic *love.*
3. *Spirit:* Indicates a spell would be beneficial for understanding universal or Goddess love, such as required in forgiveness or acceptance work.

These variances in the use of the word "love" can be applied to several other traits as well. Protection listed under *Body* would mean actual physical protection, while protection listed under *Mind* would mean protection from psychic attack from another person, and protection listed under *Spirit* would mean protection from entities other than human. Let your intuition guide you as to the proper magickal use of the herb under these circumstances. The entries are followed by traditional health uses of herbs, if any, and perhaps a fact or a bit of fun lore or myth.

Acorn (*Quercus* species)
Body: Fertility, grounding.

Mind: Growth, luck, money, popularity, safety.
Spirit: Environment, thanksgiving, wisdom.

Acorn was sacred among the Druids and represented the seed of wisdom (although it is actually a nut). As with other seeds or nuts, acorn is used for growth and spells for attracting.

Allspice (*Pimenta officinalis*)
Body: Health and healing.
Mind: Artistic talent, communication, confidence, creativity, breaking bad habits, happiness, loneliness, love, luck, marriage, banishing negativity, relationships.
Spirit: Divination, wisdom.

Allspice can be sprinkled in tea to help an upset stomach; especially beneficial if combined with peppermint tea.

Aloe (*Aloe vera*)
Mind: Growing aloe near your home serves as a charm for protection to your home.

The "gel" inside the aloe plant has long been used to soothe skin irritations such as minor burns, cuts, rashes, sunburn (when mixed with a base oil), and insect bites. Break open a stem of aloe, and gently pat the gel onto irritated area. Not to be used for deeper wounds. Sniffing aloe can help the mind relieve stress.

Amaranth (*Amaranthus hybridus*)
Body: Health and healing, self-image.
Mind: Communication, love, marriage, popularity, banishing fear.
Spirit: Thanksgiving.

Amaranth greens can be steamed for several minutes and served as greens for an occasional diuretic.
The amaranth has been related to immortality for magickal reasons and because some families (there are over fifty species of amaranth) of the plant keep their flowers for many years. Tumbleweed is a member of the amaranth family.

Anise (*Pimpinella anisum*)
   Body: Youthful appearance.
   Mind: Happiness.

   Anise seeds can be made as a tea to help with digestive problems including flatulence.
   Anise belongs to the parsley family, and is native to Egypt. The oil of anise is used for flavorings and the seeds are used in the preparation of anisette, a sweet liqueur.

Apple (*Malus rosaceae*)
   Body: Health and healing, fertility, breaking down sexual inhibitions.
   Mind: Artistic talent, creativity, communication, confidence, fear patterns, growth, leadership, luck, money, monogamy, negativity, power, prosperity, relationships, self-image, stress.
   Spirit: Environment, grounding, happiness, loneliness, love, marriage, peace, thanksgiving, understanding, wisdom.

   The pectin in apples removes the symptoms of arthritis and the accompanying pain; however, the pectin is better taken when separately purchased (as in canning pectin). Take one tablespoon per day, much as you would a vitamin.
   To receive a magickal answer to your questions, charge your apple with the conflict or question, take one bite of the apple, and then bury it. As the earth's energies enter the apple with regard to your question or problem, so too will the answer to the problem come to you.
   The apple is sacred to Venus as a symbol of love and fertility.

Basil (*Ocimum basilicum*)
   Body: Cleansing baths, health and healing, fertility.
   Mind: Anger, communication, confidence, employment, leadership, banishing fear, breaking bad habits, reducing negativity, luck, money, monogamy, popularity, protection, healthy relationships, and safety.
   Spirit: Stopping violence, blessing, calming, divination, dreams, exorcism, grounding, intuition, loneliness, love,

marriage, meditation, prosperity, increasing your psychic abilities, giving thanks, understanding, wisdom, and healing the environment.

Growing basil can produce happiness and peace in your home. Basil has many uses in the kitchen, and can reduce stress when added to foods. Fresh basil is rich in vitamins A and C.

Basil has been known as a symbol of love and courage, and has a long association with witchcraft and magick. Basil has been used in spells from banishing to drawing, to love and aphrodisiacs, to hexes which keep people away.

Basil can be added to tea for cramps, fevers, colds and flu.

Bay (*Laurus nobilis*)
> *Body:* Health and healing, fertility.
> *Mind:* Calm, communication, employment, drawing money, banishing negativity, reducing stress.
> *Spirit:* Astral projection, blessing, divination, dreams, grounding, loneliness, meditation, spirit guides/muses/teachers, thanksgiving, visions, wisdom.

Add bay leaves to bean soups to prevent gas or indigestion from the beans.

Bay is comprised of eight families with at least 2,500 species. Surprisingly, cinnamon, avocado, and camphor are within the bay families.

Bayberry (*Myrica cerifera*)
> *Mind:* Money.

Bayberry can draw money by making a sachet with it, or by burning it as incense.

Benzoin (*Styrax benzoin*)
> *Body:* Protection.
> *Mind:* Communication, confidence, creativity, banishing fear, mental focus, breaking bad habits, leadership, banishing negativity, power.
> *Spirit:* Astral projection, divination, dreams, increasing intu-

ition, meditation, peace, psychic ability, spirit guides/muses/teachers, spirituality, wisdom.

Burn crushed benzoin prior to doing intuitive magick. The connection with your astral teachers will assist with your intuition in creating new incense or magickal skills. You can also add benzoin to incense and homemade oils for intuition and guidance when using the incense.

Blackberry (*Rubus fruticosus*)
Body: Relieves tension and stress.
Mind: Stress. Will also assist with bringing energy.
Spirit: Stress.

Use the leaves for colds and fevers. The berries can be eaten to prevent anemia.
Blackberry is a member of the rose family.

Cactus (*Cactacaeae* family)
Body: Protection and safety.
Mind: Leadership.
Spirit: Grounding.

The cactus family has approximately 1,650 species, some of which are becoming extinct because of gardening popularity.
A lesson taught by cactus is that if you learn that someone isn't good for you, you can still associate with him, but you can also put up your defenses. You need not let them get close enough to do harm.

Camphor (*Cinnamomum camphora*)
Body: Can be toxic if ingested.
Spirit: Prophetic dreams, cleansing.

Can be used effectively for cold sores. Tansy leaves also contain a form of camphor.

Caraway (*Carum carvi*)
Mind: Creativity
Spirit: Protection, thanksgiving.

Chew a pinch of caraway seeds prior to studying; the seeds will increase your memory capacity. Caution: Caraway is also known as an aphrodisiac, so if it has this affect on you, you might be *distracted* from your studies!

Carnation (*Dianthus carophyllus*)
   Body: Health and healing.
   Mind: Artistic talent, communication, confidence, creativity, luck, money, popularity, success.
   Spirit: Divination, love, peace, protection, thanksgiving.

Catnip (*Nepeta cataria*)
   Body: Sleep.
   Mind: Artistic talent, calming, creativity.
   Spirit: Divination, love, peace, thanksgiving.

While catnip will excite cats, it acts as a calming, soothing herb for humans. A tea made of organic catnip and raspberry leaves will help you relax and find peaceful sleep.

Chamomile (*Chamomilla recutita*)
   Body: Health and healing, fertility, self-image.
   Mind: Anger, calming, love, money, banishing negativity, stopping violence.
   Spirit: Divination, peace, psychic ability, self-image, spirituality, thanksgiving, understanding.

As a tea, chamomile aids in sleep, stress relief, and calming the nerves, and it also helps to soothe stomachaches and cramps. Dunking a chamomile tea bag a couple of times into hot water won't do. You must steep chamomile for five minutes in a covered pot to obtain full benefits.

Cinnamon (*Cinnamomum zeylanicum*)
   Body: Health and healing, safety, sex.
   Mind: Communication, confidence, employment, banishing fear and negativity, leadership, money, popularity, power, self-image, success.

Spirit: Grounding, prosperity, protection, thanksgiving, safety in travel (astral), wisdom.

A teaspoon of cinnamon steeped with chamomile tea is effective for stopping diarrhea and any accompanying upset stomach. Add honey to taste.

Clove (*Zyzygium aromaticum*)
Body: Fertility, health and healing, protection, safety, sex.
Mind: Artistic talent, communication, confidence, creativity, employment, breaking bad habits, leadership, love, money, banishing negativity, popularity, prosperity, relationships other than romantic, self-image, stress relief, success, thanksgiving, safety during travel, stopping violence.
Spirit: Blessing, cleansing, divination, exorcism, banishing fear, happiness, intuition, loneliness, peace, psychic ability, spirituality, understanding, wisdom.

Jupiter rules clove. An excellent party drink for ten to fifteen people: Charm a single clove for each person anticipated, and add the cloves to a gallon of apple cider, simmering for at least 20 minutes. You'll never see such a group of fun, talkative, people!

Clover (*Trifolium*)
Mind: Money, monogamy, popularity.
Spirit: Exorcism, love, thanksgiving.

Clover can be added to incense for love spells which require a spiritual flavor. The spiritual essence in the clover—from the three leaves representing maiden, mother, and crone—will draw a spiritual lover to you.

Comfrey (*Symphytum officinale*)
Body: Health and healing, safety.
Mind: Loneliness, safety in travel.
Spirit: Grounding, peace, understanding.

Add comfrey leaves to your bath to ease sore muscles.

Copal (*Bursera odorata*)
Body: Health and healing, protection, sex.

Mind: Creativity, mental focus, breaking bad habits, money.
Spirit: Cleansing, divination, dreams, environment, intuition,
   meditation, spirituality, wisdom.

To assist with breaking a bad habit, hold copal in your right
hand. Visualize the bad habit as a spirit within you. Allow the
"spirit" to move into the copal, and then burn the copal on a
charcoal disc. As the smoke is released into the ethers, thank the
"spirit" for teaching you its lessons and offer it its freedom, bidding
it a loving farewell. The spirit of a habit can be constricting to you,
and to the aspect of you which has created the defense mechanism.

Coriander (*Coriandrum sativum*)
   Body: Health and healing.
   Mind: Understanding.
   Spirit: Love, protection, wisdom.

Coriander tea can help to reduce fevers. Take two teaspoons
of the seeds of the coriander and crush them. Boil a cup of water,
and place the seeds into the cup and cover for 20 minutes. Also
used to ease abdominal discomfort.

The leaves of coriander are called cilantro and used in salsas
and to flavor many dishes.

Cumin (*Cuminum cyminum*)
   Spirit: Exorcism, love.

To clear the sinuses and ease sinus headache, fill a large pot
with water and bring to a boil. Place two tablespoons of cumin
and one bay leaf into the pot and turn off the heat and cover.
When it has cooled but is still steaming, inhale the steam for at
least ten minutes.

Dandelion (*Taraxacum officinale*)
   Body: Health and healing.
   Mind: Loneliness, luck, money, relationships other than
      romantic, success.
   Spirit: Divination, thanksgiving.

Dandelion can be steamed as a green for high natural doses of vitamins A and C. Occasional use of the leaves as a tea is helpful to relieve water retention.

Devil's Shoe String (*Viburnum alnifolium*)
Body: Safety during travel.
Mind: Confidence, employment, banishing fear, leadership.

Viburnum is of the honeysuckle genus. Charge devil's shoe string for employment via a successful interview. Visualize the interview going well, then simply carry the dried root with you during the interview.

Dill (*Anethum graveolens*)
Body: Fertility.
Mind: Leadership, money, success.
Spirit: Understanding.

Use a teaspoon of dill tea for infants with colic or upset stomach. Make sure the tea is not too hot.

Dragon's Blood (*Daemonorops draco*)
Mind: Love, protection.
Spirit: Love, exorcism.

Use as incense to clear negativity from any room, as well as any minor entities which cause discomfort.

Echinechea (*Echinacea angustifolia*) (also called Snakeroot)
Body: Health and healing.
Mind: Stress relief.

A highly regarded healer, echinacea will fight infection and help to reinforce your body's ability to fight colds, flu, and bronchitis. Capsules of echinacea are now available at health stores.

Elder (*Sambucus nigra and S. canadensis*)
Body: Health and healing, protection, sleep.
Mind: Growth, leadership, money, monogamy, popularity, relationships other than romantic.

Spirit: Exorcism, peace, psychic ability, spirituality, understanding, wisdom.

Elder is sacred to Venus. Venus is known as the goddess of love and the mother of Cupid, but she was often unfaithful to her husband. Elder will teach you the wiles of unfaithfulness so that you can spot unfaithful intentions in a mate before it's too late. "It takes one to know one" is the adage that is helpful with monogamy.

Elm (*Ulmus campestris*)
   Mind: Growth, leadership.
   Spirit: Divination, growth, intuition, thanksgiving, understanding.

Dutch elm disease has seriously affected the population of elm in the United States. If the disease is caught early, the tree can be saved.

Sit with your back against an elm, close your eyes, move into alpha, and ask the elm what the weather will be.

Endive (*Cichorium endivia*)
   Spirit: Love.

Also known as chicory and used to smooth the taste of coffee.

Fennel (*Foeniculum vulgare*)
   Body: Protection, sleep.
   Mind: Loneliness, negativity.
   Spirit: Spirituality.

Florence fennel seeds can be crushed and made into a tea to alleviate nausea or an upset stomach. Steep 20 minutes.

Frankincense (*Boswellia carterii*)
   Body: Health and healing, protection, sleep, safety during travel.
   Mind: Calming, confidence, creativity, employment, banishing fear, mental focus, breaking bad habits, leadership,

loneliness, love, marriage, negativity, safety, stress relief, stopping violence.

Spirit: Astral projection, blessing, cleansing, divination, dreams, environment, exorcism, intuition, meditation, peace, power, prosperity, psychic ability, spirituality, thanksgiving, understanding, wisdom.

Frankincense can be used as the base of many incenses in order to bind the ingredients to work together.

Gardenia (*Gardenia thunbergia, G. rothmannia*)

Body: Fertility, health and healing, self-image, sex, sleep.

Mind: Artistic talent, communication, confidence, creativity, mental focus, happiness, loneliness, love, marriage, negativity, popularity, stress relief, success, stopping violence.

Spirit: Blessing, calming, cleansing, divination, dreams, intuition, meditation, peace, power, psychic ability, spirit guides/ muses/teachers, thanksgiving, understanding, wisdom.

When making a poppet, place a dried gardenia in the hands of the poppet to indicate that the poppet has been made with the highest spiritual intention and for the good of All.

Garlic (*Allium sativum*)

Body: Health and healing, protection, sex, safety during travel.

Mind: Banishing negativity, safety.

Spirit: Exorcism.

Garlic is used the world over as a near cure-all. It is taken whole, as an oil applied externally or taken internally, or made into a syrup for colds and chest maladies.

Everyone knows garlic wards off vampires.

Geranium (*Pelargonium*)

Mind: Calming, to stop violence.

Spirit: Love, protection.

Place a handful of the petals of the geranium flower in 3 cups of warm water with ¼ cup of rubbing alcohol. Stir and cover overnight (at least 12 hours). Sift the leaves and use as an after-wash toner for your face. Excellent as an astringent, and to fight acne and eczema. Follow with your favorite moisturizer.

Ginger (*Zingiber officinale*)
Body: Grounding, health and healing, sex.
Mind: Break bad habits, happiness, leadership, loneliness, love, marriage, money, popularity, relationships other than romantic, success.
Spirit: Love, prosperity, psychic ability, spirituality, thanksgiving, wisdom.

Ginseng (*Panax quinquefolius*)
Mind: Confidence.
Spirit: Love, protection, wisdom.

Ginseng has long been used as an aphrodisiac, and is also used as a stimulant. Ginseng chewing gum can be purchased at health stores, and ginseng can be a beneficial additive to your favorite iced juice drink (smoothie).

Gota Kola (*Hydrocotyl asiatica*)
Mind: Confidence, creativity.

Gota kola is a known blood purifier. Recently popularity of gota kola has produced a variety of capsules with various mixtures of herbs sold at health stores.

Hawthorn (*Crataegus oxacantha*)
Mind: Communication.
Spirit: Love, thanksgiving.

Hawthorn is a member of the rose family. The flowers are very sweetly scented, and can bring good cheer for the day to those who take the time to smell them.

Holly (*Hex aquifolium*)
Mind: Luck.
Spirit: Thanksgiving.

Holly is the traditional symbol from the plant kingdom for Yule. The fruit of holly contains two to eight one-seeded stones. To find an eight-seeded stone is highly lucky at Yule. The number 8 is associated with abundance and power, and Yule is an excellent time to bring these energies into the home for the coming harsh winter.

Honeysuckle (*Lonicera caprifolium*)
Mind: Happiness, stress.
Spirit: Thanksgiving.

Use honeysuckle in a spell if you are experiencing stress regarding a particularly painful breakup where arguments predominated the end of the relationship. It is excellent to relieve anxiety related to separation, especially if you feel betrayed and forgiveness is difficult. If memories of the separation are chronic at night and affect sleep, make a honeysuckle pillow (see Chapter VI) to break the cycle of thoughts.

Horehound (*Marrubium vulgare*)
Body: Health and healing.
Mind: Creativity, mental focus, to break bad habits, leadership.
Spirit: Dreams, intuition, spirituality, understanding.

Horehound is one of the ingredients in cough syrups and is part of the mint family. Horehound has a very bitter taste, but, used in a tea combined with sweeter herbs, horehound will help you to achieve higher levels of concentration.

Sacred to the Hebrews and Egyptians, horehound is one of the bitter herbs used at Passover celebrations.

Jasmine (*Jasminum officinale*)
Body: Sex.
Mind: Communication, employment, loneliness, monogamy, popularity, sex, stress, stopping violence.
Spirit: Blessing, cleansing, dreams, love, meditation, peace, spirit guides/muses/teachers, spirituality, visions.

The Chinese make tea with the scent of flowers being absorbed into the tea; jasmine is a particular favorite.

As a love draw, place a few drops of true jasmine essence in a hot bath. As you bathe, visualize the characteristics of your ideal love. As each characteristic comes to focus, quietly whisper, "Come to me, come to me, *humor*" (or whatever the characteristic you wish to draw) and then "come to me, come to me, *love*." Alternate each characteristic with the term "love" until the water has become too cool.

Juniper (*Juniperus communis*)
   Body: Health and healing.
   Mind: Communication, happiness, leadership, loneliness, luck, marriage, success.
   Spirit: Blessing, exorcism.

Juniper berries can be used as a diuretic and for urinary problems. Steep a teaspoon of berries in water which has been brought to a boil and cover for 20 minutes. (Not recommended for pregnant women.)

Lavender (*Lavandula angustifolia, L. officinalis*)
   Body: Health and healing, self-image, sex, sleep.
   Mind: Anger, calming, confidence, mental focus, breaking bad habits, happiness, loneliness, love, marriage, monogamy, banishing negativity, popularity, protection, relationships other than romantic, self-image, stress relief, stopping violence.
   Spirit: Blessing, cleansing, divination, dreams, environment, intuition, peace, psychic ability, spirit guides/muses/teachers, spirituality, thanksgiving, understanding, wisdom.

Burn dried lavender as an antidepressant. Lavender is excellent for making pillows (see Chapter VI) for bringing peace into your life.

If you are trying to quit smoking, carry lavender essential oil. When you become tense and desire a cigarette, take off the cap of the oil, and sniff the oil. Pass the bottle quickly across your nose (as the scent is *very* strong), but continue to inhale deeply, almost as though you are smoking. Take two more deep breaths and concentrate on a calming feeling. Your desire for a cigarette will temporarily go away. Keep repeating until you finally quit.

Lemon (*Citrus limon*)
 Body: Health and healing, self-image.
 Mind: Anger, confidence, employment, mental focus, happiness, leadership, loneliness, love, luck, banishing negativity, popularity, relationships other than romantic, stress, success, stopping violence.
 Spirit: Thanksgiving.

Lemon juice is extremely high in vitamin C. Use the juice of the lemon on salads and as a flavoring for vegetables.

Save lemon peels, and allow them to dry. Grated lemon peel is excellent to use in incense to draw pleasant energies into the home, bring personal beauty as a state of mind, regain lost youth, and fill an area with good cheer.

Lemon Verbena (*Aloysia triphylla*)
 Body: Health and healing
 Mind: To stop violence.
 Spirit: Divination, love.

Lemon verbena is part of the mint family.

Use lemon verbena in incenses to draw love, and specifically to help you become more intuitive when meeting potential lovers regarding their truest personalities.

Mandrake Root (*Mandragora officinale*)
 Body: Health and healing, safety in travel.
 Mind: Love, safety.
 Spirit: Understanding.

Although used for medicinal purposes, consult professionals as mandrake is toxic if not used correctly.

Maple (*Acer rubrum, A. saccharum, A. nigrum*)
 Mind: Loneliness, love, popularity, stopping violence.
 Spirit: Environment.

Maple branches can be used in the making of wands as they direct energy well. Be sure to thank the tree from which the branch was taken.

The maple teaches us adaptability and cycles, and that with every ending there is a beginning. The maple also teaches us to go inward, and that leaving things behind which no longer serve a purpose can take us through difficult times.

Marigold (*Tagetes lucida*)
Body: Self-image.
Mind: Communication, banishing fear, leadership, love, money, success, stopping violence.
Spirit: Banishing negativity, wisdom.

Marigolds planted around your home will keep mice away.

Marigold belongs to the largest family of flowers, Compositae, including 20,000 species which include dandelion, daisy, tansy, chrysanthemum, and black-eyed Susan. The only place that Compositae do not grow is Antarctica.

Marjoram (*Origanum majorana*)
Body: Fertility, grounding, health and healing.
Mind: Leadership, love, stopping violence.
Spirit: Understanding.

Belonging to the mint family, marjoram tea alleviates stomach problems as well as menstrual cramps and nausea.

Prior to adding to soups or recipes, charm marjoram for a happy family.

Mint (*Mentha*)
Body: Health and healing.
Mind: Leadership, money.
Spirit: Exorcism, thanksgiving.

True mint leaf tea is excellent for headaches, calming, stomachaches, and to help sleep. Add a small handful of mint leaves to a large pot of simmering water, remove from heat, and cover for 15 minutes. Use the steam to clear and soothe sinuses and to soothe a sinus headache.

Mint includes within its family many well-known herbs such as rosemary, thyme, sage, savory, and basil. Mint can be used as a substitute for these in spells if time is short. Simply ask mint to bring in the qualities of its sister or brother for the purpose of the spell.

Mistletoe (*Phoradendron flavescens*)
Mind: Communication, confidence, love, stopping violence.
Spirit: Exorcism, thanksgiving.

Mistletoe is a parasitic plant which grows on and can kill, among others, apple trees, junipers, maples, and elms.
Mistletoe can be used in exorcism as it is a parasitic plant and understands how to "draw life." At one time, mistletoe was used as an antidote against poison. The pagan practice of kissing under a mistletoe is still acceptable and even customary.

Mugwort (*Artemisia vulgaris*)
Body: Health and healing, sleep.
Mind: Creativity, health and healing.
Spirit: Astral projection, divination, dreams, intuition, meditation, psychic ability, spirit guides/muses/teachers, spirituality, understanding, visions, wisdom.

Mugwort used as a tea helps with digestion and nervous problems. Mugwort is bitter; therefore combine the dried leaves of mugwort with a more palatable plant such as chamomile and add lemon and honey. The tea may also be used for colds and flus.
Mugwort is sacred to the goddess Artemis. Mugwort can be burned to consecrate magickal tools, and to clear the mind for divination.

Myrrh (*Commiphora myrrha*)
Body: Health and healing, protection, sleep, safety in travel.
Mind: Anger, calming, communication, confidence, employment, banishing fear and negativity, mental focus, breaking bad habits, leadership, loneliness, love, marriage, peace, popularity, prosperity, safety, stress, stopping violence.
Spirit: Astral projection, blessing, cleansing, divination, envi-

ronment, intuition, meditation, psychic ability, spirit guides/ muses/teachers, spirituality, thanksgiving, understanding, wisdom.

The essential oil can be added to jojoba and rubbed into arthritic areas to ease pain associated with arthritis.

Sacred to Isis. Myrrh is excellent to use as a base for any incense, and brings intense spiritual vibrations to incense you create.

Myrtle (*Myrtus communis*)
Body: Fertility.
Mind: Love.
Spirit: Peace.

Sacred to many goddesses of love, myrtle can be used in any incense or oils created for successful love spells. Tie myrtle to the legs of a baby's crib to ensure peaceful nights for the baby—and for the mother and father.

Nettle (*Urtica dioica*)
Body: Health and healing.
Mind: Confidence.

Medicinally, nettle can be used as a benefit to many organs in the body, and it also helps with anemia owing to its many nutrients. Nettle works particularly well for the urinary tract as well as the lungs. The root has been found to help treat enlarged prostate.

Nettle has a mirroring effect. If someone has deliberately sent negative energy to you, it is better to deflect that energy and send it to the universe to be cleansed. Nettle spells, however, will send the energy to its origin.

Nutmeg (*Myristica fragrans*)
Mind: Artistic talent, creativity, banishing fear, mental focus, breaking bad habits, luck, money.
Spirit: Astral projection, blessing, cleansing, divination, dreams, intuition, meditation, banishing negativity, power, protection, psychic ability, spirituality, thanksgiving, understanding, visions, wisdom.

Nutmeg may have been one of the ingredients in Nostradamus' divination powder. Large doses of nutmeg, however, can be quite toxic. Habitually using a little charmed nutmeg in coffee or tea for the intention of building psychic powers is quite beneficial.

Nuts and Seeds (All)
Body: Fertility, sex.
Mind: Employment, growth, money, success.
Spirit: Growth, thanksgiving.

Carry seeds or nuts which you have charmed to spiritual retreats to help you with spiritual growth.

Oak (*Quercus alba*)
Body: Safety.
Mind: Money.
Spirit: Growth, spirituality, understanding.

Oak leaves can be boiled and laid on injuries to mitigate discomfort. Make sure the leaves have cooled sufficiently prior to placing them on the injured area.

Sacred to the strongest of gods, Zeus, Thor, Pan, and Hecate, the oak is a holy tree respected for its strength.

Onion (*Allium cepa*)
Body: Health and healing.
Mind: Safety in travel.
Spirit: Exorcism.

The onion can be used in similar ways to garlic for healing.

Orange (*Citrus senesis*)
Body: Health and healing.
Mind: Artistic talent, creativity, employment, happiness, marriage, popularity.
Spirit: Divination, peace, thanksgiving.

Don't use dried orange peel in a spell for love unless you definitely want marriage; these spells have a way of leaping ahead of themselves and going straight for the final commitment.

Orris (*Iris florentina*)
  Mind: Marriage, protection, relationships other than romantic.
  Spirit: Thanksgiving, understanding, visions, wisdom.

Sacred to Hera, orris root works well for hearth and home. Keeping orris root in the home promotes intuition for the "master of the house" so that he or she will know what's going on in the home.

Pansy (*Viola tricolor*)
  Mind: Peace, relationships other than romantic, stopping violence.
  Spirit: Love.

The Greeks developed *florigraphy*, which is the language of flowers. Pansies stood for thought. Sit in front of a group of pansies and meditate with them; they will assist you with deciding the best type of love for you. The information gained here can be used in poppet work or other love spells.

Parsley (*Petroselinum sativum*)
  Body: Health and healing.
  Mind: Popularity.
  Spirit: Cleansing.

Parsley is an aid to stomach and digestive ailments. Eating a sprig of parsley with dinner helps with digestion.
A handful of parsley may be used in a ritual bath for purification and cleansing purposes, and to visualize popularity and drawing people to you.

Patchouli (*Pogostemon cablin, P. patchouli*)
  Body: Health and healing, sex.
  Mind: Calming, confidence, creativity, mental focus, breaking bad habits, loneliness, love, money, banishing negativity, popularity, prosperity, stress, stopping violence.
  Spirit: Blessing, cleansing, divination, dreams, grounding, intuition, meditation, psychic ability, spirituality.

Patchouli is excellent to burn as incense in the home to clear the home of negative energies.

Peony (*Peonia officinalis*)
Body: Protection.
Mind: Protection.

Peony can be made into a steam to help soothe the nerves. Place a small handful of petals and a drop of vanilla in a quart of water which has just been removed from boiling. Cover for 20 minutes. Use as a steam with a towel over your head to keep the steam from escaping elsewhere.

Pepper (*Piper Nigrum*)
Body: Grounding.
Mind: Protection.

Using pepper in an incense to be lit during the cakes and wine portion of ritual will help to ground you.

Peppermint (*Mentha piperita*)
Body: Health and healing.
Mind: When burned as an incense or when drunk, mitigates anger, calming, loneliness, money, popularity, stress, success.
Spirit: Prosperity, spirit guides/muses/teachers, spirituality, wisdom.

Peppermint tea assists with headaches and soothes the stomach.
Dried peppermint and roses left as a potpourri at your front door will bless those who enter, as well as disallow any negative energies to enter your home.

Pine (*Pinus*)
Body: Grounding, health and healing.
Mind: Calming, confidence, mental focus, growth, luck, money, banishing negativity, peace, power, protection, safety, stress, success, safety in travel, stopping violence.
Spirit: Cleansing, environment, exorcism, growth, love, spirituality, thanksgiving, understanding, wisdom.

Place your hands on a pine tree, ask a question, and allow the energy of the answer to enter your consciousness. Sitting against a pine tree can help with backaches. Simply close your eyes and relax. Although it's a bit scratchy, placing boughs of pine in your bath will work as a money draw.

Pomegranate (*Punica granatum*)
  Body: Sex, fertility.
  Mind: Artistic talent, creativity, loneliness, love, money, power, stopping violence.
  Spirit: Psychic ability, thanksgiving, understanding, visions.

If you are in a situation in which you have difficulty understanding its purpose, charge a pomegranate to assist with your problem. Eat the pomegranate at night, knowing that as it moves through your blood, the wisdom will reach your mind and assist you with the purpose of your situation.

Poppy (*Papaver*)
  Mind: Artistic talent, creativity, money.
  Spirit: Thanksgiving.

The poppy is used to assist with sleep.

Primrose (*Primula vulgaris*)
  Mind: Luck, protection.

Primrose is a bright, early-blooming flower. To meditate with the primrose in the spring and visualize your goals for the year will bring those goals to fruition.

Raspberry (*Rubus idaeus*)
  Body: Fertility, health and healing, self-image, sex.
  Mind: Artistic talent, calming, confidence, creativity, love, marriage, banishing negativity, peace, popularity, self-image, stress, stopping violence.
  Spirit: Psychic ability.

Raspberry leaf tea can calm nerves, especially if blended with chamomile and catnip.

Raspberry leaves are a wonderful additive to any incense you create. Use them to ensure that you are doing your spells out of purest love, without intention for misuse of magickal power.

Rose (*Rosa*)
Body: Cleansing, health and healing, love, self-image, sex.
Mind: Anger, communication, breaking bad habits, love, luck, marriage, peace, popularity, self-image, stress, stopping violence.
Spirit: Blessing, cleansing, love, peace, self-image, spirituality, thanksgiving.

The rose represents love, and the various colors of the rose correspond with the chakras. Rose petals can be used in love spells to attract the purest of love to you. Rose oil baths will also work to attract love to you, as well as act as a shield against emotional ties to family squabbles.

Rosemary (*Rosmarinus officinalis*)
Body: Grounding, health and healing, safety in travel.
Mind: Calming, banishing negativity, peace, protection, safety, stress.
Spirit: Cleansing, divination, exorcism, psychic ability, spirituality, thanksgiving, wisdom.

Rosemary combined with sage creates a very strong house-blessing incense. Move through the home, blessing it and clearing it of energies belonging to previous owners.

Saffron (*Crocus sativa*)
Body: Health and healing, sex.
Mind: Mental focus, breaking bad habits, happiness, leadership, popularity, prosperity, self-image, stress, success.
Spirit: Divination, intuition, psychic ability, spirit guides/muses/teachers, spirituality, thanksgiving, understanding, wisdom.

When taken as tea or burned as incense, mitigates anger. Further, saffron sprinkled in tea can help strengthen your intuition.

Sage (*Salvia officinalis*)
Body: Grounding, health and healing, safety in travel.
Mind: Calming, communication, confidence, creativity, banishing fear and negativity, mental focus, breaking bad habits, leadership, popularity, power, protection, safety, self-imagè, stress.
Spirit: Astral projection, blessing, cleansing, divination, dreams, environment, exorcism, intuition, meditation, peace, psychic ability, spirit guides/muses/teachers, spirituality, thanksgiving, understanding, wisdom.

Sage and rosemary blended together create a good tea for soothing headaches.

Sage can be burned as incense to achieve psychic ability, visions, high meditative states.

Saint John's Wort (*Hypericum perforatum*)
Body: Health and healing.
Mind: Luck, protection, stress.

Saint John's wort has gained huge popularity as an antidepressant.

Saint John's wort has magical properties for luck, and can be burned as incense to drive away evil spirits.

Sandalwood (*Santalum album*)
Body: Grounding, health and healing, sleep.
Mind: Calming, communication, to banish fear, mental focus, leadership, loneliness, prosperity, protection, stress.
Spirit: Blessing, cleansing, divination, environment, exorcism, intuition, banishing negativity, psychic ability, spirit guides/muses/teachers, thanksgiving, understanding, visions, wisdom.

Sandalwood is used as a base for incense, and has strong spiritual vibrations which are excellent to smudge your chakras with prior to ritual.

Scullcap (*Scutellaria lateriflora*)
Mind: Peace.

Spirit: Astral projection, divination, intuition, spirituality, understanding, wisdom.

Scullcap can be made into a mist in order to assist with divination processes. Boil 1 quart of water, remove it from the heat, and add 2 tablespoons of dried scullcap. Use the mist for scrying purposes.

Spearmint (*Mentha spicata*)
Body: Health and healing.
Mind: Employment, loneliness, relationships other than romantic.
Spirit: Prosperity.

Spearmint is an excellent herb to use for tea for soothing colds and flus, especially if the lungs and breathing are affected. Spearmint can also be taken as a steam to aid in breathing, but this method works best with fresh spearmint leaves or true essential oil.

If you want to be sharp and on your toes for an interview, charge some spearmint with the specificity of doing well at the interview, and smudge devil's shoe string with spearmint smoke. As spearmint assists with mental clarity and employment, smudging the devil's shoe string will provide a "double whammy."

Strawberry (*Fragaria virginiana*)
Body: Health and healing, fertility, self-image.
Mind: Love, luck, marriage, stopping violence.

Strawberries are related to the rose. Eat plenty of well-washed strawberries early in the season to help your body adjust to the warmer weather of summer. (In general, foods eaten within their season help your body adjust to the weather conditions of that season; e.g., squash helps to adjust your body to cold weather.)

See Chapter VI to create a love draw poppet from strawberry leaves.

Sunflower (*Helianthus annuus*)
Body: Health and healing.
Mind: Eat the seeds (raw, unsalted) to mitigate anger.

Employment, growth, happiness, leadership, money, relationships other than romantic, self-image, success.
Spirit: Prosperity, wisdom.

Contrary to popular belief, sunflowers do not droop because of the weight of the flower. It is actually the aspect of one side of the flower growing faster than the other because of a growth regulator called *auxin.* Auxin is created due to unequal sunlight. The darker side grows faster, and the stem bends toward the sun.

Sunflowers boost mental self-image. Charm the seeds with an appreciation for the grandness of the flower from which they came. Then visualize the aspect of you that is grand, and which you would like to enhance, whether it be physical looks or a personality trait. Eat the sunflower seeds while visualizing this aspect of yourself growing within yourself.

Tansy (*Tanacetum vulgare*)
  Body: Health and healing.
  Mind: Artistic talent, creativity, love, stopping violence.
  Spirit: Divination.

Can be toxic if not properly used. Tansy was brought to the United States by early settlers.

Tarragon (*Artemisia dracunculus*)
  Body: Health and healing.
  Mind: Protection, to banish fear.
  Spirit: Cleansing, divination, spirituality.

Chew to mitigate halitosis (bad breath).
Blend tarragon with frankincense and myrrh to help you overcome fear regarding moving forward with your plans or future.

Thyme (*Thymus vulgaris*)
  Spirit: Cleansing, intuition, psychic ability, spirit guides/
    muses/teachers, understanding.

Thyme is of the mint family.
Thyme was used by the ancients to cure nightmares and was also thought to cure shyness. To banish gloom or worry, combine

dried thyme, grated orange peel, and benzoin in a mortar and pestle for a cheery incense which will also remove the negativity from the room as well as your mind and heart.

Tobacco (*Nicotiana*)
Spirit: Divination, environment, meditation, thanksgiving, understanding.

The first use of tobacco is thought to have been by the ancient Mayans, and from there its use spread to Native North Americans.

Tonka Beans (*Coumarouna odorata*)
Body: Sex.
Mind: Love, luck, marriage, money, stopping violence.
Spirit: Intuition.

The tonka bean, also called a coumara nut, contains coumarin, which is used in making perfumes.

Tonka beans can be charged with energy as a talisman for sexual pleasure between two people who love one another. Charge two beans representing both people, and place the beans on your night stand—assuming, of course, the sexual pleasure will take place in the bedroom!

Valerian (*Valeriana officinalis*)
Body: Sex.
Mind: Anger, money, protection, stress.
Spirit: Divination, intuition, psychic ability, spirituality, understanding, wisdom.

Valerian works well to mitigate stress and insomnia. Mix equal parts chamomile and valerian to make a tea to calm nerves and allow emotional tension to drift away.

Valerian allows you to trust again after a damaging relationship. Charge and burn valerian as a love draw with the full intention of drawing gentle love and trusting that you will get it.

Vanilla (*Vanilla planifolia*)
Body: Sleep.

Mind: Loneliness, love, monogamy, popularity, stress.
Spirit: Love.

Vanilla is from the orchid family, but the flowers of these orchids are dull in color.

Vanilla is a feminine plant sacred to the goddess Venus. It is associated with purity of intention, and will give strength when you need to "get to the bottom" of an issue regarding any secrets or misrepresentations stated behind your back.

Verbena/Vervain (*Verbana officinalis*)

Body: Health and healing.
Mind: Artistic talent, creativity, stopping bad habits, money, negativity, protection, stress.
Spirit: Astral projection, divination, exorcism, intuition, peace, prosperity, psychic ability, spirit guides/muses/ teachers, spirituality, understanding, wisdom.

Part of the mint family, vervain is helpful for creating a soothing inner self. Vervain can be combined in equal parts with chamomile and valerian for a tea remedy for tattered nerves. Honey can be added to sweeten the taste. Also helps with PMS.

Clears the home of unwanted negativity. Use whole, dry vervain and wrap string around it to make a one-inch thick bundle. Light the bundle for smudging your home to clear the energy.

Willow (*Salix alba*)

Body: Health and healing, grounding.
Mind: Anger, calming, mental focus, breaking bad habits, banishing negativity, stress.
Spirit: Cleansing, environment, spirituality, thanksgiving, understanding.

Willow bark is the source of salicin, which has now been synthesized for mass-marketed aspirin.

To sit with your back against a willow tree will soothe the nerves and calm anger, and perhaps bring a bit of understanding to the situation which is causing anger. Allow yourself to be receptive to the loving and grandmotherly affections of the willow. Use willow leaves in healing spells of any kind.

Wintergreen (*Gaultheria procumbens*)
Body: Health and healing.
Spirit: Prosperity, wisdom.

Oil of wintergreen is now manufactured synthetically, but it was originally harvested from the birch tree. Even the true oil of wintergreen is now usually synthetic. Wintergreen can be used as a local antiseptic.

Wintergreen can be used in a variety of healing spells, poppets, sachets, etc. Growing wintergreen near your front door can remove potential negative energy from your home.

Witch Grass (*Agropyron repens*)
Spirit: Divination, dreams, exorcism, intuition, meditation, psychic ability, spirituality, wisdom.

Strew witch grass around your home to make petty spirits depart. Everything good that you can think of that a witch does, witch grass does too.

Witch Hazel (*Hamamelis virginiana*)
Body: Health and healing.
Spirit: Divination.

Witch hazel is used in cosmetics, astringents, and healing salves and ointments for skin irritations.

Wood Rose (*Ipomoea tuberosa)*
Mind: Love.
Spirit: Divination, intuition, psychic ability.

Wood rose is also known as a "frozen rose" and can absorb the qualities of a rose if so charged for that purpose. In this way, you will always have a rose to work with, and you can "deprogram" the rose for its next use.

Wormwood (*Artemisia absinthium*)
Body: Health and healing.
Mind: Banishing fear, leadership.
Spirit: Divination, dreams, intuition, meditation, psychic abil-

ity, spirit guides/muses/teachers, spirituality, understanding, visions, wisdom.

Wormwood can be used to expel worms within the body.

The leaves of the wormwood are powerful psychic messengers. Fresh wormwood can cause visions when made into a pillow (see Chapter VI). The visions, however, can be in the form of intense nightmares and difficult to interpret.

Yarrow (*Achillea millefolium*)
> *Body:* Health and healing, self-image, sex.
> *Mind:* Confidence, happiness, loneliness, love, banishing negativity, stress, stopping violence.
> *Spirit:* Cleansing, environment, exorcism, thanksgiving.

Yarrow has been used to heal cuts and wounds. Achilles is said to have discovered its healing properties and treated his soldiers with the herb. To help with a cold, make a tea of equal parts of mint and yarrow, and squeeze a healthy amount of lemon into the tea. A facial steam with yarrow is excellent to smooth and cleanse the skin, as yarrow works well as an astringent.

Burn dried yarrow as an offering to Venus, the goddess of love, to bring you beauty and new love.

CHAPTER VII

Stones and Crystals

tones have represented comfort, wealth, superstition, love, and many other human interests since the beginning of recorded time. There are stones which famous lovers have given to one another now held in museums. There are also the stones that are famous in the Bible, such as mentioned in Exodus. Detailed instruction is given as to how to create Aaron's robes and breastplate. The breastplate was covered with precious stones and said to have given Aaron special powers or gifts. Stones have been used in decorating various ritual items such as athames, wands, and chalices, and the scepters of royalty were decorated in gemstones. The most famous is the British royal scepter which holds the Star of Africa, a diamond weighing 530.2 carats.

Crystals are used in computers and watches, and we receive true readable energy from them. What we will look at is the ability of stones and crystals to help us with the energy in our bodies as well as send us messages to better understand ourselves and to help us through difficult situations. Although conscious work with crystals and stones is most effective, even carrying a stone with you is helpful to activate what is needed within you to solve a problem. Diamonds illustrate this scenario well. When a couple is having difficulties in their marriage or relationship, one glance at the diamond and memories flood their thoughts of how they once loved each other and can work on that love again. To carry this scenario a bit further, the diamond which had in a manner of speaking been blessed during the wedding ceremony carries with it the program to keep the couple together. The diamond has energies to work with the couple to hold the marriage together in and of itself. It is not merely a mental/visual reminder; the diamond works on the aura to help you through a difficult situation.

Crystals and stones have various personalities. There are a wide range of stones, from jade to rose quartz to obsidian, that have very specific properties which can help us in different areas of our lives and health. Within each of those realms, however, there is a specific personality to each stone. For instance, within the family of jade, if you know that jade is a stone for dreaming, stop and think of all the different ways this can affect you. A fair comparison can be drawn with the difference in people who are like-minded. You will run the gamut in personality differences. Imagine a field of doctors and each doctor is trained in an area of expertise. There are thousands of podiatrists with similar training, yet their personalities have an effect on the way they treat you when you have a foot problem. The same is true for stones. There are many jade stones, and within those, they each carry on the same work, but also have their own personality. Define your purpose for working with a stone or gaining insight from a stone, and then find out the personality of that particular stone to see how it can suit your personal needs. It is a collaborative work between you and the stone.

The stones mentioned in the list below represent the 52 personality traits mentioned in Chapter VIII. Many of the stones have other qualities to which you can attune, but the qualities that are mentioned are in line and directly related to the traits in Chapter VIII. You will have a basic text for learning the different subtleties of each stone. For instance, amethysts and emeralds are both excellent for meditation; however, the purpose of meditation would be different. Amethyst pertains more to your wisdom-seeking nature. It is gentle, guiding, and will lead you to find the wisdom that is inside you. Emerald will help you more specifically to meditate with matters concerning the heart. It is associated with the heart and feminine strength, and its strength in meditation is to assist in this area.

☀ Healing Uses of Stones

There are many ways to use stones for healing the body, mind, or spirit. You can create charms or elixirs, or meditate with stones for effective healing of emotional issues. Healing emotional issues will trigger physical health and healing. In order to know more about healing with stones, you must first learn the chakra system. *Chakra* is an ancient Sanskrit word meaning "wheel." Chakras are power centers within the body that form a bridge between the physical and ethereal realms. The bridge is what causes health and wellness, both emotional and physical. The idea behind this is that our chakras are intricately connected to our aura and astral bodies. The aura collects energies, and those energies, good or bad, eventually affect our bodies. If we feel as though we are carrying a heavy load, or we "can't stand something," our shoulders can begin to droop. This negative attitude is first reflected in our aura, and this attitude in turn affects our heart chakra, which is the fourth chakra located in the center of the chest, and perhaps our throat chakra, which is the fifth chakra located at the Adam's apple. Before we know it, we're walking with slumped shoulders. When you are in a situation where there is lack of forgiveness, or continual anger or arguing, the illness first shows up in your aura, and in your chakras, and then in your physical body.

The seven major energy centers, located from the base of the spine to the top of your head, are like balls of energy which spin at varying speeds. These balls of energy are made up of colors, which correspond to the colors of the rainbow, which are red, orange, yellow, green, blue, indigo, and white. Become familiar with the following:

The *first major chakra* is located at the base of the spine, and the color associated with it is red. Black has also been associated with the base chakra. This is a slower-moving chakra, and its job is to show us how we are connected to the Earth, how our Earth's energy is being maintained within us, whether we will enjoy our time here. If the base chakra is healthy, then we will enjoy various earthly delights such as prosperity and a happy family life.

The *second chakra* is located approximately two inches below the navel. The color associated with this chakra is orange. The second chakra is responsible for and controls our sexual desire, whether our attitudes toward sex are healthy, and our ability to be creative and understand our creative force. When this chakra is unhealthy, the result can be problems or illness in sexual organs, problems with relationships, personal doubt of creativity, and other dysfunction associated with sex, relationships, and creativity.

The *third chakra* is located in the solar plexus, the center of the abdomen. The color associated with this chakra is yellow. This chakra is responsible for how we project our personal power into the world, and our ability to cope with various challenges and situations within the world. Executives, for instance, who are very successful have a very strong third chakra. Someone with a weak third chakra would not be able to assert his or her personal power. Stomach problems are also associated with a blocked third chakra.

The *fourth chakra* is the heart chakra. This is the connector between the spiritual realms and our physical self. The heart chakra is the midpoint between our seventh and first chakras. This chakra is located in the center of the chest, and the most common color associated with this chakra is green. Pink is also associated with this chakra. Interestingly, red (the color associated with the first chakra) and white (the color associated with the seventh chakra) create pink; it is easy to envision how the spiritual and physical mingle at the heart center. A healthy fourth chakra is responsible for your ability to love yourself, to love others, and to have an understanding of the universal love, which represents the All. An unhealthy fourth chakra might result in heart problems, a lack of self-esteem, as well as the inability to acknowledge the differences of others and accept and love everyone on the planet regardless of their race, sexual preference, religious preference, or any other things which make them different from you.

The *fifth chakra* is associated with the color blue, and it is located at the Adam's apple area of the throat. The fifth chakra is responsible for our ability to communicate. Communication is not only our ability to send words outward in the form of our thoughts, but also to receive and understand what is coming inward clearly. A person who has an unhealthy fifth chakra might not immediately understand others, or may jump to conclusions, as well as have an inability to express themselves effectively.

Probably the most well-known chakra is the *sixth chakra*, which is called the "third eye." Its color is indigo. This is the chakra associated with the sixth sense, the ability to be intuitive, the ability to perceive others' feelings, the ability for clairvoyance, ESP, and all phenomenon which are actually ours by birthright. A person with an unhealthy sixth chakra would likely be very linear, very "left-brained," very logic oriented, and unwilling to see two sides to a situation, much less understand the concept of intuition.

The *seventh chakra* is located at the top of the head. Its color is white, although gold and amethyst have also been associated with the seventh chakra. This is the chakra that connects us to our spiritual self as well as to the energy that is the All in the universe, the God and the Goddess. This chakra affects our ability to understand spiritual principles, as well as take spiritual information in and process it. This chakra is the epitome of wisdom and is the culmination of learning and healing of all the other chakras. A person with an unhealthy seventh chakra probably has no religious or spiritual connections, or could possibly have a very narrow-minded approach to religion. Headaches and other ailments associated with the head could be connected to an unhealthy seventh chakra.

Understanding that these areas can be healthy or unhealthy from our physical perspective will help you understand how best to use the stones in relation to the chakras. Actually, it is our health or lack of health that leads us to spiritual questions oftentimes. Therefore, an unhealthy chakra leading to ill health in a particular area often represents a method of learning by our physical selves. Using the stones for healing while keeping this in mind will help you to understand a methodology by which to place the stones so that they are best connected to a specific chakra. Once you have a basic understanding of how these energy areas, or chakras, affect our health, you can correlate them with what you will learn about stones and crystals. During meditation, stones can be placed on various chakras to help create healthy vibrations within the chakras in order to help heal the physical and astral bodies.

Suggestions are given with many of the stones as to where to place them in relation to healing work and the chakras. In a very general manner, using a stone that is the color of the chakra is a fairly accurate practice in order to create healing of those chakras. The dark or red stones would be placed on the base chakra area, an orange stone such as agate on the second chakra, a yellow stone such as citrine on the third chakra, a green stone such as aventurine on the fourth chakra, a blue stone such as blue lace agate or sodalite on the fifth chakra, an amethyst on the sixth chakra, and crystals for the seventh chakra.

If you are ill, it is of course always wise to see your doctor regarding any discomfort or illness, but it is also a good idea to work with other than the physical body for healing modalities. For instance, using the alpha level for visualizing yourself well while doing a stone layout which corresponds with the chakras is an excellent way to align yourself with healing energies.

Charms

Stones and crystals can be made into charms, which are items worn for magickal benefit. Charms made from stones or crystals can be simply the stone itself. To make a simple charm, project the result desired, such as protection or love attraction, into the stone, and then carry that energy with you. There are particular stones for particular results. If you want to become more intuitive, charge an amethyst during ritual with the image of yourself understanding things without knowing why, and knowing that it is your intuition and newly budding psychic abilities blossoming.

As an example, to create a charm from an amethyst during ritual, combine equal parts frankincense, sage, and mugwort, and grind them with a mortar and pestle and bless the mixture as described in Chapter VI. Light a piece of charcoal, which you can purchase at a craft shop, and place the incense on the lit charcoal. Hold the amethyst in your right hand over the smoke created by the incense. Allow the energy from the God and the Goddess to flow through you and visualize yourself as intuitive and using other than your physical senses. Allow the amethyst to be smudged by the incense, which has also been attuned to the energies of intuition. Most important, *know* that your charm will work.

You would then have a stone that is made into a charm that you can carry with you whenever you require intuition, during

Tarot card readings, if you need to know what someone is thinking during a business meeting, or any other time you require your highest intuition.

You can also place your charm, the blessed and charged stone, in a small bag, which is also called a medicine bag. Attach the bag to your person rather than just carrying the loose stone in your pocket or purse. This medicine bag can take the form of a small drawstring satchel that you can wear as a necklace, or a bag that you can tie to your belt. You can also choose to keep your medicine bag in your pocket or desk drawer.

Charms can be made out of any stone. Take any stone listed in Chapter VIII, perhaps from the list of stones to assist with anger or from the list of stones to assist with love. Visualize yourself as being calm during various situations while charging the stone with incense selected specifically to mitigate anger. One to three herbs can be ground with the mortar and pestle. You increase your commitment by smudging the stone with incense as well as visualizing your intent in the stone. For instance, if you want healing energy, select a stone and some herbs from the healing section of the lists, and create a healing charm.

Stones and crystals can also be used for tools and jewelry. You can make your personal wand by using seven different stones which correspond to the seven chakras, and embed the stones into a small branch of willow, oak, or other sacred wood to make your wand. Affix the stones in the order of the chakras, perhaps using a crystal at the tip to represent the seventh chakra. You can attach the stones and crystal with copper wire or jewelry wire. This creates a wand with excellent focus.

Using stones or crystals in your jewelry is a fine way to consciously create clearings in your aura and energy. You can purchase the gemstones with the idea in mind of what you want to achieve; emerald earrings are an excellent way to get in touch with your feminine intuition (whether you are male or female). You can also decide to find your own tumbled stones, go to a craft shop which carries jewelry-making supplies, and create your own necklace, earrings, bracelet, or any other jewelry. You are further asking your stones and crystals to be more than just decoration on you. They become part of your personality. If you are concentrating on an aspect of your personality which requires care and treatment, such as becoming less angry or expressing your anger at an appropriate time in an appropriate manner, you can make a rose quartz necklace. Some craft shops sell little beads of rose quartz and various other stones. You can actually just make a string bead necklace, or you can use a rose quartz crystal and make a necklace with it. The loving energy of the quartz near your heart chakra will allow you to understand yourself and others. Over a long period of time of wearing the necklace, change will become habit and mitigate your anger and allow you to express it in a more appropriate manner. The idea is to use stones or crystals with a specific purpose in mind. Find the trait which requires attention, and charm your jewelry to be of assistance to you.

Your use of charms, tools, and jewelry is limited to your ability to be creative. You can use any combination of stones or crystals to create a desired affect. Having pieces of jewelry containing stones which are charged for specific purposes can make a definite improvement in your life if you are open to change.

You can also carry a set of blessed stones in a small silk bag in your purse or in a pocket. The set of stones would be charged to help each of the chakras for your consistent personal balance with any emotions or ability to fend off the emotions of others. The bag will help you to align the chakra energies, which will create a healthier you both physically and mentally.

A charm can also be made specifically for banishing personal energy which you feel is no longer appropriate. Energy which you no longer require can be given to the Earth or to a body of water. This spell is performed best during a waning moon. One method of doing this is to purchase a rose quartz (tumbled or raw), which should cost no more than one or two dollars. The specific purpose of the banishing should be known, such as banishing unhealthy aspects of a relationship, or an inability to find a new job. This is a banishing technique designed to help you get rid of aspects of your life which are no longer needed. This charm works if you want to give away your procrastination, or your fear of doing something new that you've always wanted to do, or your fear of risk.

Performing this banishing during circle or ritual is best, but is not necessary. Hold the stone in your right hand. Concentrate on the energy of the circumstance moving out of your body and into the stone. Visualize the relationship with the dysfunctional person, the bad aspects of the relationship, visualize that energy literally moving away and into the stone. Carry the stone with you for twenty-four hours, making sure that any last bit of this energy which is no longer wanted is moving into the stone.

After you have completely moved the energy into the stone, bury the stone in the earth with the intent that the earth will heal those energies, and like a hologram, heal the energies within you. You can also throw the stone into the ocean, lake, stream, or any body of natural water. The energies of the water will calm the energy which you have given to the stone, as well as feed intuitive abilities to you which will help you resolve your situation or even just allow you to let it be gone from your consciousness.

Using either method, (1) carrying a charm with you or wearing charged jewelry in order to heal areas of your life, or (2) banishing the energies in yourself to a stone which will then heal a situation you no longer desire, can help you to realign with your highest good. You will be healthier both physically and emotionally while on earth.

✳ Elixirs

The qualities of any stone can be captured in liquid form. A mineral water elixir is highly effective for a variety of uses, and it is very simple to make. All you need is a glass container and whichever mineral, stone, or crystal has the appropriate quality for the purpose of the elixir. Basically, if you wish to create some blessing water, select one of the stones listed in Chapter VIII under "Blessings," such as agate, amethyst, or aquamarine. Place the stone in a glass container—preferably a jar with a lid on it—and place this water, distilled or mineral water, in the sun for up to nine days, but not less than twenty-four hours. The reflective properties of the water will draw the attributes of the stone into the water.

The steps are simple. Obtain pure water, the stone you wish to draw the energies from, and an airtight glass receptacle for the water and a stone. Charge the stone using the visualization technique of holding the stone in your right hand, and sending the purpose of the elixir into the stone. Place the stone into the water. Seal the jar tightly, and set the stone out into the sunlight and/or moonlight. The number of days can also be taken from the aspects of numerology. For instance, letting the stone remain in the glass jar for four days would bring the energy of goal setting to your stone, while letting the stone remain in the glass jar for six days would bring the energy of balance to your stone. Letting the stone remain in the jar for one day (twenty-four hours) will bring "new beginnings" energy to your elixir. The energy of the number one in this process will also create an elixir suitable for use during blessing work.

The uses of this charged water are as endless as your ability to create uses. The blessing can be used to create your circle and to do your ritual bath. You can use this water to sprinkle into your ritual bath and allow the elixir of the stone to work for its highest good in your cleansing. You can also use this water for creating a strong circle as you use water as one of the elements to seal your circle. Depending on the safety of your stone regarding toxicity to your body, you can use this elixir as a drop or two in any soups or tea you make, or any cooking where you could put a drop or two of the water into the recipe. The elixir could be used for a regular, nonritualistic bath. If you want calming during the evening, you can make an elixir specifically for this using one of the calming stones such as moonstone or selenite. Create the elixir for calming and sprinkle a little of this each time you take a bath.

This elixir can be used for any magickal workings. You may choose to use blessing water, or you can use water created specifically for a particular magickal intent. If you have created a poppet to heal a friend, you can make healing water specifically with that friend in mind. If you create a charm for prosperity with a peridot, topaz, turquoise, or any other stone listed under "Money" in Chapter VIII, you can use the elixir to bless the stone that you are using for the charm. Using prosperity water to seal the envelopes of your bills is also a good way to bless them as they go. As with charms, the uses for your elixirs are limited only to your ability to see their potential uses.

☀ Care and Cleansing of Your Stones and Crystals

Stones collect the energy of the person with whom they are in contact. It is important to cleanse this energy from the stones, or the energy of the stones can become as muddy as an unhealthy human aura and incapable of doing their highest good and highest assistance for our realm. As healing work or working with a particular individual's aura can drain the energy of a stone or crystal, the proper care and cleansing is an important part of their maintenance. There are various methods of cleansing stones. Here are discussed four ways which correspond with the four elements of Earth, water, air, and fire.

Earth Cleansing: Place the stone in a natural sack, such as a small cotton or small silk bag. Tether the bag to a small stake. Pound the stake into the ground with the sack tied to the stake. Dig a small hole, and bury the sack next to the stake. Leave the stone in the Earth for at least twenty-four hours. This will realign the stone with the natural healing abilities of the Earth, and cleanse it of any unwanted energy that has been attracted to the stone.

Water Cleansing: Place a stake into the ground near a stream of running water. Put the stone in a cloth bag, and attach it to the stake with a thin rope or fishing wire long enough to allow the bag to bob in the water. For the best water cleansing, leave the stone in the water for at least twenty-four hours. You can also simply hold the stone in the water while sending white light to it for cleansing purposes. Use your intuition as to the length of time for this procedure. Holding stones or crystals in ocean waves has a powerful cleansing effect. If you haven't access to natural sources of water, you can use running tap water to cleanse your stone. The cleanliness of your source of water isn't a strong influence. Of course clean water is preferred, but stones and crystals react to the positive energy of your care and the energy of the water. The positive energy outweighs the negativity of neglect or collected pollutants or chemicals in the water.

Air Cleansing: Light incense which you have blessed. Hold the stone over the smoke that is created by the incense, and send blessing words to the stone such as, "I do bless and cleanse this stone and dedicate it to the light and love of the Goddess, and this I do for the good of All." You can also leave the stone in full moonlight overnight.

Fire Cleansing: Allow the stone to sit in the sun and be cleansed by the energies of the sun. Fire cleansing is most effective during the equinoxes and solstices.

Over time you will develop a relationship with stones. The stones that you collect can be placed in your bath water in the morning. Just allow the energies of the stones to mingle with your own energy. You can also release what you don't want, such as anger or lack of forgiveness, into the water, and mentally state that the negative energies will return to the Earth for cleansing as you release the drain. Getting to know the stones in this manner will also help you understand your own chakra system, along with its strengths and weaknesses, and allow you to have daily contact with the stones that is highly relaxed at the time of day when you are most receptive to new input and new information.

In working with the stones on a daily basis, you will also learn how to use them for healing, how receptive various stones are for charms, what stones to put into jewelry to help you become more effective, and how an elixir feels as it is being formed. Taking a bath with your stones is similar to creating an elixir. When you learn to sense the energies of the water changing, you will begin to sense the difference between plain water and an elixir. Getting to know the stones individually like this will also help you develop your own intuition as to the personalities of various stones without having to read a book.

Use the color of a stone for determining its primary personality, and then just spend time with it, meditate with it, let it talk to you. There is a correlation between the color of stones and the color of chakras. The color of a stone is a clue to its personality. Understanding the chakras will help you understand the personality of color. Be receptive. As with scrying, don't send energy outward in order to understand the stone. Be a receptacle for information and let the stone talk to you.

Below is a list of common stones and their nature. An excellent way to judge your intuition is to purchase or find a stone without knowing its qualities. You do need to know what kind of stone or crystal it is. Hold the stone, and examine the stone closely. Write down any feelings or perceptions which come to you, and then compare them to the descriptions below. Being slightly "off" doesn't necessarily mean you are incorrect in your perceptions and intuitions, as each stone has its own resonance and qualities.

✳ Guide to Crystals, Minerals, and Stones

Agate

Description:

Agates are formed within a large spectrum of colors, including reds, oranges, yellows, browns, blues, and more. Agates can be solid, striped or spotted. Tumbled agates are popular, often inexpensive, and found in a variety of shops owing to their universality.

Key Words:

All relationships, with partner, with self, with others.

Mental/Spiritual:

Agates have many wise personalities, and it is best to attune to a particular agate through meditation to see how it best serves your forward growth. Agates are great to carry in pockets near the second chakra as this will assist in calming anger which is related to romantic relationships, specifically failed or trying relationships. As the negative aspect of anger is cleared, forgiveness is possible, and the memory of the original love and relationship replaces the anger. Placing an agate on the second chakra area and focusing on removing the hurt of past relationships will assist with healing blocks in the second chakra and related organs and aid in the forgiveness process. Forgiveness work is highly beneficial prior to entering into the next relationship as sexual intimacy with the new partner will be enriched if there is no residual anger left from the previous association.

Agates can also open you to your artistic talent, especially when working with clay, wood carving, or any three-dimensional artwork.

As these stones attune well to the second chakra, they are excellent grounding stones, as well as being great for blessing and cleansing yourself prior to any ritual or sacred rite.

Agates promote successful communication where messages are sent *and* received. As such, agates are wonderful stones to assist in banishing any fears and gaining confidence while seeking employment, specifically employment which would place you in a leadership capacity where popularity is important. Carrying an agate will assist with mental focus regarding presenting yourself well, especially helpful during the interview process.

Projecting energy into an agate will assist in breaking a bad habit. Visualize yourself free from the habit, and send that image into the stone. Let the stone know you would like to be free of the habit, that you appreciate the help given. Carry the stone with you so that energy comes to you in the form of "reinforcements" if you feel the urge to continue in your old habit.

Agates of many varieties promote an

analytical mind, and therefore rule out rash actions. For this reason, agates are excellent to carry for personal safety and safety during travel.

Place an agate on your abdomen at the location of the second chakra. Concentrate on the healing energy mingling with your own healing ability. Use standard energy-clearing practices. To banish negativity collected in agates, leave them in a waning Gemini moon for twenty-four hours.

Amber

Description:

Amber has a resinous-looking quality in a variety of brown, rust, orange, and copper colors.

Key Words:

Focus, cleansing.

Mental/Spiritual:

Simply worn as earrings or necklace, amber can enhance upper chakra efficacy. As efficacy in the third eye or sixth chakra occurs, mental focus, psychic ability, and divination abilities are enhanced. Amber earrings are great to wear during ritual if scrying or using the Tarot.

Amber is an excellent stone to facilitate prayer or visualization for environmental cleanup of our earth.

The energy of amber will banish fear and promote grounding while asking unwanted entities to leave.

Carry during travel, especially if it's a long car trip, to ensure safety and ease any negativity that might arise in the close quarters of an automobile.

Amber is an excellent stone to carry to understand difficulty with leadership or authority figures. With this understanding and seeing a given situation from the other viewpoint, you become the "leader" with regard to fixing challenges associated with abrupt leaders.

Regarding the second chakra, amber assists in creativity and easing timidity in sexual activity.

Amber is an excellent stone to meditate with for the third chakra on the solar plexus for clearing stress-related stomach problems.

Amethyst
Description:

Beautiful hues of purple, lavender, lilac all encompass the spectrum of the amethyst crystal. Amethyst can also be purchased in tumbled and polished form.

Key Words:

Loving, knowing.

Mental/Spiritual:

To meditate with an amethyst on your third eye will calm anger, relieve stress, and bring understanding as to why the anger is present with a possible solution.

Amethyst is excellent for pursuits involving mental focus and the improvement of sixth chakra or third eye activity such as astral projection, divination, dreams, intuition, meditation, psychic abilities, and help with better sensing whether information you receive is from your higher self or from spirit guides, muses, or astral teachers. Working with the amethyst in this regard takes on a spiritual edge, and allows you to see the spiritual and loving reasons for honing these skills, rather than allowing you to "perform" them merely because these skills are dramatic. Use of the amethyst in this regard brings an understanding that developing yourself spiritually first will naturally bring these skills as you become open to spirit.

Amethyst will allow you to fully see, from all aspects, the reason for an addiction, and the lessons any addiction has to offer. Understanding an addiction to personal loneliness and the lessons it has to offer is also a gift of the amethyst. Amethyst assists you in understanding negative thoughts about yourself which could subconsciously create distance in or even sabotage love, relationships, or marriage.

Blessing and cleansing your home or office with an amethyst being used as a director of energy will create a peaceful and calm environment. Meditating with an amethyst regarding a difficult or trying situation while being thankful for the predicament will bring the wisdom for the purpose of the situation showing up in your life as a spiritual learning tool.

An amethyst is excellent to carry for protection against emotional stress brought into an area by others. Amethyst is also excellent to visualize the energy of a protective shield around you while banishing unwanted entities and directing them toward the light.

This stone assists in alleviating headaches and in facilitating sleep.

Directing energy into a cleansed amethyst during an Aquarian moon to change a negative relationship into a positive one will bring excellent results. Visualize the outcome you desire, and send that energy into the amethyst, then carry the amethyst with you. It is also excellent to send energy into the stone to banish world violence; place the stone on your altar or sacred area to send focused energy.

Aquamarine
Description: The aquamarine is pale blue to blue-white in color.

Key Words: *Calm communication.*

Mental/Spiritual: When placed on the throat chakra, the peaceful, calming message of aquamarine will help you with calm communication, especially when tempers or anger have been the prior means of communication or lack thereof. Aquamarine will also assist in mental focus as well as intuition during communication and conversations to the point of near psychic ability.

A stone of calm spirituality, the aquamarine will softly guide you during meditation to receive messages that you require to grow spiritually. This spiritual growth will bring understanding and wisdom, which in turn brings happiness and a strong sense of inner peace when you know you are on the right path. Although not necessarily a stone for astral projection, aquamarine will facilitate "traveling" during meditation.

The aquamarine is a good stone for blessing and cleansing.

The aquamarine is a calming stone and will relieve the stress associated with breaking a bad habit.

Aquamarine can be carried in the

workplace, especially during meetings when you are the speaker because of its emphasis on communication and calming influence. Aquamarine will guide you when speaking or leading a meeting so that the message you are sending will be received by the recipients.

Aquamarine is excellent for safety, and especially wonderful for travel across water.

Place an aquamarine in an evening bath to help you get to sleep and maintain a peaceful, restful sleep for the evening. If you have a mild headache, lying down with an aquamarine on your sixth chakra will help to soothe the headache.

Aventurine

Description:

A lovely green stone in various shades of a pine-colored green.

Key Words:

Happy heart stone.

Mental/Spiritual:

When placed on the heart chakra, aventurine will create a space for happiness, removing angry feelings and replacing them with joy, true joy which might make you giggle! Aventurine is excellent for cleansing in the area of personal heart issues.

Allow the aventurine to soothe your spirit prior to doing art. If you are allowing yourself to move to a "dark place" to be creative, aventurine probably isn't the stone for you; however, if you are working with light, aventurine is an excellent stone to create playfulness in the light of your work.

Via meditation with aventurine on

your heart chakra, you can be shown personal patterns which have created blocks to your prosperity in the form of money.

Because aventurine helps with a "happy heart," carrying this stone near your heart chakra will assist in your efforts to draw friendly, like-minded people to you, and help you with your personal efforts at popularity. This popularity is not merely for the sake of gathering people, but to create genuine friendships. This will help with your confidence in dealing with people, leadership qualities, and of course lighten loneliness. The new, like-minded "family" around you will assist in relieving stress.

Aventurine works well to banish a cold that has settled into the chest. Place the aventurine on your heart chakra with several small crystals pointed toward it to amplify the power, and meditate while visualizing your lungs clearing and while breathing green light into your lungs for healing.

Bloodstone

Description: The color of bloodstone is green, with bits of red which appear to be "bleeding through."

Key Words: *Fear be gone!*

Mental/Spiritual: The only thing constant in life is change. Bloodstone will help you realize that current changes are for your personal spiritual growth and evolution, as well as banish the fear that sometimes is associated with change or the unknown.

Bloodstone will help you successfully make the changes needed in your life.

Bloodstone is also wonderful for grounding during periods of change; the red color of the stone assists with connecting to the healing properties of the earth, while the green assists with your heart's understanding of the need for this form of healing.

Bloodstone helps you during "life travels" to journey safely, as it softens the emotional impact of these life travels.

Bloodstone is an excellent stone to facilitate prayer or visualization of environmental cleanup of our earth.

To relieve stress (especially if brought on by major changes in your life), while lying down, place one bloodstone between the heels and one bloodstone just above the head. Next, place a crystal above the bloodstone that is above your head, pointing toward the bloodstone and your seventh chakra. This will bring the healing energies of heart and base chakras throughout your body, calming you and bringing the needed answers to take action on the particular situation which is causing the stress.

Blue Lace Agate
Description:

Blue lace agate is a lovely sky-blue stone with wavy lines of milky-white moving through it.

Key Word:

Communication.

Mental/Spiritual:

Sometimes it is exceedingly difficult to communicate your feelings to someone who is grieving or mourning, or someone who is ill herself. Words can seem so trite and meaningless. Blue lace agate is an excellent stone to carry if you need strength to console someone and bring a degree of calm and peace to her, or allow her to talk to you from her heart.

Blue lace agate also opens the veil to your spirit guides, helping you to differentiate between your thoughts and those of your spirit guides and teachers. Opening this veil will help your guides better attune you with your intuition and psychic ability.

Although blue lace agate does not directly help you with popularity, because of its ability to help with your style of communication and saying the right thing, it will guide your words to assist you in not alienating anyone with harsh words, thereby helping you to keep the friends you have and cultivate more friends. It will also allow you to understand the process of communication more clearly, bringing confidence that you are seeing the other person's point of view, which will help you communicate more wisely.

Meditating with blue lace agate will bring out the nurturing, feminine aspects of self to minister to the self, bringing you closer to deity and the knowledge that being alone doesn't necessarily mean that we are lonely.

Blue lace agate is an excellent stone for mental focus, especially the "mind over matter" strength of will needed to break bad mental habits. Included in "bad mental habits" is negative self-talk, such as "I can't . . . ," which impedes personal growth. Blue lace agate can help change your habitual internal negative self-talk, a dysfunctional form of communicating to the self.

To help heal a sore throat, meditate with the blue lace agate on your fifth chakra. As you inhale, visualize that the air you breathe in is a soothing blue color which heals your throat.

Water is an especially strong element to purify negative energies collected in the blue lace agate. Simply run water over the blue lace agate, letting the collected negative energy run down the drain and then be healed by the Earth.

Bornite
Description:

Also known as "peacock rock" because of the beautiful iridescent colors reminiscent of those in peacock feathers. These colors include varying shades of turquoises, blues, greens, and blue-greens.

Key Word:

Self-image.

Mental/Spiritual:

Bornite, or peacock rock, will enhance your self-image. Not only will carrying bornite allow others to "suddenly" see the best in you, which will in turn increase your popularity and heighten your sense of self-image, but it will also make you aware of good qualities in yourself which you have overlooked in the past. An enhanced self-image, and therefore a happier spirit, will open opportunities for you to create steps toward your personal idea of success.

Bornite is also a stone of luck, especially in the form of being creative about being in the right place at the right time.

As these positive changes take place, you will experience a confidence that promotes personal growth in the form of advancement on the physical level.

Bornite will help you to connect with the heart center of your spirit guides and teachers, a means of learning more about their personalities.

To relieve stress, place some bornite which has been cleansed of negativity on a table in front of you. Take a piece of paper, and write down all the things that cause stress in your life. Hold the bornite in your left hand, and the piece of paper in your right. Feel yourself receiving from the bornite the energy you need to clear the stress out of your life; let it move through your body and into your right hand and into the paper. Visualize all the things causing stress receiving the energy to be cleansed and transformed. Fold the paper several times to "bond" the good energy to the stressful items in your life. Put the paper in a small pouch, then bury the pouch while asking the Earth to cleanse the items and remove the stress.

Calcite

Description: Calcite comes in a variety of beautiful colors including clear, a variety of reds, a variety of yellows, as well as a variety of blues.

Key Words: *Spiritual awareness.*

Mental/Spiritual: Calcite is a highly spiritual stone, helping you to become aware of your hidden talents. White calcite can be used to create a circle for ritual, a circle which will make you aware of the energy of forces present who are there to help you. These are good conditions under which to scry for divination purposes during ritual.

White calcite will assist with astral projection and psychic pursuits. This stone helps with seeking higher spiritual awareness, truly giving thanks, receiving understanding of the purpose of negative situations in our life, and therefore attaining the wisdom necessary to deal with those situations. White calcite can be used for blessing and cleansing your home and ridding it of any unwanted entities or energies.

Blue calcite will heighten your intuition, and allows you to attain deeper levels of meditation and become aware of your spirit guides, muses, or teachers. This stone will banish negativity from a selected environment, bringing a sense of calm and peace to the environment. This, in turn, relieves stress.

Green calcite works well to allow peaceful dreams during sleep. If so programmed, it will also bring meaningful dreams which contain messages of how to solve problems in your life. Green calcite is also excellent for breaking bad eating habits, as it works on the aspect of yourself which requires eating as a sense of comfort.

Orange calcite will bring out your artistic nature.

Red calcite will make you more aware of your connection with the Earth, creating a higher level of personal safety and safety while traveling.

Calcite of any color is excellent for facilitating prayer or visualization of environmental cleanup of our earth.

The various colors of calcite can be placed on the corresponding chakras to augment healing meditations for the organs or area in harmony with those chakras.

Carnelian

Description: Carnelian is a murky, opaque stone in various colors of rust, orange, dark gold, and orange/browns with smoky darker lines running through the stone.

Key Words: *Energy, balance.*

Mental/Spiritual: Carry a carnelian in your pants pocket close to where it can influence your second chakra to keep your emotions balanced.

Carnelian is outstanding for creative and artistic endeavors of all kinds, including gaining employment in acting and theatre production. Such employment includes pursuit of directing and producing as carnelian also aids in leadership skills. Because it is combined with the ability to banish fear as well as achieve success, carnelian will help you gain the confidence to market your work and yourself in this field. Carnelian is especially helpful in understanding the strength of "team work" and a team effort in theatre.

Carnelian is excellent for blessing and

cleansing the physical body, and removing qualities that create loneliness and impede your ability to relate to others, whether it be business relationships, relationships with friends, or your ability to relate to the one you love. This cleansing will also remove blocks to finding an appropriate mate for marriage. Carnelian also maintains a balanced relationship whereby two can remain monogamous during their relationship. As carnelian is an excellent stone for the second chakra, not only relationships but the sexual organs are affected by the healthy energy; it therefore also promotes fertility.

Carnelian is an excellent stone for meditation. While meditating, project energy into the stone for items already mentioned, as well as projecting protection during physical and athletic pursuits, banishing negative dreams and nightmares, and drawing money to you.

Carnelian is an excellent stone for grounding, and as you are grounded while using carnelian, you will feel that you are able to distribute energy more efficiently, and therefore not have "highs and lows" during the day.

Carnelian facilitates prayer or visualization of environmental cleanup of our earth.

Meditation with carnelian on your second chakra while visualizing freeing this area of negativity and filling it with white light and creative forces will help you work toward a healthier physical condition.

Cat's Eye

Description: When polished, cat's eye is a satiny-appearing stone in varying colors of golden browns with markings which give the appearance of a cat's eye.

Key Words: *Forward movement.*

Mental/Spiritual: Just as a cat will take action when hungry and pounce on its prey, the cat's eye represents forward movement and action. If you find yourself in a "stuck place" that doesn't seem to be working for your highest good, cat's eye will help you move toward your goal with confidence, intuition, and success. Meditation with cat's eye will also assist you in learning the reason you became stuck in the first place.

Cat's eye is an excellent stone for leadership. This stone will assist with keeping your eye on the goal for the group endeavor, a strong leadership quality.

In a manner of speaking, cat's eye is also good in the leadership capacity regarding who's the boss in your home. Carrying cat's eye while banishing unwanted entities shows that you mean business.

As cat's eye helps with second chakra work, it assists with creativity blocks and sexual blocks, as well as blocks about being creative sexually!

Meditate with two cat's eyes, one on your second chakra, and one on your third eye, in order to intuit any problems or blocks in the second chakra.

Citrine

Description: Crystals and stones range from palest of yellow to a vivid gold to a rich topaz/ brown color.

Key Word: *Self-realization.*

Mental/Spiritual: Citrine is a stone that teaches happiness, but that happiness is a result of clearing the third chakra so that you can finally realize that you are in control and that you create your personal power. Citrine teaches that you are in charge of your destiny, and that it's not external, outside factors dictating your life's path. Citrine is also a stone representing personal responsibility. You make your luck by being in the right frame of mind. Citrine teaches that we are all valid as individuals, and if we are open, we create our own confidence, self-image, success, power, leadership skills, money, and prosperity. Citrine alleviates the stress of the bad habit of feeling "out of control," and allows us to move forward in a positive fashion knowing that confidence and success are ours. If you are seeking employment, these valuable lessons are paramount to getting the job.

Citrine helps with your intuition, specifically with recognizing the "gut feeling" aspect of intuition.

As citrine helps to clear the third chakra, it is an excellent stone to carry to remove any anger involving power struggles, and to carry for protection during those power struggles. Communication regarding power will come from pure intent when citrine is carried.

Citrine facilitates mental focus during visualization meditation, especially if you are seeking wisdom through meditation.

For blessing and cleansing an area, meditate with a citrine to clear your third chakra of any personal "debris" and visualize bright yellow light washing over your third chakra. Once you feel the energy of your power center, proceed to take in energy from the universe as you inhale, and then exhale, imagining good, clean, blessed energy moving through your solar plexus to the room around you. Fill the room with the newly found energy.

If you are lonely, citrine will help you understand the purpose of your loneliness, and show you how to banish negative thoughts of yourself. This will open the door to friendships, and you will begin to see yourself in a new light. The new light is also the way new friends will begin to see you.

Citrine aides in any disorders related to the third chakra.

Some maintain that it is not necessary to cleanse a citrine; however, it is certainly beneficial to occasionally hold the stone in your right hand. Visualize Goddess or universal light and love moving through your seventh chakra, and then down through your arm, through to the citrine, while thanking the citrine for its guidance.

Copper
Description: Copper!

Key Word: *Success.*

Mental/Spiritual: Copper removes blocks that have kept you from achieving your highest goals and your personal idea of success and prosperity. Accompanied by the removal of these blocks is the removal of any previous fears associated with the forward movement necessary to achieve your goals. Realize that fear associated with success is also a spiritual block.

Copper will help the artistically gifted to generate ideas.

If you are feeling "scattered," copper will help to ground and center you. This aspect of copper is especially helpful if grounding and centering are needed during stressful situations if you are in management or a position of leadership.

Copper helps to ease sexual inhibition and to remove learned attitudes or guilt toward sex, allowing you to be more comfortable with your partner.

Copper is an excellent metal to facilitate prayer or visualization of environmental cleanup of our earth.

It is said that a copper bracelet will help ease the pain of arthritis as well as soothe tendon strain caused by computer work.

Coral
Description: Coral, actually a marine invertebrate, is found in a variety of colors, shapes, and sizes.

Key Words: *Psychic pursuits.*

Mental/Spiritual: Coral is an excellent "stone" to have on your altar while doing magick, or to place in the west of your circle as a representation of the element of water. As coral comes from our queen mother source of the water element, the sea, there is much "water energy" within the core of this substance. Water energy includes intuition, creativity, and peace. Put the two together, meaning the creative and intuitive energies of coral as well as working with it in circle, and you can see how your visualization for magickal workings will increase and become strikingly clear.

Place coral in a warm bath at night. While bathing, visualize falling asleep quickly and sleeping well throughout the night. You will be assured of a restful sleep.

Diamond

Description: A mineral with a range of colors, with white (clear) being the most well known.

Key Word: *Love.*

Mental/Spiritual: The diamond is a stone of Universal Love, as it can transmute fear (the opposite of love) into understanding, and negativity into wisdom, bringing peace to a situation. While meditating with a diamond resting on your seventh chakra, visualize blessing and cleansing a "negative" situation. Realize that you have power over the situation, and that any situation you encounter was designed by you to raise your consciousness and bring yourself in tune with growth in your personal spirituality.

When focused on the seventh chakra, the diamond can also assist in showing the metaphysical purpose for anger as relates to a particular situation.

The diamond is beneficial to all chakras, and is especially helpful to the sixth and seventh chakras working in unison. The diamond is therefore a prime candidate to help you understand that psychic ability, astral projection, divination, and healing are truly gifts from the universe. To believe otherwise is the work of our ego.

When specifically directed, the diamond enhances safety and protection when clearing a home of unwanted entities.

The diamond is a stone of new beginnings and can bring confidence and success to new endeavors or new employment, and will assist with leadership skills if you are new and inexperienced in a position of authority. The diamond will also bring success in drawing money and prosperity to you.

Creativity comes from the right brain, and mental focus comes from the left. The diamond will promote the functioning of these two sides of the brain as "willing" to communicate with one another. Bringing these two sides of the brain together will help you accomplish creative endeavors in a disciplined and focused manner.

The diamond will help you realize that loneliness comes from your personal separation from the Goddess, the God, and Universal Energy, and that being "alone" does not necessarily mean that you need be "lonely." In this regard, the diamond will assist with bringing personal happiness that precludes the idea that being alone does mean being lonely. Our ability to love ourselves is directly related to our ability to love others. The diamond teaches that as we heal our ability to love ourselves fully, we become open to new relationships, romantic or otherwise, opening the opportunity for new friends of like ilk. The diamond assists in our ability to see in ourselves old patterns which kept us from seeing how we relate to ourselves, others, and the universe, hence opening us to new possibilities. For this reason, the diamond is also excellent for romantic relationships and marriage. If fertility energy is desired, the diamond can help to call the Fates to your favor in the fertility process because of its "creativity" and "beginnings" energy.

If someone you love is about to travel and he owns a diamond, visualize his safe return and project that image into the diamond to ensure he does return safely.

As relates to "beginnings," the diamond will assist in thwarting personal violence in its beginning stages.

To lessen the pain of a tension headache, hold the diamond to your sixth chakra and visualize white light pouring into your head and erasing all pain.

Emerald
Description:

A brightly colored gemstone which is actually a form of the mineral beryl having sufficient chromium present in it to create the bright green color for which it is famous.

Key Words: *Feminine strength.*

Mental/Spiritual: The emerald is the epitome of loving feminine energy. It can assist with realizing whether anger is associated with matters of the heart. Hold an emerald at the heart chakra, and if a particular person comes to mind, continue with meditation to heal emotions or do forgiveness work where anger toward this person is concerned.

The feminine energy of emerald will help you to understand the true meaning of strength. Feminine wisdom, understanding, creativity (a form of creation), spiritual growth, intuition, and leadership are highly misunderstood feminine qualities. Aggressiveness and prosperity in the material world have been valued as strength since the advent of patriarchal society. The emerald will help you to value the strengths of femininity.

When placed with jade under your pillow, the emerald will help you use your dreams for divination purposes.

The emerald will help you to understand the true meaning of love and marriage. This gemstone will aid in identifying reasons for the lack of relationship or loneliness, the reason for your current relationship, or unrest within your relationship.

Channeling prosperity energy through an emerald for the purpose of blessing a business will help to draw money to the business. If your business is in a previously leased shop, it is also an excellent way to clear (exorcise) the space of previous nonprosperous, negative business "residue."

Working and meditating with the emerald on your heart chakra will assist with abating stress, while bringing calm and peace. As you develop a stress-free, calm, peaceful personality, you will draw people with like intentions to you.

The emerald facilitates group meditations to stop world violence, especially by focusing the energy on individual violence-prone areas.

If you have problems with fertility, place an emerald on the second chakra with three small crystals pointing downward, one from the heart down to the solar plexus, one from the solar plexus down to the second chakra, and one pointing directly to the emerald. Meditate with the stones in this position to understand the metaphysical reasons behind the lack of fertility, as well as give insight as to steps to take to remove any blocks in that area.

This stone will help males who wish to understand feminine qualities, either those feminine aspects within themselves, or communicating with sisters, mothers, wives, and lovers. Either wear an emerald ring, or scry with an emerald for a specific challenging area regarding balance and femininity.

Fossil

Description:

Fossils are the remnants of animals or plants left in limestone, sandstone, or shale, or which have been trapped in tar, amber, or ice.

Key Word:	*Completion.*
Mental/Spiritual:	None of the properties in Chapter VIII focuses specifically on the special ability of the fossil, the ability to assist with completion. As the fossil is an animal or plant that perhaps met an untimely death, the struggle for life is inherent within the fossil. The fossil therefore represents the cycle of life. As the struggle gives way to healing from the Earth energies, and then surfaces again as the new fossilized structure, the cycle of completion is also represented. Fossil can therefore help you with understanding and accepting when an issue is ready to close and heal in your life, perhaps a relationship or a job. If these have not been fully processed in your mind and heart, the fossil can help you put to rest the ever-important forgiveness process. Plant fossils resonate a reassuring and feminine healing energy, while animal fossils resonate a masculine take-action healing energy.

Garnet

Description:	Whether polished stone or gemstone quality, garnets are formed in a variety of colors. Although the most popular or traditionally known hue is red, garnet is formed in an array of browns, greens, and yellows, and can also be either clear (common) or black.
Key Words:	*Healthy relationship.*
Mental/Spiritual:	The garnet will help to banish negativity and fear where love, relationships, and

marriage are concerned. If your previous experience with relationships has been negative, the garnet will help you understand what proper relationship is, and also allow your intuition to reign supreme in finding a healthy relationship. This permits you to seek happiness in a relationship and teaches that you can learn from joy as well as grief and sorrow. Although a relationship is not meant to alleviate loneliness, as only an individual can alleviate her own loneliness, the garnet's ability to help you seek a like-minded partner will help to mitigate loneliness of that nature. From a spiritual perspective, the garnet will also clear energies within you to allow you to see the divine within a partner, even during moments of stress or anxiety within a relationship.

If you are currently in a relationship which you perceive to be negative, the garnet will assist you in knowing the underlying causes for an unhealthy relationship and the responsibility you must take for your part in an unhealthy relationship.

The garnet will also assist you with healthy, monogamous sexual practices which lead to healing unity between two people rather than using sex as a manipulative endeavor. Because the garnet encourages healthy sexual relationship, if fertility is desired, this healthy attitude will help to remove any metaphysical blocks associated with the fertility process.

The garnet will enhance confidence in

any matter, and is also beneficial for enhancing confidence in leadership situations.

Regarding money and prosperity, the garnet will help to remove the stress that is perceived to be the necessary reaction to lack of money. With this stress removed, it will then be easier to visualize the prosperity you deserve.

The garnet is a terrific stone to assist one with resurrecting or even restoring old friendships. Visualize the friendship taking root again, and focus that intention into the stone. Visualize smiles upon contact, then make contact with the friend from your past, and you will find he is very receptive to you. Once contact has been made, cleanse the stone if you wish to repeat the procedure.

The garnet will assist with the development of personal gifts and talents whether they be artistic, talents helping people, in business pursuits, or other gifts. In other words, the garnet will amplify what you do best.

The garnet is an excellent stone to facilitate prayer for or visualization of environmental cleanup of our earth, as well as stopping world violence while promoting world peace.

For back problems, direct energy into several small, tumbled garnets to assist with healing your back. Next, place the garnets in a very warm bath. While you relax in the bath with the garnets, meditate and visualize the stones pulling the negative energy out of your back, as though streamers of negative energy are leaving your body and moving into the stones. After you are finished with the visualization and the bath, place the garnets into a cloth bag and bury in the Earth for cleansing for at least seven days.

Geode

Description:

Geode is a more or less round stone of various sizes with crystals on the inside. Often sold as a stone which you later crack open to find the crystals yourself. The crystals are formed as water seeps in and minerals are left behind.

Key Word:

Understanding.

Mental/Spiritual:

See *Agate* for further information as agate and geode have comparable energies.

Geode brings with it energies of change, and therefore energies of growth. This stone assists in breaking habits or banishing negativity that is no longer necessary for growth as the lessons have been learned yet the habits linger. If the lesson has been learned on an intellectual level, the geode will help you to *know* the lesson from a heart level. For instance, knowing smoking is bad for your health is an intellectual understanding; knowing smoking is bad for your health because it blocks your spirit from growing and does not honor your sacred body is an understanding from a heart level.

The agate is an excellent stone for the analytical mind. The geode takes the analytical ability one step further, and helps you to understand things on many different levels. It combines analytical capabilities with intuition and wisdom. This combination could perhaps bring visions or great symbolism during meditation. If you imagine the crystalline structures inside a geode reflecting back to the other side of a geode, the answers to questions will come to you on different levels much as the geode reflects back at itself from many directions. This form of reflection enables spiritual advancement and success.

The geode also carries with it the wisdom that prosperity is not only monetary. Prosperity can come in the form of friends, family, loving pets, a great work environment, or gifts and talents. The geode teaches you how to appreciate these other forms of prosperity in order that you feel less monetary lack.

As the geode assists with better communicating between the left brain and the right brain (intuition influencing logic), an excellent mental/intuition exercise is to lie down with a geode placed on your third eye. Visualize the inside of your head as an empty void. Pose a question. Note how you "hear" the question in your head. This is focused thinking. Now, allow yourself to "hear" thoughts from this one question from many directions within your head, similar to hitting a pool ball and having it hit many sides of a pool table. This emulates the refractive properties inside of a geode. You'll be surprised at the "new" answers you receive to the question posed.

Gold
Description:

Gold is a bright yellow or gold metal with a high sheen.

Key Word: *Confidence.*

Mental/Spiritual: Gold is connected to the astrological sign of Leo as well as the third chakra. Just as you would perform magick during a Leo moon for confidence, leadership, power, and success, so too would you develop a meditative relationship with gold in order to seek results related to these characteristics. Be aware, though, that gold is a great teacher in this regard, and sometimes the lessons can be difficult.

Gold is related to success on the material level, and is therefore associated with material and monetary gain.

Wearing charged gold for an interview will enhance your possibilities for success in gaining employment if it is meant to be. Gold will also bring understanding as to why you are blocking yourself from gaining employment as well as further define the purpose of your struggle. As gold also assists with both mental focus and Leo energy, it is an excellent tool to help you "sell yourself" to the prospective employer.

If you have been in a challenging situation regarding love or marriage, or lack thereof, gold will assist you with understanding the purpose for that lack or loneliness. Gold will also give you the courage to seek new avenues previously not sought in order to find love. If a previous relationship was violent, gold will also help to direct you to a relationship without violence as it will teach self-love.

The saying goes that gold can't buy

you happiness, but it certainly resonates with a happy and thankful energy. Gold will help you to be thankful for the way the Goddess and the Universe have brought lessons to you to become a better person, and therefore create a happiness innate in a contented life. Gold also teaches the wisdom to be happy and contented with what you have, thereby erasing the seeming need for sorrow for what you do not have.

Wear gold with you for safety during travel—just don't flash it around in dangerous areas!

Gold is an excellent metal for meditation with the third (power) chakra. As personal power is often misunderstood and sometimes out of balance because of our patriarchal society, meditate with gold on your third chakra to better understand the purpose of personal power and the difference between healthy and unhealthy personal power. Then, move the gold to the heart chakra to bring the energies of the power center to your heart chakra. Become aware of the strength you feel there. Concentrate on a particular situation where you feel a lack of power, and see what ideas come to you when your power is centered from the heart.

Hematite
Description:

Hematite is a very dense, smooth, lustrous silver-colored mineral.

Key Words:

Calming, harmony within self.

Mental/Spiritual:

Hematite teaches harmony within self and brings the understanding that you are doing the best you can with a given situation, taking into consideration your life circumstances and your knowledge and ability to handle a situation at any given moment. As you become self-accepting and learn that we are all doing the best we can, inner conflict will give way to inner harmony. If, however, your goal is to come to terms with your past, hematite can gently bring to the surface old anger you have had toward another or yourself. Because of this, it is a superb stone to assist with healing the past.

Hematite is a fabulous stone for grounding. Merely carrying hematite in your pocket near your base chakra will bring wonderful, immediate grounding results. Grounding is an excellent way to keep you in the "now" rather than in the past or future. As hematite keeps you in the now, it will banish fear, reduce stress, and then calm you regarding future or past events. As the future does not exist in the present, hematite teaches that there is no need to allow fear to enter your thoughts and create anxiety based on something that does not yet exist.

Carry hematite to calm stressful situations and banish negativity and protect you from negativity in your environment. Placing hematite in an area which resonates with negative energy will clear the area of that energy. Remember to cleanse the stone often if it is used for either of these purposes as hematite very quickly absorbs energy like a sponge absorbs water.

If you are attempting to overcome emotional habits such as anger or defense mechanisms such as sarcasm, hematite will gently remind you of your intention to release any habit which is no longer necessary for your spiritual growth.

Hematite will help you to draw love into your life which could lead to marriage. If monogamy has been a problem in past relationships, hematite will help you to find love that will remain true to the relationship if that is your goal.

Meditation with a group focusing energy into a hematite for stopping violence in the world is definitely beneficial to the world.

Just as hematite will help you understand yourself and learn to appreciate yourself, so too will it help you to intuitively understand others. If you are going into a situation where you wish to understand others, such as a business meeting or in a group where you are teaching or passing on information, charge a hematite with the thought that you will understand the group that you are about to encounter. This is a powerful charge as you might actually see the individuals understanding and then experience "déjà vu" as the visualization or charge actually occurs, bordering on divination.

Herkimer Diamond

Description:

The herkimer diamond is an incredibly clear crystal which resembles a diamond.

Key Words:

The seeker's crystal.

Mental/Spiritual:

The herkimer diamond will assist you during meditation to help you discover answers to life issues you purposefully examine. Questions regarding your personal actions or life choices are particularly effectively answered.

Simply carrying the herkimer diamond will also bring you luck in a general manner.

To allow the herkimer diamond to assist you with answers to your questions about your personal actions or life choices, lie back and place a herkimer diamond on your third eye. Gently inhale, then visualize the energy of the crystal moving through your third eye and into your brain, or more specifically, your thought patterns. Once you feel the energy of the herkimer within your thoughts, completely visualize a situation which has become a life choice of yours. Allow yourself to ask, "Why?" You will receive the answer in the form of, for example, seeing a person who is prominent in your life appear in the picture. This will give a clue that your life choice has to do with learning a lesson with that individual. Seeing someone during a meditative state such as this would have to do with either healing that relationship (forgiveness) or learning to let go (acceptance). Either lesson is a strong one.

Jade

Description:

Jade is a stone with a color range of dark forest green to palest ivory.

Key Words:

To dream.

Mental/Spiritual:

Jade can assist with answers in dreams as to how to solve anger, and provide loving answers as to how to mitigate the anger, or the source of the anger can be made apparent if it is unknown. A jade stone can be charged in order to be able to pursue psychic work through your dreams, and in your dreams, you can charge the stone to bring your spirit guides, muses, or teachers to you, as well as do divination work regarding the future, or becoming more intuitive while dreaming. You can charge the stone to bring any answers to you during your dreams, and also use visualization and the alpha level to help you work with the energy of the jade stone to understand your dreams fully.

Our dreams allow us to work through the problems we've had throughout the day. They also allow our mind time for free-form activity in order to solve those problems, sort them out, or categorize them. You can charge a jade to help you understand those processes. Use alpha in conjunction with jade to assist in any area, whether to bring creativity, to banish negativity from your life, to show you how to mitigate any loneliness you might be experiencing. Use alpha in conjunction with jade to find love and/or marriage, as well as find the reasons for the lack thereof. You can use alpha in conjunction with jade to find answers to any facet of your life, and allow your brain time to solve any problem in your life.

As you make better use of your sleeping patterns, you will make progress in your personal life. You will then begin to develop a sense of peace and experience less stress through these practices. Certainly restful sleep in and of itself will alleviate stress.

The jade stone will help you to work with the psychic aspect of yourself, and help you to understand that the psychic is connected to the spiritual aspect of yourself.

Jade will cleanse a room just by being in the room. You can use jade to bless any area, whether it is your car, an office, or a room within your home.

Jade is an excellent stone for stopping violence or anger within your home. If there are troubled parties, place a piece of jade under each pillow. Charge the jade stones so that they become matching pieces of the same energy. Hold two jade stones within your hand and visualize the parties reconciling, and then place the jade under each of their pillows. Solutions will come to both parties as to how to resolve the problems and forgive one another. Harmony will be restored.

Jasper

Description:

Jasper is a stone with a wide range of color. Siberian jasper has red and green bands. Egyptian jasper ranges from yellow to brown. There is also a form of jasper which is actually "agate jasper," and some bloodstones actually contain red jasper.

Key Word:

Confidence.

Mental/Spiritual:

Jasper has the ability to bring confidence to you in any situation. Because of this, in regard to moving forward with a personal goal, jasper can banish your fear and help you to move forward with your goal.

Jasper also helps in a marriage to keep the marriage monogamous, or in a relationship to keep any two people monogamous. Jasper is also an excellent stone for fertility; this fertility can be in the form of monetary gain, ideas, or any other area where something new is to be born.

As jasper helps with goals, it's a good idea to carry jasper and charge it for a particular goal. For instance, if you want to have a different physical appearance, picture what you wish to look like, within reason, of course, and project that image into the jasper. Charge the jasper with your new look. Simply carry the jasper in your gym bag if physical fitness is one of the methods to gain your new look. If you have a goal of moving toward a higher business situation within a company, charge the jasper with how you would like to advance within the company, and then keep the jasper on your desk or in the desk drawer. Perhaps you want to become a better driver. Picture yourself handling all driving situations quickly, reasonably, and well, and charge the jasper with this image. Leave the jasper in your car. These give you a few ideas for how to use jasper for goal setting. The idea is to have the goal, charge the jasper with the projected idea of your goal, then carry the jasper in a place which is most conducive to that goal.

Lapis Lazuli

Description: Lapis lazuli is a midnight blue stone with flecks of silver or white running through it.

Key Words: *Psychological strength.*

Mental/Spiritual: Lapis lazuli can help you align with your personal happiness. Because of this, it is an excellent stone to help you understand how you can best present your personality in the world. It helps with leadership in this regard, assisting you with the ability to talk to people, talk within a group setting, lead people, and project your happiest self, which also will show a sense of confidence.

Lapis lazuli works well as earrings as it will then be within the realm to influence your third eye and assist with intuition, psychic ability, meditation, and spirituality. Lapis lazuli works on your ability to be happy; this happiness also teaches you how to be open. When you are open, you can then become more intuitive and psychic, as well as being more open to spiritual matters.

Lapis lazuli is excellent for placing on your fifth chakra and concentrating on healing a sore throat. In general, lapis lazuli can also help you heal a blue mood, and will assist with exorcising any negativity within you. The negativity exorcised can be in the form of getting rid of the "monkey on your shoulder." Once the monkey is gone, you will see things from a brighter perspective.

Lodestone

Description:

Also called *magnetite,* lodestone is a black stone which is a common ore with a metallic luster, although some stones seem not to have much luster. Lodestone is a natural magnet.

Key Words:

Mental clarity.

Mental/Spiritual:

Lodestone is an excellent stone for communication, mental focus, and can also help you use linear thinking, straight logical thinking, in order to attain that which you strive for. Lodestone is great to carry for meetings, tests, and anything which requires logic. Regarding meetings, lodestone will assist in guiding meetings, and helps with leadership skills during such meetings. Conversely, lodestone assists with intuition and psychic abilities and gaining insight in the spiritual realm. Because it is an excellent stone for communication, it helps the left and right sides of the brain work together toward a common goal. If you are communicating with someone, you will understand the logic behind the communication, as well as have intuition about what might be going on "behind the scenes."

Regarding love, lodestone can help bring the kind of love to you that is conducive to communication, where you will be right for one another and share the same ideas. Lodestone will help you draw like-minded love to you, and work toward a monogamous relationship. For partnerships, lodestone helps you work toward a common goal and meet your objectives together. These objectives are perhaps earthy as far as monetary or family matters.

Lodestone will protect you when you carry it with you during a meeting or in a situation where communication is paramount to solving a problem. It will protect you from those who would normally attack verbally. In other words, it will calm a situation to the point where you can talk to one another without apprehension of being attacked verbally.

Magnetite   See *Lodestone.*

Malachite
Description: Malachite is a green mineral which has also been used as a pigment. Malachite has a beautiful luster when polished, and has been used widely as a gemstone since ancient times.

Key Word: *Understanding.*

Mental/Spiritual: As we go through various situations in our life, malachite helps us understand the reason for the changes within our lives. For instance, if we become ill, malachite will help us understand the reason for the illness, whether it is a common cold or something more serious. Malachite can help us banish negativity associated with the disease, and therefore continue learning from and understanding the disease.

Malachite helps us with our higher self, giving us the intuition and psychic ability to understand that self. In other words, our higher self would be able to tell us directly the purpose for being sick.

To meditate with malachite while you are not well will help you to see clearly, perhaps even in a vision situation, the reason for any changes you are experiencing. Malachite will help you understand that you are safe during these travels via shedding the cocoon through your health and healing process.

Malachite is a wonderful stone to carry if you are trying to let a seemingly negative entity know how to find its way to the light. Malachite will help transfer the negative energies of that entity into loving energy, and actually help you to teach the entity to move toward loving light, although this is quite advanced work.

Marble

Description: Marble can be a combination of dolomite and calcite. Marble can be highly polished and is primarily used for building and art in the form of statuary. Marble has a veined quality as other elements run through the calcite to form the veins.

Key Word: *Strength.*

Mental/Spiritual: Marble has a long history dating back to ancient Greece. Statues and pillars were made of marble. The pillar can be seen as a metaphor for what marble can do for our metaphysical selves and our understanding of our spiritual selves. Marble is a very earth-centered stone, and can bring very earth-centered traits into our lives. Leadership, power, prosperity, and success can all be gained through meditation with marble. Also, we can learn what we need to do to grow in our personal evolution to gain these things if that is our goal.

Marble also assists with keeping us calm during transitions and growth, helps us work toward success and prosperity, and helps us understand the pillar of strength within us.

Keep marble in a room where someone is ill if you need to be strong for that person. It allows you to be strong enough to listen to the person's feelings regarding illness, rather than avoiding that kind of talk, as is so common. We can also mentally note our personal fears regarding illness.

Marcasite

Description: Marcasite has similar composition to pyrite, and is identified by its metallic luster.

Key Word: *Self-understanding.*

Mental/Spiritual: Marcasite will assist you to find what is good within yourself and bring it out for the world to see how shiny you are! The reflective, shiny surface of marcasite is an excellent example of how we are mirrors of all that has come to us. Marcasite assists with artistic talent, the artistic talent being something within us that *must* shine forth. Marcasite can assist with leadership in the artistic realm, such as directing or choreography. It also helps us break bad habits as these habits are no longer needed to let everyone know who we truly are. These bad habits can be in the form of the way we harm ourselves, such as smoking or drinking, but they can also be the bad habit of defense mechanisms which are no longer needed such as sarcasm. Marcasite is a wonderful healing stone regarding personal cleansing, and will help you clear away that which is no longer needed.

Like hematite, marcasite is an excellent stone to draw to you the love which could lead to marriage of someone who is like-minded. As we reflect the mirror image of ourselves outward, that is what we will attract to us. This helps us to understand that those whom we attract into our lives are also acting as our personal teachers and guides as far as lessons we need to learn to better understand ourselves. In understanding ourselves, we can understand others. From understanding our personal actions and the actions of others, therein we gain true wisdom.

Marcasite helps to allow the process of sleep to become more natural if it has been difficult in the past. During this sleep, dreams will come which will help to act as a catalyst to understanding your personal spirituality and enhance your intuition. The dreams will be indicative of your potential spiritual goals.

If you are experiencing a lack of money, meditation with marcasite can show you ways to bring money into your life more readily.

To meditate with marcasite can assist you in stopping violence. Send energy toward violent people so they can look within themselves to understand where their violence is coming from.

Meteorite

Description: A composite of iron and nickel, with traces of cobalt and silicates. It is now believed that meteorites are actually asteroids. The stones generally have a pitted surface.

Key Words: *Broaden horizons.*

Mental/Spiritual: Meditation with meteorite can help us to understand that if we move outside our normal day-to-day lives, there are opportunities available to us. There are opportunities beyond our natural scope of life as we understand it that can bring us higher understanding. One aspect of higher understanding is divination, and therefore, meteorite is excellent to carry with you while doing many forms of divination, whether it be for the Tarot or scrying, or for pendulum work or dowsing. Being receptive is the key to divination—rather than sending energy outward, receive energy inward. Meteorite is a wonderful stone to assist with receptivity. Just as we receive the meteor as a gift, so too can we receive information from external sources as a gift.

Mica

Description: There are several types of mica which share the common characteristic of forming in thin-layered sheets, and mica is formed in various colors depending on the mineral which combines with it.

Key Word: *Self-understanding.*

Mental/Spiritual:

Mica is a reflective stone. It is also a stone which will help us understand ourselves better, and reflect what we send outward back to us. This will help us understand what we're sending out. In this regard, mica works well for grounding and banishing fear, and cleansing that which is no longer necessary in order to become whole. Mica assists with dreams. If consciously directed into mica, dreams will come to you which will teach you about yourself and help you to understand yourself better.

Meditation with mica will help us better define who we would require in a love relationship or in a marriage relationship. Being able to define our needs will help to draw to us specifically who we require. The reflective properties of mica also let us intuitively know whether the love we have drawn to us is correct for our growth and well-being. As mica heals us on many levels, we are free to learn spiritual lessons more pragmatically as they come to us, rather than experiencing the events in our lives as emotional.

Moonstone
Description:

Moonstone is a beautiful white stone which looks like the full moon when polished.

Key Words:

Hearth and home.

Mental/Spiritual:

The key words for emerald are feminine strength, and these could very well be the key words for moonstone. The difference is that the emerald is of the loving, feminine energy of the earth, while the moonstone is of the loving, feminine energy of water.

The loving and feminine energy of moonstone can act as mother and guidance as to why anger might be showing itself in your life.

As moonstone is a water stone, and a feminine stone, it can help with intuition, meditation, psychic ability, as well as connect you with your spirit guides and teachers. This feminine, water energy is also a very strong protective energy. Moonstone can take the protection of the lioness with her cubs and assist you in protecting your family, your children, and the love that remains in your family, as well as the love that remains in your marriage. The feminine water energy of this stone also helps you to give thanks for your family and understand the lessons that they can bring to you. In this regard, moonstone helps you to understand the wisdom of living a simple life with a loving family.

Whether you are male or female, this feminine water energy will help you in the blessing and calming of your home life, help you to be creative as far as making your home the best it can be. Moonstone also helps with fertility, and the release of stress within your home. Having moonstone in your home also acts as a conductor to peace within your home, and helps with the healing of family situations which are unhealthy. The peace which the moonstone brings can also bring peace within the house that helps to stop household violence if the stone is charged for this purpose.

The moonstone is an excellent stone to bring the higher self energies of the seventh chakra down into the sexual and creative energies of the second chakra. In this regard, if you meditate with moonstone, it will help you to understand the reasons for any discomfort in the second chakra area, which does include sexuality and creativity.

Whether you have a family or not, the moonstone can help your home become a place of refuge and peace, as well as bringing strong spiritual vibrations into your home. This can help you feel better about yourself and your home life, and create a better self-image as your home becomes a place of peace and tranquillity. Your home will draw people to it as you actually find yourself less shy about inviting someone to a place that you have filled with love.

Moonstone will help you visualize the purpose of the home, and the way your home should be, and the vibrations within the home.

Obsidian

Description: Dark and nearly translucent, obsidian is formed from the magma of volcanoes. Obsidian is most often black, but also forms in an array of reds and browns.

Key Words: *Ruthless teacher.*

Mental/Spiritual: If any stone epitomizes the phrase "tough love," that stone is obsidian. In its ability to cleanse negativity from your psyche, it will go through anything it needs to do in order to do that. To work with the obsidian, be warned. Lessons will come to you seriatim in order to give you a better understanding of what needs work. Although lessons may seem harsh when working with an obsidian, they are never more than you can handle. However, just as lifting too heavy a weight causes sore muscles, there are repercussions to learning the lessons of the obsidian which can be like living on an emotional roller coaster.

Further, the obsidian has almost a sense of humor about the lessons it teaches. Along with the learning, you will have intuition bordering on psychic instances as to what will come up to teach you these lessons, but you will also have the wisdom to know what these lessons are for and why they come into your life.

When you are carrying an obsidian, your spirit guides are fully aware of these aspects of the stone, and will work with you to banish any fear resulting in the lessons that you are going to be learning. Carrying an obsidian will help to ground you. Grounding you will correlate your system with the Earth's system, and this makes the lessons easier. You will find that you more readily understand any divination or visions with regard to lessons that you need to learn.

Meditation with the obsidian will help you to understand current situations in your life and understand their purpose.

Obsidian works to protect you during exorcism of negativity.

Obsidian is an excellent stone to facilitate prayer or visualization of environmental cleanup of our Earth.

Obsidian, Snowflake

Description: Black obsidian with white material included which looks like white snowflakes.

Key Words: *Balance, seventh and first chakras.*

Mental/Spiritual: The snowflake obsidian carries with it the same qualities as obsidian; however, because of the pale snowflake pattern on this obsidian, the wisdom and spirituality make it a gentler stone with which to work. Further, meditation with the snowflake obsidian helps you realize your uniqueness in the world, and eventually will bring about your unique purpose in the world.

Onyx

Description: Onyx is a mineral comprised of chalcedony and opal, commonly occurring in a lustrous black or black layered with white, and also occurring in other colors layered with a white/cream.

Key Word: *Leadership.*

Mental/Spiritual: The onyx is an excellent stone for leadership, success, and confidence. Wearing an onyx ring on the left hand helps one to receive information regarding the best course of action within a leadership situation. Onyx also assists in cultivating your popularity. It shows you the flaws within yourself which need to be healed and reconciled in order to stop anything which prohibited you from making new friends and acquaintances. The onyx helps with loneliness in this regard as you come to understand why you have been blocking your highest good for bringing like-minded people into your life.

This new knowledge is a form of growth as to the fact that bringing new people into your life will promote personal growth as we learn from others through conversations and, yes, their mistakes, and our ability to grow is given in the exchange of friendship.

The onyx also allows protection in the form of creating the proper type of friends that will best assist your personal growth.

Meditation with the onyx assists in your ability for visions and divination. Carrying onyx with you is an excellent way to tap into your affiliation with the Earth, which resonates with that aspect of the All within the universe. Tapping into the Earth for these purposes is an excellent grounding tool.

Opal

Description: Opal forms in a variety of colors from black to white, with a strong diversity of transparency and luster. A chief characteristic of opal is the many colors within the stone.

Key Word: *Peace.*

Mental/Spiritual: The energy of the opal, because of the many colors within the white stone, and turning the stone and being able to see the various colors, helps us realize that, although we are one soul, there are many facets to our being, and many "colors" to us which have different emotions.

Opal is a stone of peace and calming. This calm allows you to overcome that which has prevented peace with relationships with others and reduce stress related to relationships with others. Meditation with opal helps with intuition and understanding regarding the love that is the All and spirituality because of the spectrum of colors within the opal reflecting within its self.

Further, because of the many colors reflected in the opal, it is an excellent stone for mental focus, allowing the attributes of each of the chakras to become fully integrated within your mental self. This mental focus helps you during meditation regarding health and healing meditations.

The opal will assist you with difficulty sleeping if you place the opal on your third eye and use the flower-opening visualization discussed in Chapter V, to help you achieve the alpha state and then see yourself falling asleep.

The opal helps to stop violence of a racial nature. The many colors imbedded within one stone teach us that many can live together regardless of the differences.

Opal is also a stone of love. When charged with the energies of a request to draw marriage and relationship to you, the opal can help to bring to you a person who is as multifaceted as you.

Opal, Fire
Description:

Opaque stones with a color range from red to yellow. Commonly used in making jewelry.

Key Word:	*Passion.*
Mental/Spiritual:	The attributes of opal apply to the fire opal, but added to these are passion and luck.
Peacock Rock	See *Bornite.*
Pearl **Description:**	The pearl is an abnormal growth formed by mollusks which have been invaded by a foreign object. Pearls come in a variety of shapes including round, pear, bell, or drops. The colors include white, black, rose, and cream.
Key Word:	*Intuition.*
Mental/Spiritual:	Pearl is a stone of calming and intuition. It is a stone of bringing love back into a marriage, as well as bringing peace into the home. Pearl is excellent to visualize the stopping of any violence; however, it does not mitigate the reason behind the violence, the anger or the fear, but rather covers the violence until such time as it is safe to investigate the reasons for the emotions. The lesson received in this is that, just as the grain of sand in an oyster produces the material needed to create the pearl, the same idea applies to stopping violence. The pearl will help to ease the situation; however, the initial "grain of sand" that caused the situation is still present.

Pearls are excellent for blessing situations which are new, or for blessing new beginnings, such as marriages (which is why they are so popular to wear with wedding dresses!). A situation which is new can also include newborn infants, or new relationships. The pearl gives these situations a fresh start regarding purity of intent.

Pearls are also excellent to meditate with for the genesis of something new regarding fertility, and that can be personal fertility for actual childbirth, or fertility in crops, or fertility in ideas. Pearl is an excellent stone for communication and will help to calm a situation so that true communication can take place, which is both receiving and sending the communication. Pearl heals blocks in the third eye and assists with intuition. Meditate with a pearl on the sixth chakra in order to find the purpose for the block that exists there.

As the pearl is a water element stone, it can dowse the fire energy of anger. Wearing the pearl on the left hand will create receptivity as to the lesson needed for feeling anger.

Peridot

Description: A translucent yellow-green gem.

Key Word: *Self-love.*

Mental/Spiritual: Peridot is a stone that works well with self-image in regard to understanding the reason for our masks. The masks we wear include various masks for who we are at home, who we are at work, who we are at school, and peridot helps us to integrate these different people so that we can bring forth the truest sense of ourselves. Peridot helps immensely with honesty in love or marriage situations, as well as honesty in communication.

Peridot brings about personal intuition regarding the face masks that we have created. Peridot gives us the ability to cleanse ourselves and to seek our spiritual selves in order that we can go forward with our personal talents and creativity without the masks and blocks that we created to keep us from knowing our full potential. Meditation with the peridot will assist in all of these endeavors regarding finding our true selves and removing these masks.

The peridot will also help with a psychic ability regarding seeing other people's masks and the reasons behind them. In doing this, it will help you to understand the reason for the masks, and also give you an understanding that there are many layers to people, and that each person has put on a mask in defense of something that has happened in the past. In this regard, peridot shows us that we do not need as much protection from people as we previously thought; people are working toward personal health and healing, and their masks serve a point and a purpose toward that goal.

Peridot helps with money and prosperity of all kinds. Prosperity comes in the form not only of money, but of friends, popularity, personal accomplishment, good feelings toward your self. Prosperity can come in the form of items and lifestyle we desire. Peridot helps us to understand that a particular lifestyle might not be what we originally thought prosperity meant.

Peridot is also a stone of the heart cha-kra. The soft green with the hint of yellow shows us our personal power within our heart. Peridot helps us be open to remov-ing violence within our life, whether it is the violence we see on television or the violence that actually does us harm.

Petoskey Stone

Description: A stone in a variety of grays which has the appearance of an "eye" when polished. Particularly found in Michigan.

Key Words: *Sixth chakra.*

Mental/Spiritual: The petoskey stone is a stone of divina-tion, spirituality, and creativity, which helps us work toward being able to see more clearly through the third eye. The pattern on the stone resembles eyes, and these patterns are indicative of our ability to work with the stone and our third eye. Seeing with the spiritual influence through the third eye brings wisdom and shows that the loving energy of the earth working through our third eye is not indicative of something we need, but rather a gift to us that we can offer in love. The petoskey stone is a stone of protection. Carrying it with you will help you see potential danger, and allow you to avoid that danger.

Petrified Wood

Description: Petrified wood is actually a stone, usually agate or crystal, which has replaced the original wood. Petrified Forest National Park in Arizona contains petrified wood from the Triassic Period; the original trees grew approximately 240 million years ago.

Key Words: *Personal strength.*

Mental/Spiritual: As petrified wood has weathered the course of time, and as it was once physically alive in the form of a tree, it brings us the lessons of leadership regarding our ability to adapt, change, and gain strength with time. This is a survival mode that helps us to become something new, to be transformed, and to change our old programming.

Petrified wood is excellent to facilitate prayer or visualization of environmental cleanup of our earth. Visualize our Mother Earth to become strong, like the coating of the "stone."

Platinum
Description: Platinum has been used in Europe since at least the early sixteenth century, but platinum in its pure form could not be separated from other metals until the early nineteenth century. Platinum is a gray-white metal.

Key Word: *Confidence.*

Mental/Spiritual: Platinum, one of the most precious metals on earth, teaches us confidence and leadership. Confidence normally comes with experience and age, and knowing that we can move through things without harm and that mistakes often lead to lessons that lead to success. Platinum, however, helps to leap through this aging process associated with leadership, and shows us that we can be confident leaders prior to weathering the storms of experience.

Platinum is also a reflector which can show us how we can draw money into our lives. Money is a form of energy which flows through our pockets as a symbol of energy that moves between individuals on the earth. Like blocks in our personal energy within our bodies, there are blocks where energy is not moving on the earth between individuals, and this shows up in the form of lack. Platinum can help us understand how we might potentially be creating a block within our current perceived form of energy, which is money. Platinum lets us know our responsibility to not creating these energy blocks.

Pyrite

Description:

Pyrite is also known as "fool's gold," and is a brassy, yellow metallic stone. Prospectors have mistaken this mineral for gold, hence its nickname.

Key Word:

Wisdom.

Mental/Spiritual:

Pyrite is a stone of leadership and wisdom. Similar to the traits of platinum, where wisdom and the wisdom to lead are normally gained through age, pyrite allows you to see your flaws and clear the flaws that would cause you to make mistakes in a leadership situation. Removing these flaws assists you in making appropriate decisions in a leadership position.

Quartz
Description:

Quartz, or silicon dioxide, is one of the most common minerals, and one of the primary components of sand. The following discusses clear quartz in crystal form.

Key Word: *Everything.*

Mental/Spiritual:

If you have a challenge with controlling anger, gaze into a quartz crystal and visualize yourself as calm and responding to situations with assuredness and tranquillity. This will program the crystal to assist you with a more serene nature and reaction to everyday events.

Quartz is an excellent stone to facilitate prayer or visualization of environmental cleanup of our earth.

Quartz has many uses, and it can be a conductor in the laying on of stones between the stones. Use a double-terminated quartz pointing as a conductor between two points of stones. For instance, if you have an agate on your second chakra and a citrine on your third chakra, placing a double-terminated quartz crystal, which is a crystal with a point on both ends, in between those two will help draw the energies of the chakras together.

Keeping this in mind, the quartz crystal for the base chakra is excellent in healing, anger, creating your personal confidence, and mitigating fear in any given situation. When pointed downward, the clear quartz crystal can ground you and align your first chakra with the energies of the earth. The quartz crystal can bring the earthly requirement for money into your life. It will help bring protection to you if needed on a physical level, and will provide safety, including safety while traveling. The grounding of the first chakra will also relieve stress associated with trying to move forward and not living in the "now."

Meditation with the quartz crystal on the second chakra will assist with fertility and clearing any negativity regarding your reproductive organs. It will also assist with breaking bad habits associated with creativity. If you are feeling creative and you thwart your creativity through use of alcohol, drugs, food, or cigarettes, the meditation with the quartz on the second chakra will help to banish those negative habits. Meditation with a quartz crystal on the second chakra will heal relationships on all levels, including relationships other than romantic. It will also serve as a guide with regard to removing any blocks toward sexual behavior.

Meditation with a quartz crystal on the third chakra will assist with employment and personal growth regarding your ability to move forward with your personal power in the world. It will help with your leadership ability as you learn to express your personal power, as well as mitigate any stomach problems if you use the alpha level meditations to banish negativity in the third chakra. Quartz crystal will assist the third chakra with your idea of prosperity. The third chakra will also help with your success and endeavors regarding finding individuals who will help you make your way in the world.

Meditation with a quartz crystal on the

fourth chakra will help with regard to your personal happiness and your self-love in regard to obtaining that happiness. It will help you mitigate loneliness when you understand that your self-love will create your own best friend, and therefore leave no room for loneliness. Meditation with the quartz crystal on your heart chakra helps with love, marriage, and monogamy within that marriage, as well as banishing any negativity with regard to past relationships and expectations placed on present relationships based on those past relationships. This allows you to move forward with peace and clearing the way for healthy relationships. Meditation with quartz crystal on the heart chakra also assists with popularity as you become healthier and more self-assured. You will draw people to you as your self-image is enhanced by personal love. After consistent heart chakra crystal work, don't be surprised if strangers seem friendlier.

Meditation with the quartz crystal on your sixth or throat chakra helps with your communication with others, as well as creating mental focus so that you can properly communicate with others. It is also excellent for the ability to offer thanks and to communicate your thanks to whoever needs it most. The thanks can be to a personal friend on the physical level, or the thanks can be to the deities.

The sixth chakra meditation with the quartz crystal helps in divination and dreams, as well as being able to work with exorcism with regard to visualizing a clean environment within your home.

Meditation with a crystal on the third eye will help you to see any areas on your body that need healing, whether you feel physical symptoms or not. This meditation can bring guidance as to which chakras require healing work to avoid potential illness. Further, as the chakras are healed, any potential or realized illness associated with those chakras will also be healed. Meditation with the quartz crystal on the sixth chakra assists with allowing your intuition to bud and grow, as well as assisting with meditation. This process allows your psychic abilities to come forth more readily. These psychic abilities also help you come to know your spirit guides or muses or teachers (some call these angels). Understanding that you can accept the gifts of knowledge from your spirit guides will assist with your ability to experience visions.

Meditation with the quartz crystal on your seventh chakra will allow you to understand the truest meaning of blessing. Blessing is sending your energy into an object, a home, or a person, in order to fill it or him with the light of the universe or Goddess, and remove negativity from an object or person. In this regard, quartz crystal also helps with cleansing. That cleansing can be through blessing or through cleansing the environment of hostile energies or energies which we perceive as negative. Meditation with a quartz crystal on the seventh chakra helps open the chakra to spiritual matters as it allows your seventh chakra to open to the lessons that we have from the universe and from the God and from the

Goddess. It helps us to understand the reasons for violence, to know that violence is part of the process of our learning here on the physical plane, and to recognize that violence is necessary by all participants in order to overcome lessons and work through karmic consequences. In other words, meditation with the quartz crystal on the seventh chakra assists us in accepting the reasons behind violence, and this acceptance actually works to mitigate violence through the power of love. When we do not feed a situation with worry or anger, we are not allowing it to gain power on the physical level.

Rhodochrosite

Description:

Rhodochrosite is beautiful when tumbled and polished, exhibiting an array of colors from pink to red with a variance of colors within each stone, including "earth tone" colors such as browns and oranges.

Key Word:

Peace.

Mental/Spiritual:

Rhodochrosite is a stone which allows you to create a bridge between the heart chakra and the second chakra. This bridge is helpful in love and marriage situations, as well as being helpful in relationships other than romantic—for instance, relationships with parents, siblings, and children. Rhodochrosite also assists in creating a bridge between the fourth and the second chakras with regard to your attitudes toward sex. This bridge provides an understanding of the purpose of sex, which is the coming together of two people to create a whole. This is the purpose of our being on earth—to become whole again; whole meaning healthy.

Rhodochrosite also helps us realize that love must be present with sex; otherwise sex is merely a vapid physical act. To take sex to a higher plane, sexual encounters with the one we love provide a sense of personal strength. Further, rhodochrosite helps us understand the loneliness we feel after sex with a person we do not love, as that situation only creates a scenario for a power play where one individual is sure to be a loser in the game.

Rhodochrosite is a stone for the home, creating peace in a situation and realizing the purpose of maintaining healthy energy within the home. This results in personal growth and creates happiness. Happiness within our home creates ripples. As we go out into the world with our happiness reflecting on others, their attitudes then change and flow outward, and so on.

Rhodochrosite is also an excellent stone for artistic talent and creativity, and it helps us to love and accept our talents, and therefore make the circle of being creative. This is another method of becoming whole as we realize our purpose here.

Rhodochrosite helps in relieving stressful and even violent situations within the home. This understanding of love can lead to health and healing between the heart chakra and the second chakra, where oftentimes mixed signals and mixed learning can create unhealthy attitudes and therefore an unhealthy body.

Carrying a rhodochrosite in a shirt pocket close to your heart chakra will help you remain calm in situations where you would normally be angry.

Rhodonite
Description:

Rhodonite exhibits an array of colors from pink to red with a variance of colors within each stone, including "earth tone" colors such as browns and oranges.

Key Word:

Home.

Mental/Spiritual:

Rhodonite has quite similar energies to rhodochrosite; however, the difference is that it is more of an Earth element stone which creates happiness within the home. Rhodonite is an excellent stone to bless a house when a new family moves in or when newlyweds occupy their first home together. Rhodonite will project love and happiness within the home.

Rhodonite is also an excellent stone to keep on an altar to continually project the stopping of violence or war within the world. Send your positive energy into the stone along with visualizations of world peace, and the stone will send the energies to combine with all those who are visualizing world peace.

Rhodonite mitigates loneliness and, in doing so, helps you to reach out to others regarding your personal fears, problems, or weaknesses in order that you can be shown that you need not be alone on your life path.

Rose Quartz

Description:

Rose quartz is without definite crystal form, and is popularly sold as tumbled stones in a range of pink to deeper rose colors.

Key Word:

Love.

Mental/Spiritual:

The statement has been made that all things boil down to either fear or love. Rose quartz allows the removal of all fear in order that only love remains. Rose quartz is a master of bringing love into your life in many forms, whether in the form of creating happiness, allowing creativity through love, allowing growth through love, allowing healing through love, mitigating loneliness by removal of fear, or allowing peace into your life. Rose quartz also gently brings you the love of friendships and relationships other than romantic. Rose quartz can heal all wounds, including the wound of believing that you are not good enough for any given situation or person. Therefore, rose quartz also boosts self-image.

As love is the basis for all things, all energy that moves through the universe, bringing more love into your life through the use of the rose quartz and through meditation with the rose quartz calms your life as it clears out areas of negativity in your life that are associated with fear. Rose quartz brings courage, and also brings protection in the form of understanding that there is no incorrect path. There are many varying trails along the major path of life, but all trails lead to the same place. It is this wisdom that brings the true essence and understanding of the strength of love into your life. This understanding will also reduce stress.

Rose quartz can help in the most obvious aspects of love—looking for a partner, looking for a marriage partner, and finding one who is in harmony with your heart in order to create a life partner situation.

Rose quartz is excellent for cleansing, especially in cleansing the energies in yourself. It is an excellent stone to place in a ritual bath in order to do self-blessing and self-cleansing prior to ritual.

Rose quartz also can help to bring money into your life. Simply charge your self-worth into the stone, and then release it to trust that you will receive money. Rose quartz will help you realize that you are worth the earthly things in the world that make it a loving place.

Rose quartz will also assist with the exorcism of any unwanted nonspecific energies or entities within your home. This exorcism consists of transforming an entity into a loving being, and releasing the being into the light of the universe. This act will remove the entity from your presence, and allow growth for that entity.

As with rhodonite, rose quartz is an excellent stone to place within your home to remind you to send energy outward to stop violence within the world. That energy will move throughout the world, and join with all those who are in prayer and meditation for peace.

If there is tension or anger in your

home, place a cleansed and cleaned rose quartz in rice for a meal (being careful to remove the stone when finished cooking!). As the rice is eaten, it will soothe the tension or anger in the home.

Ruby

Description:

The only mineral harder than the ruby is the diamond. Rubies come in a variety of shades of red to a deep indigo. Minerals which are not rubies are often sold as such; even rose quartz is sold as the Bohemian ruby, with the Siberian ruby actually being part of the tourmaline family.

Key Words:

Feminine, mother.

Mental/Spiritual:

The ruby is a stone of love, particularly feminine love, and represents the love a mother has for her child. In this regard, the ruby is an excellent meditation stone for males when bonding with a newborn child. This stone will help them understand feminine love and get in touch with their nurturing aspect.

The ruby is a stone for protection. This energy is associated with your base chakra and your intuitive ability. You will understand a situation and know how to protect yourself because of your awareness of danger.

The ruby will help you break bad habits. It is a stone that has a deep connection with the heart chakra, and will show you how any bad habit is not in line with your highest good and with your heart. This stone will help you to realize that your personal power comes from your heart, as opposed to believing it comes from your mind and will. When you realize that the source of true personal power comes from your heart chakra, courage becomes natural.

The ruby is an excellent stone to assist with your leadership skills. Once you have used the ruby to perceive your personal power and to hone your intuition and understanding, it is natural for your leadership skills to become enhanced.

The ruby assists with your relationships with others—family, friends, or spouse—and therefore has the ability to assist with healing and marriage. This stone helps you understand the reason for misalignment between two people within a marriage.

Meditation with the ruby will assist you with understanding whether a marriage should continue. It will assist you with the fact that the end of a marriage does not necessarily equal loneliness, but rather a blossoming of your own creativity for you to step out into the world as a single entity rather than relying on a relationship. This also helps in your leadership skills.

The ruby assists with personal artistic talent, allowing your heart to open up to your creative abilities with art in any form, whether creative art such as drawing or two-dimensional art, or three-dimensional art in the form of theatre or dance.

The ruby also helps you to realize that violence is not necessary in your life and can remove violent features of your life, as well as any personal tendency you might have toward violence.

Sandstone

Description:

Sandstone looks like it sounds. Imagine making a snowball with sand. It is a sedimentary rock made of compressed sand with a naturally occurring binding product such as silica. Polished sandstone is a shiny copper color, and used readily in jewelry.

Key Words:

Peaceful sleep.

Mental/Spiritual:

Sandstone, when highly polished, shows that there are many parts that make up a whole, and therefore is an excellent teacher with regard to spirituality. Sandstone can show us the wisdom of the fact that there are many of us who make up a whole, that we are individuals yet still part of the All. Sandstone is also excellent for helping to induce sleep when sleep is troubled by worrying. Sandstone helps you to see the bigger picture, to see solutions rather than feeling overwhelmed by so many things that keep you from sleeping.

Sandstone is an excellent communication stone. As you look at this stone and know that there are many pieces that make up the stone, you can understand that our ability to communicate is actually small on the level which we communicate verbally or written. We have the ability to be in communication with the All.

Another use for sandstone is to draw out artistic talent as you are able to take the understanding that you have with communication with the God and the

Goddess, and take your artistic talent and be able to express it to more people.

Sapphire

Description: Sapphires are a form of corundum, which occurs in a variety of transparent colors; deep blue is the color of the true sapphire. Colors such as yellow and pink also manifest, but these are impurities in the corundum.

Key Word: *Tranquillity.*

Mental/Spiritual: Sapphire has calming energy which is conducive to meditation as well as relieving stress. Sapphire emanates strong, loving energies, and helps you to understand or achieve a calm love that is peaceful and blissful, even conducive to marriage. Sapphire assists in banishing negativity in a relationship or allows you to intuitively see negativity that would result in a current or potential relationship. It is also an excellent stone to assist with communication, an important aspect of any relationship.

Sapphire assists in helping you find your spiritual partner and a partner who will walk with you on your spiritual path. Your intuition in finding this partner will be keen while working with sapphire.

Sapphire is excellent for mental focus when it is used for magickal works regarding moving to alpha. This mental focus will assist you with your psychic abilities and your abilities to contact your spirit guides and teachers.

Sapphire assists with your ability to lead, and helps you to understand the path toward successful leadership.

Sapphire assists in protecting you from people who choose not to be led. In other words, the group that you will lead will be inspired by you when you work with sapphire for leadership purposes.

Sapphire can highlight your artistic abilities and talents and bring to the surface that which may be hidden by your personal blocks resulting from a lack of self-esteem. Sapphire is good for blessing a new relationship regarding keeping communication open with that relationship, whether that relationship is with business partners, with parents, with siblings, or with children. Sapphire also assists with your sex life, which can be opened by realizing your quest for other as healthy.

Another important aspect of sapphire is its ability to draw people to you; however, it isn't as choosy regarding the *type* of people. Meaning that, rather than drawing like-minded people, sapphire will draw a wide spectrum of people who might come into your life for various purposes and to teach you various things. This can be perceived as popularity; however, it is more along the lines of gaining friends for learning purposes.

Sapphire can be charged to stop violence.

Sapphire, Black

The black sapphire is an excellent stone for getting in touch with your base chakra, which assists in grounding.

Sapphire, Star

The star sapphire carries the qualities of sapphire, but helps you to put your eye on a goal, and to achieve it.

Sapphire, Green

Along with the qualities of sapphire, the green sapphire assists you in understanding about spiritual ego. It is possible to get to a point in your spirituality where you are egotistical because you feel superior to those who don't have your understanding. The green sapphire will help you be grounded in your heart center, and know that we are all on a path and all learn our lessons at different times.

Selenite
Description:

This stone is named after the moon, and is reminiscent of the moon's transparent quality on a clear night. The transparent quality of selenite is such that, in the past, large sheets of it were used to serve as glass.

Key Words:

Psychic work.

Mental/Spiritual:

Selenite helps you to better communicate with your spirit guides and teachers in order to have them assist with your psychic abilities, your intuition, and your ability with divination. Selenite helps you to understand your dreams, as well as to work with visions. Selenite assists in achieving sleep in order that dreams will have sleep that includes memory of dreams.

Selenite is therefore an excellent stone to have present during divination work with Tarot cards or with scrying. Further, selenite can be used to create a circle of stones for ritual.

Selenite assists with meditation in order to get in touch with your spirit guides and teachers. This work will help you better understand your soul's purpose. Understanding your soul's purpose will bring wisdom. This wisdom, for those who have been seeking their soul's purpose for quite some time, will bring peace and calm into your quest for spirituality. In this regard, selenite helps you understand that we all do the best we can at any given time, and that our spiritual path is one that moves like a roller coaster. There will be fast times and slow times, fast spiritual growth and slow spiritual growth, on our spiritual path. Understanding this growth pattern will also further bring calm and peace to your spiritual quest.

Selenite can banish negativity, and therefore works to exorcise negativity within your home or other place. Selenite will protect your home. Place selenite near the door and envision its protective shield moving around your entire home.

Selenite can be used on your altar as a form of thanksgiving. Selenite is an excellent stone to help you break bad habits, as well as understand the reasons for those bad habits. We can often stop a bad habit without realizing why we had it in the first place.

Shell
Description:

Shells are formed in a variety of shapes and colors. The shell discussed here is the abalone, which is large with a multi-colored iridescent interior.

Key Word:	*Blessing.*

Mental/Spiritual: The abalone shell is a wonderful tool to use for blessing. When you place sage in a shell, and burn the sage for blessing, you are combining the four elements and considering the strength of the four elements, it is one of the strongest blessings you can perform. The sage represents the Earth element, the smoke represents the air element, burning the sage to create the smoke represents the fire element, and the shell itself represents water.

Carrying sage in a shell for blessing your circle works extremely well. Using the shell with the sage in it to smudge your home for cleansing and blessing helps you use your intuition in sensing the flow of energy within your home.

Silver

Description: Silver was once reserved for those who worshipped the moon and for ritual use. Silver is a precious metal which is luminous and white/gray in color. Silver is also the best-known metal conductor of electricity.

Key Word: *Intuition.*

Mental/Spiritual: Silver is an excellent conductor, not only for electricity but for energy from other stones as well. For this reason, silver is great to use in making jewelry in order to magnify the traits of any of the jewels, gems, stones, or crystals that you intend to wear as earrings, necklace, rings, toe rings, ankle bracelets, bracelets, belts, etc. Silver assists you with getting in touch with your intuition, helps you understand your spirituality, and offers a soft, feminine quality of the moon energies in regard to your intuition and spirituality.

Silver works well as a pendulum chain for divination purposes. Combined with most stones, silver helps to magnify their abilities. Having a rose quartz crystal at the end of a silver chain for your heart chakra will truly help to clear the heart chakra to help you be open to love and marriage. Wearing a jade pin set in silver will help to further enhance jade's ability to protect. Silver is a conductor of protection as is jade, and the two combined create a higher degree of protection.

Because silver is a feminine entity, it is also conducive to your personal creativity, whether that creativity is artistic, or represents creativity in romantic situations or in health and healing.

Silver also opens you to other worlds which will teach you not to be lonely. There are many planes for you to discover in order to seek out friendship and seek out your personal strength. Anytime you receive the wisdom of personal strength, loneliness is mitigated. We each have the ability to decide whether to be lonely or not.

Silver is an excellent conductor with other stones to stop violence. When used in conjunction with a crystal, silver can project nonviolence in any situation, whether it be violence in the home, inner-city violence, or world violence. Wear silver as a reminder that we must first be peaceful within ourselves and have faith in our peace with ourselves before the world can become a peaceful place.

Smoky Quartz

Description: A form of quartz which is lustrous and transparent, it is also called cairngorm stone. The color ranges from smoky yellow to very dark brown.

Key Word: *Fun.*

Mental/Spiritual: Smoky quartz carries with it the elements of clear quartz crystals; however, it also brings with it a sense of fun. Smoky quartz helps you with the ability to make studying and learning fun, and realize that growth in your mind is actually a form of fun for your mind.

Smoky quartz brings a sense of fun to sex. It brings a sense of romping and relaxation when directed toward the second chakra, and brings you back to the playfulness of youth in the bedroom. Meditate with smoky quartz on the second chakra and visualize your partner and you engaging in creative and playful sex without inhibitions. Just as any visualization will bring the astral to the physical, visualization with a smoky quartz will bring the astral images of playful sex into the physical realm of your bedroom.

Smoky quartz also assists with gaining employment. Lie on the floor with your hands at your sides, one smoky quartz on the floor above your head, and one smoky quartz on the floor below your feet. If you have them, place two more smoky quartz beside your hands. You will then have placed yourself in a diamond-shaped grid of smoky quartz. Visualize yourself performing well during an interview and then actually working in the job you desire. The smoky quartz will cleanse any energy within you that does not resonate with your visualization. This cleansing could come in the form of suddenly understanding the blocks you have set up that prevent you from achieving the employment you desire.

Sodalite

Description:

Most well known as a dark blue stone which has creamy white veins running through it, sodalite can also be shades of yellow and red, with combinations of red and blue creating purple. Lustrous when tumbled and polished.

Key Word:

Communication.

Mental/Spiritual:

Carrying sodalite with you allows you communication of the sort which is blended with spirituality. This communication is guided communication from the universe, and assists with removing all masks and being able to talk to people from your heart. This removing of masks allows you to be honest with people with whom you previously hadn't been honest. Be warned, however, that relationships can fall away that are no longer necessary when you become honest. Those relationships were only supporting the aspect of you which wore masks.

As these relationships might perhaps leave your realm, you begin to have an understanding of your personal sense of self. Therefore, your self-image is strengthened by drawing people to you who understand the importance of honesty. Sodalite therefore mitigates loneliness regardless of the physical friends around you, as you have an understanding of the purpose of friendship and growth within those friendships.

Sodalite breeds within you confidence, and that confidence is evident to those you meet, whether they be friends or business acquaintances. Sodalite breeds mental focus. The mental focus combined with confidence creates successful business ventures and a business mind. It is a looping circle; your mental focus creates confidence, which creates success, which in turn allows you higher mental focus.

Sodalite is wonderful for use during meditation and when visualizing and working within alpha. Sodalite also helps you to talk to your spirit guides, muses, or teachers. Sodalite is helpful in allowing you to use that meditative form of communication for the loved ones in your life, and creating communication with the one you love in order to express yourself fully without fear of being misunderstood. Sodalite works with your psychic abilities and intuition with regard to communication. It is also a beneficial stone for divination when the divination is dependent on your spirit guides for communication.

Sodalite enhances your creativity. This

creativity comes from being able to express yourself effectively through the medium of art.

Sugilite

Description:

Sugilite ranges from pink to purple which almost looks black.

Key Word:

Peace.

Mental/Spiritual:

Sugilite emanates a peaceful energy, this peace being a happy kind of peace which can go forth within your home. Sugilite also emanates an understanding for this peace with regard to correlating that peace with the all-knowing peace of the universe. This understanding promotes personal growth, and this personal growth toward peace and a peaceful nature allows you to understand that all is right with the universe regardless of current circumstances or situations.

Sugilite is a stone of luck—not the kind of luck for going to Vegas and winning millions, but the kind of luck that comes from expecting good things to happen to you. This sunny stone, if worn or carried, will help you to draw luck to you simply by being in a better frame of mind and receptive to that which would make you happy.

Assists in showing the purpose for anger, as well as showing you how to take the anger to your heart to better understand the origin of your feelings.

Tiger Eye

Description:

Tiger eye is a fibrous stone which has bands of a lighter color running through bands of a darker color. Dark blue or navy stones have lighter blue bands. Dark brown stones have bronze-colored bands through them. The effect is somewhat striped looking.

Key Word: *Power.*

Mental/Spiritual: Tiger eye is an Earth element stone which will assist you with confidence, power, and success. These qualities will come from an inner assuredness which clears your third chakra power center in order to know how to go forward without being aggressive. It is the confidence that is gained when you are walking and doing and being in right mind, right action, and right thinking.

Tiger eye can be used to make a charm for employment by charging the stone with confidence and success in the interview process.

Tiger eye can be used for prosperity work, but be aware that the prosperity can come in many forms, not merely monetary. Prosperity can come in the form of friendships, understanding, having a life that is good.

Tiger eye is also a stone for protection.

Topaz
Description: Gemstone-quality and desired topaz is commonly yellow to almost brown; however topaz can also be colorless, green, blue, or red.

Key Word: *Teacher.*

Mental/Spiritual:

Topaz is a stone with high spiritual vibrations. Working with topaz through meditation can put you on a path which will promote very fast spiritual growth. Topaz is a strong stone to use for getting in contact with your spirit guides and teachers, and this contact will help you to have an understanding of the spiritual realm, the astral realm, and lead to the wisdom that is gained through a spiritual life.

Topaz increases your desire for studying things spiritual, increases your desire to learn how to use your intuition, and increases your desire to learn about your psychic abilities that are yours by birthright. Topaz will also give you incentive for learning about how to have visions during divination work such as scrying.

Regarding the business world, topaz aligns with your power center, your third chakra, to magnify your confidence and creativity in business endeavors. This confidence will lead to your sense of personal power, which will bring business relationships that lead to your success. This confidence, power, and success will also lead to prosperity in the form of money. Using the topaz will help you to be successful in the business realm for the highest good of all, rather than for lack of understanding about greed on earth. Working with this higher consciousness in the business realm will also bring you luck in business from the aspect of expecting good things to happen to you.

Working with topaz can teach you how to be happier with life in general, the happiness stemming from having forward-moving goals to work toward.

Topaz will banish loneliness and negativity from your life. As you create a new, confident you, there is less room for a counterproductive you, which would draw negativity and loneliness.

Topaz assists with centering and balancing, which will help you to break habits which contribute to poor health. In this regard, topaz will help to protect you from yourself and any habits that are counterproductive to healing.

Topaz, Blue

Description: Valued as a gem, and becoming more popular in jewelry in the last several years, blue topaz crystalizes in a variety of colors of palest blue to deep blue. This stone is also available tumbled and polished rather than cut, an excellent way to obtain this gemstone with less expense.

Key Words: *Calm communication.*

Mental/Spiritual: Along with the qualities of yellow topaz, blue topaz also works with your throat chakra in order to communicate and calm you, as well as help you with meditation. This meditation will bring understanding regarding how to better communicate with others.

Tourmaline

Description: Used for jewelry, tourmaline comes in a variety of colors, including pink, red, green, blue, and black. Tourmaline can also be purchased as raw stone, which is quite effective.

Key Word: *Banishing.*

Mental/Spiritual: Tourmaline is an excellent stone to actually absorb negativity, whether it be in the form of ill health or entities which you do not want in your home.

Tourmaline can be placed on sore muscles to literally draw out the soreness of those muscles, drawing out the pain.

Tourmaline is excellent for cleansing. Resting a tourmaline on your third chakra while meditating will draw negative energies out of your aura.

Tourmaline can be used for banishing fear, especially if the fear is being expressed in a fear of forward movement or goals.

Tourmaline can be used for grounding, and helping you to connect with the healing energies of Mother Earth.

Protection from situations where people attack you verbally can be charged into a tourmaline stone. Tourmaline will help you shield yourself from that negative energy, and will help you understand that the negativity coming in your direction belongs to the people who are sending it. This, if used in a work situation, can certainly reduce the stress of that environment.

Tourmaline allows your intuitive and divining states to expand, as well as the mental focus required for intuitive work. On the home front, tourmaline will assist with keeping your relationships monogamous.

Tourmaline, Green	Along with the banishing qualities of tourmaline, green tourmaline allows you to show your heart in all matters while doing the banishing rather than acting in anger.
Tourmaline, Pink	Pink tourmaline allows you to banish traits within you that do not support clean-up of the Earth or make you *feel* as though your small efforts in this regard are not helpful. If you have procrastinated in setting up a personal recycling program in your home, for example, pink tourmaline will nudge you in the right direction to take action. Pink tourmaline will show you what you can personally do to help the Earth, and will help you to understand that your seemingly small efforts truly carry weight.
Tourmaline, Black	Black tourmaline assists you in removing pain within your body. Simply place the black tourmaline with the strands of the stone pointing away from your body, and the tourmaline will pull out the energy which is causing discomfort. This discomfort can also be stress in your shoulders. Place black tourmaline on your shoulders to pull out stress, and soothe muscle soreness related to stress in the neck and shoulder area.
Turquoise **Description:**	Turquoise is a stone which ranges in color from blue and blue-green to green. Turquoise has been found in jewelry from ancient Egypt, as well as in ancient Aztec civilizations. Robin's egg blue is the most sought-after color for jewelry.

Key Word: *Spirituality.*

Mental/Spiritual: Turquoise brings a strong sense of spirituality into your life. This spirituality has
a strength which can change your life
completely if you are open to the change.
This change can come in the form of
psychic work coming into your life in
order to become more aware of the spiritual realms. This psychic work can be
perfected through meditation. Meditation with turquoise will bring strength
and intuition. You become able to heal
others, as well as work with divination
and helping others see what has perhaps
been hidden from them.

Your spiritual teachers and guides will
assist you in this spiritual growth. Turquoise, when placed on the third eye,
assists with visions, and can help to turn
knowledge into wisdom, as this knowledge is applied to your daily life, creating
the wisdom.

Turquoise brings tranquillity and
peace into your life. Peace will come
attached to relationships, whether the
relationships are with business partners,
parents, siblings, or children. This peace
can also extend to relationships in love
and marriage, and the peace comes from
knowing that there is harmony within
your home, and proper communication
with those you love. This communication
and peace relieve stress and create a happy
mood within the home.

Turquoise energy is expansive and
opening, which allows you to take in
information regarding spirituality, and
this information can be in the form of

dreams. The dream and sleep world will further help you understand where your spiritual path currently leads.

Turquoise assists with study and mental focus, helping you to remember what you read or study in order to take in the information and process it. As the information is processed, it helps you to better understand new information.

Turquoise will work as a protective agent. This protection comes in the form of knowing you are right, and that continuing on the right path will help you to gain assistance from others who are right thinking. This in itself is a form of power. This power will allow you to travel safely through difficult situations, not only learning lessons, but banishing negativity. As each lesson is learned, the negative association with that lesson is removed from your life.

Turquoise helps cleanse and purify your home. This cleansing exorcises any unwanted entities or energies within the home.

Your artistic talents can be enhanced through meditation with turquoise. This stone will open your receptive channels to heed words from your muses in order to help you flow with energy from the universe and the God and the Goddess to better communicate your artistic talent outward.

Turquoise assists with popularity, allowing and drawing like-minded spiritual people to you. Turquoise will not allow you to draw violence to yourself. Be aware, however, that you must be receptive to nonviolent living if the stone is to work. The popularity that turquoise draws will help to mitigate perceived loneliness, and help you to understand that overcoming it comes not from friendships, but from the realization that you are never truly alone.

Meditating with turquoise and charging a stone with the visualization of money and prosperity will bring these into your life. Turquoise also assists in understanding the process of giving thanks, and is especially beneficial for thankfulness regarding prosperity.

Ulexite

Description:

A milky white mineral which can act as a magnifying glass.

Key Word:

Knowing.

Mental/Spiritual:

Simply carrying ulexite with you will help you understand others, understand the motives behind their words, and help you see whether they are being honest with you, and whether they believe your words. In this regard, ulexite is excellent for honest communication, with no barriers, and will give you the strength to call someone on their lack of honesty.

Ulexite assists with psychic endeavors, helping with mental focus which will heighten your intuition. Ulexite assists with your ability to read the subtlest body language, which you might not otherwise have seen, in order to effectively communicate. The communication is in the form of being able to receive the thoughts of another individual. With this skill comes an understanding of others' ability to communicate, and how we are all guarded in our communication. This understanding will bring a wisdom of how to best communicate with others.

Ulexite can be used for astral projection, especially toward a person who needs to feel your energy, for healing purposes or strength or working with that individual to calm her regarding your intentions.

Ulexite works with your creative centers through your third eye. If you are working toward a creative project, whether it be creativity at work or in the home, ulexite will help you to best understand how to open your creative centers to be as creative as you possibly can.

Ulexite helps with visions. Place the ulexite on your third eye. Ask a particular question, and note the visions that move through your mind while concentrating on the ulexite. These visions might be in the form of world events or they can be personal events. This meditation with ulexite can be considered a form of divination.

Place ulexite under your pillow along with a jade stone to help with dreams. Your dreams can become tools to help you understand the purpose of your dreams and the meaning behind them. Ulexite will assist you in your meditation skills in order to calm you and learn lessons regarding what can be gained through meditation in a body/mind/spirit circumstance.

Zircon

Description:

Zircon is a translucent mineral which comes in a variety of colors including all the chakra colors of red, orange, yellow, green, blue, purple, and white (or clear).

Key Word:

Creativity.

Mental/Spiritual:

Zircon enhances creativity in all endeavors, and helps you to understand that creativity is part of the process that helps you get in touch with your feminine side. Zircon also allows your creativity to be open and expansive, helping you move about confidently with new thoughts, and new ideas. Your openness will encourage people to agree with you regarding these new thoughts and ideas. In this regard, zircon inspires a gregarious attitude so that all those involved in a project know that you are working for the good of All.

CHAPTER VIII

Guide to Spells

Following is a list of 52 common reasons for doing magick. Along with the list you will find information as to when to perform a spell, which herbs to use, which stones to use, and what colors to use if color is relevant to the type of magick you are doing.

For instance, if you wanted to do a spell to increase your intuition, you would find out that the color purple would be a good candle color to use, gardenia oil and frankincense could be used to bless the candle, and you would perform the spell during a Scorpio moon or on a Tuesday. Depending on the specific *type* of intuition (i.e., intuition in business or intuition on whether friends are true, or general intuition), you could select a stone with the personality that resonates with that aspect of intuition, charge that stone during your candle magick, and then carry the stone with you when needed.

The categories of spell information are explained as follows:

Color: The color mentioned is useful to know when making poppets, doing candle magick, visualizing, selecting an altar cloth, or any other number of reasons where color will be useful to enhance your magick. A specific color is also helpful to wear if you simply want to enhance a certain aspect within yourself. If you want to become aware of prosperity consciousness, wear green. If you want to boost someone's self-image, send pink or gold flowers.

Plants: Some of the plants listed for each purpose can be ground with a mortar and pestle to make incense, sewn into a poppet, grown in your home to produce the desired effect, or in the case of common household herbs, sprinkled on your food to create the desired effect. Each plant carries with it a different aspect of the listed characteristic. For instance, if you are doing a spell for artistic talent, raspberry will help you to remove doubt where personal ability is concerned, but allspice will help you to be aggressive in your artistic endeavors if you're feeling a little daring. Look up the plant in order to be sure that you are selecting the one best suited for your needs.

Stones: The stones may be used to amplify candle magick as mentioned in Chapter III, or may be charged for a specific purpose to carry with you or give as gifts or charms. As with the plants, many stones are listed for a particular characteristic. Each stone functions slightly differently when applied for that purpose. For instance, blue lace agate is excellent for calming someone else through your enhanced ability to communicate, while amethyst will calm you if you're angry or are experiencing any kind of anxiety.

Astrological Sign: The astrological sign listed suggests the best time to perform magick. If you wish to do magick for world peace, do it when the moon is in Aquarius. If you are trying to banish or get rid of something, such as a habit, do magick when the moon is waning. If you are trying to manifest or bring something to you, perform magick when the moon is waxing, or growing. Of course, the full moon is an optimum time of energy to do most any kind of magick. The astrological sign is good to consider when doing nonmagickal things as well. A first date with someone, for example, would be advantageous during a Taurus moon, a notoriously romantic time.

Planet: The influence of a planet on magickal workings is listed for you to better coordinate when to perform spells.

Day of the Week: The most propitious day of the week for doing magick is listed. If you must do a spell without consideration to the moon, the day of the week would be a good second substitute.

Element: If you are a fire sign, perhaps fire magick or candle magick works best for you, or scrying in fire works best for you. However, to pay attention to the element which corresponds to the astrological sign is a good way to select the type of magick to perform for a particular desired outcome. For example, to perform a love spell (that has been agreed to), it would be more beneficial to perform Earth magick such as making a poppet. This would then correspond to the sign of Taurus. The elements suitable for suggesting types of magick are listed.

Direction: Although this is not necessary, it has proven helpful to pay particular attention to the direction involved in the spell when casting a circle. For instance, calling the north watchtowers *and* visualizing help from Taurus at the same time creates stronger energy for Earth magick.

 Lists

Anger (To Govern)
  Colors: Red, Yellow
  Plants: Basil, Chamomile, Lavender, Lemon, Myrrh, Peppermint, Rose, Saffron, Sunflower, Valerian, Willow
  Stones: Agate, Amethyst, Aquamarine, Aventurine, Carnelian, Citrine, Diamond, Emerald, Hematite, Jade, Moonstone, Pearl, Quartz, Rhodochrosite, Rhodonite, Rose Quartz, Sodalite, Sugilite
  Astrological Sign: Aries
  Planet: Mars
  Day of the Week: Tuesday
  Element: Fire
  Direction: South
Astral Projection
  Colors: Silver, Purple, White, Black
  Plants: Bay, Benzoin, Frankincense, Mugwort, Myrrh, Nutmeg, Sage, Scullcap, Vervain
  Stones: Amethyst, Aquamarine, Calcite, Diamond, Ulexite
  Astrological Sign: Scorpio
  Planet: Pluto
  Day of the Week: Tuesday
  Element: Water
  Direction: West

Artistic Talent

Colors: Pale Blue, Orange, White

Plants: Allspice, Apple, Carnation, Catnip, Clove, Gardenia, Nutmeg, Orange, Pomegranate, Poppy, Raspberry, Tansy, Vervain

Stones: Agate, Aventurine, Calcite, Carnelian, Copper, Garnet, Marcasite, Peacock Rock, Peridot, Rhodochrosite, Ruby, Sandstone, Sapphire, Turquoise

Astrological Sign: Libra

Planet: Venus

Day of the Week: Friday

Element: Air

Direction: East

Blessing

Colors: White, Silver, Gold, Green

Plants: Basil, Bay, Clove, Frankincense, Gardenia, Jasmine, Juniper, Lavender, Myrrh, Nutmeg, Patchouli, Rose, Sage, Sandalwood

Stones: Agate, Amethyst, Aquamarine, Calcite, Carnelian, Citrine, Diamond, Emerald, Jade, Moonstone, Pearl, Quartz, Rose Quartz, Sapphire, Smoky Quartz

Astrological Sign: Cancer

Planet: Moon

Day of the Week: Monday

Element: Water

Direction: West

Calming

Colors: Blue, Silver, Pink, Green, White

Plants: Basil, Bay, Catnip, Chamomile, Frankincense, Gardenia, Geranium, Lavender, Myrrh, Patchouli, Peppermint, Pine, Raspberry, Rosemary, Sage, Sandalwood, Willow

Stones: Amethyst, Blue Lace Agate, Blue Topaz, Calcite, Emerald, Hematite, Marble, Moonstone, Opal, Pearl, Sapphire, Selenite

Astrological Sign: Libra

Planet: Venus

Day of the Week: Friday

Element: Air

Direction: East

Cleansing

Colors: Blue, Green, White, Black

Plants: Basil, Clove, Copal, Frankincense, Gardenia, Jasmine, Lavender, Myrrh, Nutmeg, Patchouli, Pine, Rose, Rosemary, Sage, Sandalwood, Tarragon, Thyme, Willow, Yarrow

Stones: Agate, Amethyst, Aquamarine, Aventurine, Calcite, Carnelian, Citrine, Diamond, Hematite, Jade, Marcasite, Mica, Obsidian, Peridot, Quartz, Rose Quartz, Tourmaline, Turquoise

Astrological Sign: Aquarius

Planet: Uranus

Day of the Week: Wednesday

Element: Air

Direction: East

Communication

Colors: Red, Blue, Yellow

Plants: Allspice, Amaranth, Apple, Basil, Bay, Benzoin, Carnation, Cinnamon, Clove, Gardenia, Hawthorn, Jasmine, Juniper, Marigold, Mistletoe, Myrrh, Rose, Sage, Sandalwood

Stones: Agate, Aquamarine, Blue Lace Agate, Blue Topaz, Citrine, Emerald, Lodestone, Pearl, Peridot, Quartz, Sandstone, Sodalite, Turquoise, Ulexite

Astrological Sign: Gemini

Planet: Mercury (not during retrograde)

Day of the Week: Wednesday

Element: Air

Direction: East

Confidence

Colors: Yellow, Purple

Plants: Allspice, Apple, Basil, Benzoin, Carnation, Cinnamon, Clove, Devil's Shoe String, Frankincense, Gardenia, Ginseng, Gotu Kola, Lavender, Lemon, Mistletoe, Myrrh, Nettle, Patchouli, Pine, Sage, Yarrow

Stones: Agate, Aventurine, Blue Lace Agate, Carnelian, Cat's Eye, Citrine, Diamond, Garnet, Gold, Jasper, Onyx, Platinum, Quartz, Sodalite, Tiger Eye, Topaz

Astrological Sign: Leo

Planet: Sun
Day of the Week: Sunday
Element: Fire
Direction: South

Creativity

Colors: Orange, Green, White, Silver
Plants: Allspice, Apple, Basil, Benzoin, Caraway, Carnation, Catnip, Clove, Copal, Frankincense, Gardenia, Gotu Kola, Horehound, Mugwort, Nutmeg, Orange, Patchouli, Pomegranate, Poppy, Raspberry, Sage, Tansy, Vervain
Stones: Amber, Bornite, Carnelian, Cat's Eye, Coral, Diamond, Emerald, Jade, Moonstone, Opal, Peridot, Petoskey Stone, Rhodochrosite, Rose Quartz, Ruby, Silver, Sodalite, Topaz, Ulexite, Zircon
Astrological Sign: Pisces
Planet: Neptune
Day of the Week: Thursday
Element: Water
Direction: West

Divination

Colors: Black, Silver, Purple, White
Plants: Allspice, Basil, Bay Laurel, Benzoin, Carnation, Catnip, Chamomile, Clove, Copal, Dandelion, Elm, Frankincense, Gardenia, Lavender, Lemon Verbena, Mugwort, Myrrh, Nutmeg, Orange, Patchouli, Rosemary, Saffron, Sage, Sandalwood, Scullcap, Tansy, Tarragon, Tobacco, Valerian, Vervain, Verbena, Witch Grass, Wood Rose, Wormwood
Stones: Amber, Amethyst, Aquamarine, Blue Topaz, Calcite, Diamond, Emerald, Hematite, Jade, Marcasite, Meteorite, Moonstone, Obsidian, Onyx, Petoskey Stone, Selenite, Silver, Sodalite, Tourmaline, Turquoise, Ulexite
Astrological Sign: Scorpio
Planet: Pluto
Day of the Week: Tuesday
Element: Water
Direction: West

Dreams

Colors: White, Indigo, Purple

Plants: Basil, Bay Laurel, Benzoin, Copal, Frankincense, Gardenia, Horehound, Jasmine, Lavender, Mugwort, Myrrh, Nutmeg, Patchouli, Sage, Witch Grass, Wormwood

Stones: Amethyst, Calcite, Carnelian, Emerald, Jade, Mica, Moonstone, Selenite, Turquoise, Ulexite

Astrological Sign: Pisces

Planet: Neptune

Day of the Week: Thursday

Element: Water

Direction: West

Employment

Colors: Brown, Orange, Green

Plants: Basil, Bay Laurel, Cinnamon, Clove, Devil's Shoe String, Frankincense, Jasmine, Lemon, Myrrh, Nuts, Orange, Spearmint, Sunflower

Stones: Agate, Carnelian, Citrine, Diamond, Gold, Smoky Quartz, Tiger Eye

Astrological Sign: Virgo

Planet: Mercury

Day of the Week: Wednesday

Element: Earth

Direction: North

Environment

Colors: Green, Brown, Black

Plants: Acorn, Apple, Basil, Copal, Elm, Frankincense, Lavender, Maple, Myrrh, Pine, Rose, Sage, Sandalwood, Tobacco, Willow, Yarrow

Stones: Amber, Bloodstone, Calcite, Carnelian, Copper, Garnet, Jasper, Obsidian, Petrified Wood

Astrological Sign: Earth Signs: Taurus, Virgo, and Capricorn

Planet: Earth

Day of the Week: Friday

Element: Earth

Direction: North

Exorcism

Colors: Purple, Green, White, Black

Plants: Basil, Clove, Clover, Cumin, Dragon's Blood, Elder, Frankincense, Garlic, Juniper, Mint, Mistletoe, Onion,

Pine, Rosemary, Sage, Sandalwood, Vervain, Witch Grass, Yarrow

Stones: Amber, Amethyst, Calcite, Cat's Eye, Diamond, Emerald, Jade, Lapis Lazuli, Malachite, Obsidian, Rose Quartz, Selenite, Tourmaline, Turquoise

Astrological Sign: Scorpio

Planet: Pluto

Day of the Week: Tuesday

Element: Water

Direction: West

Fear (To Banish)

Colors: Black, White, Red, Pink

Plants: Amaranth, Apple, Basil, Benzoin, Cinnamon, Clove, Devil's Shoe String, Frankincense, Marigold, Myrrh, Nutmeg, Sage, Sandalwood, Tarragon, Wormwood

Stones: Agate, Amber, Bloodstone, Carnelian, Copper, Diamond, Garnet, Hematite, Jasper, Mica, Obsidian, Quartz, Tourmaline

Astrological Sign: Leo

Planet: Sun

Day of the Week: Sunday

Element: Fire

Direction: South

Fertility

Colors: Orange, Green, White, Silver

Plants: Acorn, Apple, Basil, Bay Laurel, Chamomile, Clove, Dill, Gardenia, Marjoram, Nuts, Raspberry, Strawberry

Stones: Carnelian, Diamond, Emerald, Garnet, Jasper, Moonstone, Opal, Pearl, Quartz

Astrological Sign: Cancer

Planet: Moon

Day of the Week: Monday

Element: Water

Direction: West

Focus (Mental)

Colors: White, Black, Yellow, Purple

Plants: Benzoin, Copal, Echinacea, Frankincense, Gardenia, Horehound, Lavender, Lemon, Myrrh, Nutmeg, Patchouli, Pine, Saffron, Sage, Sandalwood, Willow

Stones: Agate, Amber, Amethyst, Aquamarine, Blue Lace Agate, Citrine, Diamond, Gold, Jade, Lodestone, Opal, Quartz, Sapphire, Sodalite, Tourmaline, Turquoise, Ulexite

Astrological Sign: Aries

Planet: Mars

Day of the Week: Tuesday

Element: Fire

Direction: South

Grounding

Colors: Black, Red

Plants: Acorn, Apple, Basil, Bay Laurel, Cactus, Cinnamon, Comfrey, Ginger, Marjoram, Patchouli, Pepper, Pine, Rosemary, Sage, Sandalwood, Willow

Stones: Agate, Amber, Bloodstone, Carnelian, Copper, Hematite, Mica, Obsidian, Onyx, Tourmaline

Astrological Sign: Taurus

Planet: Venus

Day of the Week: Friday

Element: Earth

Direction: North

Growth

Colors: Green, Gold, Red, White, Brown

Plants: Acorn, Apple, Elder, Elm, Nuts, Oak, Pine, Sunflower

Stones: Bornite, Diamond, Emerald, Geode, Marble, Onyx, Quartz, Rhodochrosite, Rose Quartz, Sugilite

Astrological Sign: Taurus

Planet: Venus

Day of the Week: Friday

Element: Earth

Direction: North

Habits (To Break Bad Habits)

Colors: Black, White, Blue, Green

Plants: Allspice, Basil, Benzoin, Clove, Copal, Frankincense, Ginger, Horehound, Lavender, Myrrh, Nutmeg, Patchouli, Rose, Saffron, Sage, Vervain, Willow

Stones: Agate, Amethyst, Aquamarine, Blue Lace Agate, Calcite, Citrine, Geode, Hematite, Jade, Marcasite, Ruby, Selenite, Topaz

Astrological Sign: Aquarius
Planet: Uranus
Day of the Week: Wednesday
Element: Air
Direction: East

Happiness

Colors: Pink, Gold, White

Plants: Allspice, Anise, Apple, Basil, Clove, Gardenia, Ginger, Honeysuckle, Juniper, Lavender, Lemon, Orange, Saffron, Sunflower, Yarrow

Stones: Aquamarine, Aventurine, Bornite, Citrine, Diamond, Garnet, Gold, Lapis Lazuli, Quartz, Rhodochrosite, Rhodonite, Rose Quartz, Topaz, Turquoise

Astrological Sign: Sagittarius
Planet: Jupiter
Day of the Week: Thursday
Element: Fire
Direction: South

Health/Healing

Colors: Green, Pink

Plants: Allspice, Aloe, Amaranth, Apple, Calendula, Carnation, Catnip, Chamomile, Cinnamon, Clove, Comfrey, Copal, Coriander, Dandelion, Echinacea, Elder, Frankincense, Gardenia, Garlic, Ginger, Horehound, Juniper, Lavender, Lemon, Lemon Verbena, Marjoram, Mint, Mugwort, Myrrh, Nettle, Onion, Orange, Parsley, Patchouli, Peppermint, Pine, Raspberry, Rose, Rosemary, Saffron, Sage, Saint John's Wort, Sandalwood, Spearmint, Strawberry, Sunflower, Tansy, Tarragon, Vervain, Willow, Wintergreen, Witch Hazel, Wormwood, Yarrow

Stones: Agate, Amber, Amethyst, Aquamarine, Aventurine, Bloodstone, Blue Lace Agate, Calcite, Carnelian, Citrine, Copper, Diamond, Garnet, Jade, Lapis Lazuli, Lodestone, Malachite, Marble, Marcasite, Moonstone, Opal, Pearl, Peridot, Quartz, Rhodochrosite, Rose Quartz, Topaz, Tourmaline, Turquoise

Astrological Sign: All. Each sign rules over an area of the body generally as follows: Aquarius = calves and ankles, Aries = face and head, Cancer = chest and stomach, Capricorn =

knees, Gemini = arms and hands, Leo = upper back and
spine, Libra = lower back and kidneys, Pisces = feet, Sagittarius = thighs and liver, Scorpio = reproductive organs, Taurus = throat and neck

Planet: All
Day of the Week: All
Element: All
Direction: All

Intuition

Colors: Purple
Plants: Basil, Benzoin, Clove, Copal, Elm, Frankincense, Gar-
denia, Horehound, Lavender, Mugwort, Myrrh, Nutmeg,
Patchouli, Saffron, Sage, Sandalwood, Scullcap, Thyme,
Tonka Beans, Valerian, Vervain, Witch Grass, Wood Rose,
Wormwood
Stones: Amethyst, Aquamarine, Blue Lace Agate, Calcite,
Cat's Eye, Citrine, Coral, Emerald, Garnet, Geode, Hema-
tite, Jade, Lapis Lazuli, Lodestone, Malachite, Marcasite,
Mica, Moonstone, Obsidian, Opal, Pearl, Peridot, Quartz,
Sapphire, Selenite, Silver, Sodalite, Topaz, Tourmaline,
Turquoise, Ulexite
Astrological Sign: Scorpio
Planet: Pluto
Day of the Week: Tuesday
Element: Water
Direction: West

Leadership

Colors: Purple, Gold, Copper, Yellow, Red, White
Plants: Apple, Basil, Benzoin, Cactus, Cinnamon, Clove,
Devil's Shoe String, Dill, Elder, Elm, Frankincense, Ginger,
Horehound, Juniper, Lemon, Marigold, Marjoram, Mint,
Myrrh, Saffron, Sage, Sandalwood, Sunflower, Wormwood
Stones: Agate, Amber, Aquamarine, Aventurine, Carnelian,
Cat's Eye, Citrine, Copper, Diamond, Emerald, Garnet,
Gold, Lapis Lazuli, Lodestone, Marble, Marcasite, Onyx,
Petrified Wood, Platinum, Pyrite, Ruby, Sapphire, Topaz
Astrological Sign: Leo
Planet: Sun
Day of the Week: Sunday

Element: Fire
Direction: South

Loneliness

Colors: Pink, Green, Copper, Gold, White, Black

Plants: Allspice, Apple, Basil, Bay Laurel, Clove, Comfrey, Dandelion, Fennel, Frankincense, Gardenia, Ginger, Jasmine, Juniper, Lavender, Lemon, Maple, Myrrh, Patchouli, Peppermint, Pomegranate, Sandalwood, Spearmint, Vanilla, Yarrow

Stones: Amethyst, Aventurine, Blue Lace Agate, Carnelian, Citrine, Diamond, Emerald, Garnet, Gold, Jade, Moonstone, Onyx, Quartz, Rhodochrosite, Rhodonite, Rose Quartz, Ruby, Silver, Sodalite, Topaz, Turquoise

Astrological Sign: Aquarius

Planet: Uranus

Day of the Week: Wednesday

Element: Air

Direction: East

Love

Colors: Pink, Red, Green

Plants: Allspice, Amaranth, Apple, Basil, Carnation, Catnip, Chamomile, Clove, Clover, Coriander, Dragon's Blood, Endive, Frankincense, Gardenia, Geranium, Ginger, Ginseng, Jasmine, Lavender, Lemon, Lemon Verbena, Maple, Marigold, Marjoram, Mistletoe, Myrrh, Orris, Pansy, Patchouli, Pine, Pomegranate, Raspberry, Rose, Strawberry, Tansy, Tonka Beans, Vanilla, Wood Rose, Yarrow

Stones: Agate, Amethyst, Carnelian, Diamond, Emerald, Garnet, Gold, Hematite, Jade, Lodestone, Marcasite, Mica, Moonstone, Opal, Pearl, Peridot, Quartz, Rhodochrosite, Rhodonite, Rose Quartz, Ruby, Sapphire, Silver, Sodalite, Turquoise

Astrological Sign: Taurus

Planet: Venus

Day of the Week: Friday

Element: Earth

Direction: North

Luck

Colors: Gold, Blue

Plants: Acorn, Allspice, Apple, Basil, Carnation, Dandelion, Juniper, Lemon, Nutmeg, Pine, Rose, Strawberry, Tonka Beans

Stones: Bornite, Citrine, Herkimer Diamond, Fire Opal, Lapis Lazuli, Marcasite, Sodalite, Sugilite, Topaz

Astrological Sign: Sagittarius

Planet: Jupiter

Day of the Week: Thursday

Element: Fire

Direction: South

Marriage

Colors: Pink, Red, White

Plants: Allspice, Amaranth, Apple, Basil, Frankincense, Gardenia, Ginger, Juniper, Lavender, Myrrh, Orange, Orris, Raspberry, Rose, Strawberry, Tonka Beans

Stones: Amethyst, Carnelian, Diamond, Emerald, Garnet, Gold, Hematite, Jade, Marcasite, Mica, Moonstone, Opal, Orris, Patchouli, Pearl, Peridot, Quartz, Rhodochrosite, Rhodonite, Rose Quartz, Ruby, Sapphire, Silver, Turquoise

Astrological Sign: Taurus

Planet: Venus

Day of the Week: Friday

Element: Earth

Direction: East

Meditation

Colors: Blue, White, Silver, Indigo, Purple

Plants: Basil, Bay Laurel, Benzoin, Copal, Frankincense, Gardenia, Jasmine, Lavender, Mugwort, Myrrh, Nutmeg, Patchouli, Sage, Tobacco, Witch Grass, Wormwood

Stones: Amethyst, Aquamarine, Blue Topaz, Calcite, Carnelian, Citrine, Diamond, Emerald, Herkimer Diamond, Jade, Lapis Lazuli, Mica, Moonstone, Obsidian, Onyx, Peridot, Quartz, Rose Quartz, Sapphire, Selenite, Sodalite, Topaz, Turquoise, Ulexite

Astrological Sign: Aquarius

Planet: Saturn

Day of the Week: Saturday

Element: Air

Direction: East

Money

Colors: Green, Gold, Brown

Plants: Acorn, Apple, Basil, Bayberry, Bay Laurel, Carnation, Chamomile, Cinnamon, Clove, Clover, Copal, Dandelion, Dill, Elder, Ginger, Marigold, Mint, Nutmeg, Nuts, Oak, Patchouli, Peppermint, Pine, Pomegranate, Poppy, Sunflower, Tonka, Valerian, Vervain

Stones: Agate, Amber, Aventurine, Carnelian, Citrine, Diamond, Emerald, Garnet, Gold, Lodestone, Marcasite, Peridot, Platinum, Quartz, Rose Quartz, Topaz, Turquoise

Astrological Sign: Capricorn

Planet: Saturn

Day of the Week: Saturday

Element: Earth

Direction: North

Monogamy

Colors: Black, Pink, White

Plants: Apple, Basil, Clover, Elder, Jasmine, Lavender, Scullcap, Vanilla

Stones: Carnelian, Garnet, Hematite, Jasper, Lodestone, Quartz, Tourmaline

Astrological Sign: Libra

Planet: Venus

Day of the Week: Friday

Element: Air

Direction: East

Negativity (To Banish)

Colors: Black, Blue, White

Plants: Allspice, Apple, Basil, Bay Laurel, Benzoin, Chamomile, Cinnamon, Clove, Fennel, Frankincense, Gardenia, Garlic, Lavender, Lemon, Marigold, Myrrh, Nutmeg, Patchouli, Pine, Raspberry, Rosemary, Sage, Sandalwood, Vervain, Willow, Yarrow

Stones: Agate, Amber, Amethyst, Calcite, Carnelian, Citrine, Diamond, Emerald, Garnet, Geode, Hematite, Jade, Malachite, Obsidian, Quartz, Rose Quartz, Sapphire, Selenite, Topaz, Tourmaline, Turquoise

Astrological Sign: Cancer

Planet: Moon
Day of the Week: Monday
Element: Water
Direction: West

Peace

Colors: Silver, Blue, Purple, White, Pink
Plants: Apple, Basil, Benzoin, Carnation, Catnip, Chamomile, Clove, Comfrey, Elder, Frankincense, Gardenia, Jasmine, Lavender, Myrrh, Orange, Pansy, Pine, Raspberry, Rose, Rosemary, Sage, Scullcap, Vervain
Stones: Amethyst, Aquamarine, Blue Lace Agate, Calcite, Coral, Diamond, Emerald, Garnet, Jade, Moonstone, Opal, Pearl, Quartz, Rhodochrosite, Rose Quartz, Sapphire, Selenite, Sugilite, Turquoise
Astrological Sign: Aquarius
Planet: Saturn
Day of the Week: Saturday
Element: Air
Direction: East

Popularity

Colors: Blue, Green, Brown
Plants: Acorn, Amaranth, Apple, Basil, Carnation, Cinnamon, Clove, Clover, Elder, Gardenia, Ginger, Jasmine, Lavender, Lemon, Maple, Myrrh, Orange, Pansy, Patchouli, Peppermint, Raspberry, Rose, Saffron, Sage, Vanilla
Stones: Agate, Aquamarine, Aventurine, Blue Lace Agate, Bornite, Carnelian, Citrine, Diamond, Emerald, Garnet, Jade, Onyx, Peridot, Quartz, Sapphire, Sodalite, Turquoise
Astrological Sign: Aquarius
Planet: Saturn
Day of the Week: Saturday
Element: Air
Direction: East

Power

Colors: Purple, Red, Orange, Copper, Gold, Yellow
Plants: Apple, Benzoin, Cinnamon, Frankincense, Gardenia, Nutmeg, Pine, Pomegranate, Sage
Stones: Citrine, Diamond, Gold, Marble, Quartz, Ruby, Tiger Eye, Topaz, Turquoise

Astrological Sign: Leo
Planet: Sun
Day of the Week: Sunday
Element: Fire
Direction: South

Prosperity

Colors: Green, White, Copper, Gold

Plants: Apple, Basil, Cinnamon, Clove, Frankincense, Ginger, Myrrh, Patchouli, Peppermint, Saffron, Sandalwood, Spearmint, Sunflower, Vervain, Wintergreen

Stones: Citrine, Copper, Diamond, Emerald, Garnet, Geode, Gold, Marble, Peridot, Quartz, Tiger Eye, Topaz, Turquoise

Astrological Sign: Capricorn
Planet: Saturn
Day of the Week: Saturday
Element: Earth
Direction: North

Protection

Colors: Black, Blue

Plants: Aloe, Basil, Bay Laurel, Benzoin, Cactus, Caraway, Cinnamon, Clove, Copal, Coriander, Dragon's Blood, Elder, Fennel, Frankincense, Geranium, Garlic, Lavender, Myrrh, Nutmeg, Orris, Pepper, Pine, Primrose, Rosemary, Sage, Saint John's Wort, Sandalwood, Valerian, Vervain

Stones: Agate, Amethyst, Carnelian, Citrine, Diamond, Hematite, Jade, Lodestone, Moonstone, Obsidian, Onyx, Peridot, Petoskey Stone, Quartz, Rose Quartz, Ruby, Sapphire, Selenite, Silver, Tiger Eye, Topaz, Tourmaline, Turquoise

Astrological Sign: Leo
Planet: Sun
Day of the Week: Sunday
Element: Fire
Direction: South

Psychic Ability

Colors: Silver, Black, White, Purple

Plants: Basil, Benzoin, Chamomile, Clove, Elder, Frankincense, Gardenia, Ginger, Lavender, Mugwort, Myrrh, Nutmeg, Patchouli, Pomegranate, Raspberry, Rosemary, Saffron, Sage, Sandalwood, Thyme, Valerian, Vervain, Witch Grass, Wood Rose, Wormwood

Stones: Amber, Amethyst, Aquamarine, Blue Lace Agate, Calcite, Diamond, Jade, Lapis Lazuli, Lodestone, Malachite, Moonstone, Obsidian, Peridot, Quartz, Sapphire, Selenite, Sodalite, Topaz, Turquoise, Ulexite

Astrological Sign: Scorpio

Planet: Pluto

Day of the Week: Tuesday

Element: Water

Direction: West

Safety

Colors: Gold, White, Red

Plants: Acorn, Basil, Cactus, Cinnamon, Clove, Devil's Shoe String, Frankincense, Garlic, Mandrake, Myrrh, Oak, Pine, Rosemary, Sage

Stones: Agate, Amber, Aquamarine, Bloodstone, Calcite, Diamond, Gold, Malachite, Turquoise

Astrological Sign: Aries

Planet: Mars

Day of the Week: Tuesday

Element: Fire

Direction: South

Self-image

Colors: Pink, Gold, Green

Plants: Amaranth, Apple, Chamomile, Cinnamon, Clove, Gardenia, Lavender, Lemon, Marigold, Raspberry, Rose, Saffron, Sage, Strawberry, Sunflower, Yarrow

Stones: Bornite, Citrine, Jade, Moonstone, Peridot, Rose Quartz, Sodalite

Astrological Sign: Leo

Planet: Sun

Day of the Week: Sunday

Element: Fire

Direction: South

Sex

Colors: Red, Orange

Plants: Apple, Cinnamon, Clove, Copal, Gardenia, Garlic,

Ginger, Lavender, Nuts, Patchouli, Pomegranate, Raspberry, Rose, Saffron, Tonka Beans, Valerian, Yarrow
Stones: Agate, Amber, Carnelian, Cat's Eye, Copper, Garnet, Moonstone, Quartz, Rhodochrosite, Sapphire, Smoky Quartz
Astrological Sign: Scorpio
Planet: Pluto
Day of the Week: Tuesday
Element: Water
Direction: West

Sleep

Colors: Silver, Blue, Purple, White
Plants: Catnip, Chamomile, Elder, Fennel, Frankincense, Gardenia, Lavender, Mugwort, Myrrh, Sandalwood, Vanilla
Stones: Amethyst, Aquamarine, Blue Lace Agate, Calcite, Coral, Jade, Marcasite, Moonstone, Opal, Quartz, Sandstone, Selenite, Turquoise
Astrological Sign: Virgo
Planet: Mercury
Day of the Week: Wednesday
Element: Earth
Direction: North

Spirit Guides/Muses/Teachers

Colors: Silver, Blue, Purple, White
Plants: Bay, Benzoin, Gardenia, Jasmine, Lavender, Mugwort, Myrrh, Peppermint, Saffron, Sage, Sandalwood, Thyme, Vervain, Wormwood
Stones: Amethyst, Blue Lace Agate, Bornite, Calcite, Jade, Marcasite, Moonstone, Obsidian, Quartz, Sapphire, Selenite, Sodalite, Topaz, Turquoise
Astrological Sign: Scorpio
Planet: Pluto
Day of the Week: Tuesday
Element: Water
Direction: West

Spirituality

Colors: White, Silver, Blue, Purple
Plants: Basil, Bay, Benzoin, Chamomile, Clove, Copal, Elder,

Fennel, Frankincense, Gardenia, Ginger, Horehound, Jasmine, Lavender, Mugwort, Myrrh, Nutmeg, Oak, Patchouli, Peppermint, Pine, Rose, Rosemary, Saffron, Sage, Scullcap, Tarragon, Valerian, Vervain, Willow, Witch Grass, Wormwood

Stones: Amethyst, Aquamarine, Calcite, Copper, Diamond, Emerald, Garnet, Geode, Jade, Lapis Lazuli, Lodestone, Marcasite, Mica, Moonstone, Obsidian, Opal, Peridot, Petoskey Stone, Quartz, Sandstone, Sapphire, Selenite, Silver, Topaz, Turquoise

Astrological Sign: Sagittarius

Planet: Jupiter

Day of the Week: Thursday

Element: Fire

Direction: South

Stress

Colors: Blue, White, Pink, Green

Plants: Aloe, Apple, Basil, Bay, Blackberry, Chamomile, Clove, Echinacea, Frankincense, Gardenia, Honeysuckle, Jasmine, Lavender, Lemon, Myrrh, Patchouli, Peppermint, Pine, Raspberry, Rose, Rosemary, Saffron, Sage, Saint John's Wort, Sandalwood, Valerian, Vanilla, Vervain, Willow, Yarrow

Stones: Amethyst, Aquamarine, Aventurine, Bornite, Calcite, Citrine, Emerald, Garnet, Hematite, Jade, Moonstone, Opal, Rhodochrosite, Rose Quartz, Sapphire, Sodalite, Tourmaline, Turquoise

Astrological Sign: Libra

Planet: Venus

Day of the Week: Friday

Element: Air

Direction: East

Success

Colors: Orange, Copper, Gold, Green

Plants: Carnation, Cinnamon, Clove, Dandelion, Dill, Gardenia, Ginger, Juniper, Lemon, Marigold, Nuts, Peppermint, Pine, Saffron, Sunflower

Stones: Bloodstone, Bornite, Carnelian, Cat's Eye, Citrine,

Copper, Diamond, Geode, Gold, Marble, Onyx, Quartz, Sapphire, Sodalite, Tiger Eye, Topaz
Astrological Sign: Capricorn
Planet: Saturn
Day of the Week: Saturday
Element: Earth
Direction: East

Thanksgiving

Colors: White, Green
Plants: Acorn, Amaranth, Apple, Basil, Bay, Caraway, Carnation, Catnip, Chamomile, Cinnamon, Clove, Clover, Dandelion, Elm, Frankincense, Gardenia, Ginger, Hawthorn, Honeysuckle, Lavender, Lemon, Mint, Mistletoe, Myrrh, Nutmeg, Nuts, Orange, Orris, Pine, Pomegranate, Poppy, Rose, Rosemary, Saffron, Sage, Sandalwood, Tobacco, Willow, Yarrow
Stones: Amethyst, Calcite, Gold, Moonstone, Opal, Quartz, Selenite, Silver, Turquoise
Astrological Sign: Any
Planet: Any
Day of the Week: Any
Element: All
Direction: All

Travel

Colors: Gold, Black, Red, White
Plants: Basil, Cinnamon, Clove, Comfrey, Devil's Shoe String, Frankincense, Garlic, Mandrake, Myrrh, Oak, Pine, Rosemary, Sage
Stones: Agate, Amber, Aquamarine, Bloodstone, Calcite, Diamond, Gold, Malachite, Turquoise
Astrological Sign: Sagittarius
Planet: Jupiter
Day of the Week: Thursday
Element: Fire
Direction: South

Understanding

Colors: Silver, Brown, Blue, White
Plants: Apple, Basil, Chamomile, Clove, Comfrey, Coriander, Dill, Elder, Elm, Frankincense, Gardenia, Horehound,

Lavender, Mandrake, Marjoram, Mugwort, Myrrh, Nutmeg, Oak, Orris, Pine, Pomegranate, Saffron, Sage, Sandalwood, Scullcap, Thyme, Tobacco, Valerian, Vervain, Wormwood

Stones: Amber, Amethyst, Aquamarine, Blue Lace Agate, Blue Topaz, Calcite, Carnelian, Citrine, Diamond, Emerald, Garnet, Geode, Gold, Hematite, Jade, Malachite, Marcasite, Obsidian, Quartz, Rhodochrosite, Rose Quartz, Sapphire, Selenite, Sodalite, Sugilite, Topaz, Tourmaline, Turquoise, Ulexite

Astrological Sign: Sagittarius

Planet: Jupiter

Day of the Week: Thursday

Element: Fire

Direction: South

Violence (To Stop)

Colors: Red, White, Black, Pink

Plants: Basil, Chamomile, Clove, Frankincense, Gardenia, Geranium, Jasmine, Lavender, Lemon, Lemon Verbena, Maple, Marigold, Marjoram, Mistletoe, Myrrh, Orris, Pansy, Patchouli, Pine, Pomegranate, Raspberry, Rose, Strawberry, Tansy, Tonka Beans, Yarrow

Stones: Amethyst, Diamond, Emerald, Garnet, Gold, Hematite, Jade, Marcasite, Moonstone, Opal, Pearl, Peridot, Quartz, Rhodochrosite, Rhodonite, Rose Quartz, Ruby, Sapphire, Silver, Turquoise

Astrological Sign: Taurus

Planet: Venus

Day of the Week: Friday

Element: Earth

Direction: North

Visions

Colors: Purple, Silver, White

Plants: Bay, Jasmine, Mugwort, Nutmeg, Orris, Pomegranate, Sandalwood, Wormwood

Stones: Calcite, Geode, Jade, Malachite, Mica, Moonstone, Obsidian, Onyx, Quartz, Selenite, Topaz, Turquoise, Ulexite

Astrological Sign: Scorpio

Planet: Pluto
Day of the Week: Tuesday
Element: Water
Direction: West

Wisdom

Colors: Blue, Yellow, White

Plants: Allspice, Apple, Basil, Bay, Benzoin, Cinnamon, Clove, Copal, Coriander, Elder, Frankincense, Gardenia, Ginger, Ginseng, Horehound, Lavender, Marigold, Mugwort, Myrrh, Nutmeg, Orris, Peppermint, Pine, Rosemary, Saffron, Sage, Sandalwood, Scullcap, Sunflower, Valerian, Vervain, Wintergreen, Witch Grass, Wormwood

Stones: Agate, Amethyst, Aquamarine, Blue Lace Agate, Calcite, Citrine, Diamond, Emerald, Geode, Gold, Marcasite, Moonstone, Obsidian, Petoskey Stone, Pyrite, Quartz, Rose Quartz, Selenite, Topaz, Turquoise, Ulexite

Astrological Sign: Sagittarius
Planet: Jupiter
Day of the Week: Thursday
Element: Fire
Direction: South

Bibliography

The Holy Bible, King James Version (1611). Cleveland, OH: World Publishing Co.

Adler, Margot. *Drawing Down the Moon*. Boston, MA: Beacon Press, 1979, 1986.

Andrews, Ted. *Animal-Speak: The Spiritual and Magical Powers of Creatures Great and Small*. St. Paul, MN: Llewellyn Publications, 1994.

Blum, Ralph H. *The Book of Runes*. New York: St. Martin's Press, 1993.

Brennan, Barbara Ann. *Hands of Light: A Guide to Healing Through the Human Energy Field*. New York: Bantam Books, 1988.

Brennan, Barbara Ann. *Light Emerging: The Journey of Personal Healing*. New York: Bantam Books, 1993.

Buckland, Ray. *Advanced Candle Magick*. St. Paul, MN: Llewellyn Publications, 1996.

Budapest, Z. *Summoning the Fates*. New York: Harmony Books, 1998.

Cabot, Laurie and Tom Cowan. *Power of the Witch: The Earth, the Moon, and the Magical Path to Enlightenment*. New York: Delta Books, 1989.

Campion, Kitty. *A Woman's Herbal*. London: Leopard Books, 1987.

Cheetham, Erika. *The Final Prophecies of Nostradamus*. New York: Perigee Books, 1989.

Cunningham, Scott. *Cunningham's Encyclopedia of Magical Herbs*. St. Paul, MN: Llewellyn Publications, 1997.

Cunningham, Scott. *The Complete Book of Incense, Oils & Brews*. St. Paul, MN: Llewellyn Publications, 1998.

Cunningham, Scott. *Wicca: A Guide for the Solitary Practitioner.* St. Paul, MN: Llewellyn Publications, 1996.

Farrar, Janet & Stewart. *The Witches' Goddess.* Custer, WA: Phoenix Publishing, Inc., 1987.

Greer, Mary K. *Tarot Constellations: Patterns of Personal Destiny.* North Hollywood, CA: Newcastle Publishing Co., Inc., 1987.

Grimassi, Raven. *The Wiccan Mysteries.* St. Paul, MN: Llewellyn Publications, 1997.

Hollis, Sarah. *The Country Diary Herbal.* London: Claremont Books, 1990.

Melody. *Love is in the Earth: A Kaleidoscope of Crystals.* Wheatridge, CO: Earth-Love Publishing House, 1991.

Millman, Dan. *The Life You Were Born To Live.* Tiburon, CA: H J Kramer, Inc., 1993.

Moses, Jeffrey. *Oneness: Great Principles Shared By All Religions.* New York: Fawcett Ballantine Books, 1989.

Pennick, Nigel. *The Pagan Book of Days.* Rochester, VT: Destiny Books, 1992.

Raphaell, Katrina. *Crystal Enlightenment: The Transforming Properties of Crystals and Healing Stones, Vol. I.* Santa Fe, NM: Aurora Press, 1985.

Raphaell, Katrina. *Crystal Healing: The Therapeutic Application of Crystals and Stones, Vol 2.* Santa Fe, NM: Aurora Press, 1987.

Raphaell, Katrina. *The Crystalline Transmission: A Synthesis of Light, Vol. 3.* Santa Fe, NM: Aurora Press, 1990.

Ravenwolf, Silver. *To Ride a Silver Broomstick: New Generation Witchcraft.* St. Paul, MN: Llewellyn Publications, 1996.

Silva, J., Miele, P. *The Silva Mind Control Method.* New York: Pocket Books, 1977.

Simms, M.K. *The Witch's Circle.* St. Paul, MN: Llewellyn Publications, 1994.

Stein, Sandra Kovacs. *Instant Numerology.* North Hollywood, CA: Newcastle Publishing Co., 1986.

Tierra, Michael. *The Way of Herbs.* New York: Pocket Books, 1998.

Whitcomb, Bill. *The Magician's Companion.* St. Paul, MN: Llewellyn Publications, 1997.

Wolff, Robert Paul. *About Philosophy.* Englewood Cliffs, NJ: Prentice-Hall, Inc., 1981.

Wood, Robin. *The Robin Wood Tarot*. St. Paul, MN: Llewellyn Publications, 1995.

Woolfolk, Joanna Martine. *The Only Astrology Book You'll Ever Need*. Lanham, MD: Scarborough House, 1990.

Zukav, Gary. *The Seat of the Soul*. New York: Simon & Schuster, 1989.